COMMUNICATIONS OPT-IN FORM

LSTM
LIVERPOOL SCHOOL
OF TROPICAL MEDICINE

We are so grateful for your support, thank you! As a supporter, we will contact you to keep you updated about LSTM and your areas of interest. You can choose which communications you receive and how you would like to receive them by ticking the boxes below::

General Newsletters ☐   Annual Report(s) ☐   Fundraising Communications ☐
(mainly digital)   Donor Report ☐

Please select how you would like to receive this information:

post ☐   email ☐   SMS ☐   telephone ☐

We would also like to keep you updated about events and how you may support us further. If you **prefer not** to receive this additional information, please tick here ☐

Title: _____   Forename: _____

Surname: _____

Address: _____

_____

_____   Postcode: _____

Phone: _____   Mobile: _____

Email: _____

Privacy Policy

LSTM is committed to good fundraising practice and as a valued supporter of LSTM, we take your privacy very seriously in all our interactions with you. We have recently updated our privacy policy to reflect this. A full privacy statement can be found at www.lstmed.ac.uk/about/fundraising.

We will retain your details for the purposes of LSTM's engagement with its stakeholders, which will include general communications. We may collect names, addresses, telephone numbers, business details, bank account details (where you have provided these), tax status for the purposes of collecting Gift Aid, and record of your interactions with us (e.g. event attendance). Your details may be shared with third parties who LTSM has carefully selected to undertake mailings and surveys on our behalf. If you change your mind, you can unsubscribe at any time or if you want to update or amend your personal information or if you have questions about the above information, you can contact us: Liverpool School of Tropical Medicine, Pembroke Place, L3 5QA. Telephone: 0151 705 3272 Email: fundraising@lstmed.ac.uk

☐ **Please tick this box to confirm that you have read and understood this privacy statement.**

Thank you for completing this form.

You can return it in the Freepost envelope provided or to: Billy Dean, Liverpool School of Tropical Medicine, Pembroke Place, Liverpool, L3 5QA.

Registered with
FUNDRAISING
REGULATOR

CAPTIVE ARTISTS

the unseen art of British Far East prisoners of war

by

Meg Parkes MPhil, Honorary Research Fellow,
Liverpool School of Tropical Medicine;

Geoff Gill, Emeritus Professor of International Medicine,
Liverpool School of Tropical Medicine;

Jenny Wood, formerly art curator,
Imperial War Museums

Front cover
Left: My tent in Changi (after van Gogh) 1942, by Padre F. H. Stallard
(©courtesy Stallard family)
Centre: Tropical ulcer, Thailand, by Gunner P. Meninsky (©courtesy IWM)
Right: Embroidery, Thailand 1943, by Gunner J. B. Chalker
(©courtesy G. Chalker-Howells)
Bottom: View from my bed, Hut 3 Changi Gaol July 1944, by
Lt J. W. B. White (©courtesy Aldridge family)

Back cover
Top: Inside hut, Thailand, by Pvt. B. E. Ferron (©courtesy S. Smith)
Bottom: Tropical butterfly, Thailand, by medical officer Capt. R. S. Hardie
FMSVF (©courtesy the Bird family)

Inside front flap
Wooden carving of kingfisher, Java 1942, by medical officer
Fl/Lt F. R. Philps (©courtesy the Philps family)

First published in 2019
by Palatine Books
Carnegie House
Chatsworth Road
Lancaster LA1 4SL
www.palatinebooks.com

Copyright © Meg Parkes, Geoff Gill and Jenny Wood

British Library Cataloguing-in-Publication data
A catalogue record for this book is available from the
British Library

Paperback ISBN 13: 978-1-910837-28-3

Designed and typeset by Carnegie Book Production
www.carnegiebookproduction.com

Printed and bound by Cambrian Printers

Contents

Dedication

Captive Artists is dedicated to Far East prisoner of war (FEPOW) artists of all nationalities, especially the British FEPOW artists uncovered by the art enquiry revealed in this book. Their courage and determination, combined with artistic and creative skill, to secretly record exactly what they wanted the viewer to see, gives the reader a glimpse of the Far East prisoner of war experience during the Second World War.

It is also dedicated to the memory of war historian Dr Clare Makepeace, Fellow of Birkbeck College London. Clare cared deeply about how the history of war captivity was researched, written and shared. Her contribution to future learning and understanding in this field is immense.

List of Artists

Akhurst, Basil Parry 'AKKI'
Alexander, Stephen Crighton
Audus, Leslie John
Bagnall, Stanley Evelyn
Barnes, Ronald David
Beckerley, John
Bettany, Desmond
Bevan, Gerald Archibald Johnstone
   'Archie'
Bird, Godfrey Victor
Brazil, Robert Guthrie
Burch, Edward
Cameron-Smith, Hamish Ninian
Chalker, Jack Bridger
Clarke, Derek
Clarke, Donovan 'Don'
Clement, John Francis

Coxhead, Geoffrey Shervill
Cullen, Walter
Duncan, Andrew Atholl
Elsey, Herbert
Elwell, Francis Kenneth
Excell, John
Ferron, Basil Elvin
Forbes, Wyndham Kinloch
Gale, John Kendell
Gamble, Robert James
Gee, Geoffrey Barlow
Gimson, George Stanley
Green, Maurice Charles
Hardie, Robert Stevenson
Hardy, Mike
Harris, John
Harrison, George William

Holdsworth, Charles Gilbert

James, Cholton Noel

Kemp, Jack Ernest

Kingsley, Harold 'Harry'

Kinmonth, Maurice Henry

Margarson, Fred

Meninsky, Philip

Mennie, John George 'Jack'

Milner-Moore, Aubrey Robert

Mitchell, Alfred Cromar

Munton, Geoffrey Charles

Newman, Reginald

Norways, William George 'Bill'

Old, Ashley George

Peach, Alfred Nowell Hamilton

Philps, Frank Richard

Pickersgill, Cecil Douglas

Power, Norman Hickey 'Freddie'

Pritchard, Norman H.

Pyment, Desmond Arthur

Ransome-Smith, Frederick William
  Henry 'Smudger'

Rawlings, Leo Oscar

Reid, Claude McLaren

Rivron, Malcolm Boakes

Rogers, Robert Roland

Russell, Stanley Kay

Scott-Lindsley, Mervyn

Searle, Ronald William Fordham

Silman, Harry

Spencer, Rex

Spittle, Ronald John 'Jack'

Stacy, Eric Francis

Stallard, Frederick Hugh 'Fred'

Strange, Stanley

Teale, Donald Eric

Thrale, Charles

Toze, Alan Vernon

Upton, Herbert Cooper

Wade, Tom Henling

Warren, Charles Stanley

White, John Wilbye Benson

Wilder, William Carthew 'Will'

Wilson, Thomas 'Toss'

Young, Alexander McGowan

Foreword by Stephen Walton
Imperial War Museums

In the Introduction to his book *To The Kwai – And Back: War Drawings 1939–1945* (first published in 1986) Ronald Searle, perhaps one of the best-known artistic recorders of the Far East prisoner of war (FEPOW) experience, wrote that during his captivity he had convinced himself that his mission *"was to emerge from the various camps, the jungle and finally prison, with a 'significant' pictorial record that would reveal to the world something of what happened during those lost and more or less unphotographed years"*. Searle had volunteered for the Army before the start of the Second World War, as a *"somewhat weedy scholarship student"* at the Cambridge School of Art, so his credentials as a budding professional artist were already established well before his experiences of Japanese captivity began. However, as with most of his fellow-captives, nothing prepared him for the relentless horror of those experiences, especially in the disease-ridden camps along the route of the infamous Burma–Thailand Railway which claimed the lives of almost 7,000 British POWs alone. That he managed to make and retain several hundred drawings in these conditions seems little short of miraculous. At the time, Searle's artistic activities served him *"as a mental life-belt"*. Forty years later, he could look on these works of art as *"the*

*graffiti of a condemned man, intending to leave rough witness of his passing through,
but who found himself – to his surprise and delight – among the reprieved"*.

Most of the Far East POWs whose artwork is featured in the present book did
not achieve Searle's postwar fame and public acclaim. They remained very
private men whose personal experiences, writings and drawings were mostly
known only to their immediate families and friends, and sometimes not even to
those until after their deaths. Nevertheless, many of them would undoubtedly
have identified with Searle's observations on art as a *"mental life-belt"* amidst the
disorientating, dehumanising and destructive conditions which threatened to –
or did – overwhelm them. They were indeed 'condemned men' who felt the need
to bear witness to and preserve a record, if at all possible, of the nightmarish
life they were forced to live. The majority of POW artists in this book were
fortunate to be able to count themselves *"among the reprieved"*, their artworks
often serving as a memorial to the men who could not do so.

What strikes even the most casual viewer of the artworks reproduced in
this book is the remarkable variety of their form, purpose, content and style.
There are cleverly-observed caricatures of FEPOW 'characters', humorous
cartoons of many aspects of camp life, evocative sketches, crayon drawings and
watercolours of camp structures and of the landscapes in which the prisoners
worked and moved, exquisite representations of some of the exotic insects,
birds, animals and plants which the POWs encountered, images drawn from
their memories of home, detailed plans of houses and other things they dreamed
of constructing when (if) they returned there, posters and programmes for
camp entertainments, and much more besides. It is sometimes easy to forget
that these works were indeed created by 'condemned men' whose lives could at
any time be – and so often were – catastrophically changed or ended altogether
by tropical disease, starvation, brutal treatment and overwork, day after
relentless day. Some of the other artworks serve as a shocking reminder of this
– the literally clinical drawings of ulcered limbs, wasted and distorted human
frames, improvised surgical equipment. They all in their own myriad ways
speak directly to us of their creators' desire to record the reality of what they saw
and experienced, to capture the beauty that existed alongside the bestial, the
humour and humanity alongside that which dehumanised. This art was also a
form of resistance and defiance, an assertion that the prisoners remained human

beings despite the best efforts of most of their captors to reduce them to less. Rarely have art and survival been so intimately linked.

This is an important book which interprets the FEPOW experience in new and often unexpected ways. It reveals the remarkable artistic and observational talent which flourished in the most adverse and unlikely circumstances, and amongst otherwise 'unremarkable' men – ordinary soldiers, fathers, husbands, brothers, who have left us with a scattered but rich visual record which fully deserves to be pulled together and brought into the light of public understanding. Hopefully this 'enquiry' will act as a catalyst and inspiration for the identification and preservation of further hidden works of FEPOW art.

Stephen Walton
Senior Curator
Second World War & Mid 20th Century
Imperial War Museums

"We are perhaps a unique colony, having amongst us men skilled in all the arts ..."

—Padre Eric Cordingly

Introduction

This collaborative book charts the Liverpool School of Tropical Medicine's (LSTM) Far East prisoner of war (or FEPOW) art enquiry. Since 2012 LSTM has been seeking out previously unrecognised artwork created by British FEPOW artists in captivity during the Second World War. Except for a handful of well-known artists, most of the men so far identified as artists are unknown to researchers or to the public. To date, over 65 artists and more than 500 pieces of artwork have been identified. Some FEPOW were trained artists, many were not. They created fine art studies, landscapes, cartoons, caricatures and portraits, in pencil sketches, pen and ink studies and watercolours. There is undoubtedly more artwork to be found.

This book is richly illustrated in colour throughout. There is a mini biography in a box next to the first illustration by each artist. This information helps readers to identify members of units, regiments, squadrons, places of captivity, as well as giving dates of birth and death and where each man was from. There is a full list of all these newly-recognised artists in Section IV.

The re-launched Captive Memories website (www.captivememories.org.uk) also has a comprehensive art section, showing more work by these artists, such is the volume of material that has come to light. Visual references are a vital component to better understanding the history of neglect, degradation and survival in hundreds of Allied prisoner of war camps scattered across thousands of miles of Southeast Asia and the Far East.

Why did so much artwork, created secretly and kept hidden during captivity, remain hidden for decades after liberation? Why was is created in secret? And why is so little known about the artists? Were they trained or just keen amateurs with a creative gift? These are some of the questions that we shall explore in this book.

For the benefit of those coming to this history for the first time some explanation is necessary. Relating to the need for secrecy, from the outset FEPOW knew the keeping of any form of record or to have writing materials, was generally not allowed. If found in possession of these items, or diaries, medical notes and drawings, they could expect punishment to be both swift and dire. Those who did keep records did so at great personal risk.

This was summed up by the Commanding Officer of the 2nd Battalion (Btn) The Loyal Regiment, Lieutenant Colonel Elrington DSO MC, who survived captivity in Singapore and Korea. In his handwritten Foreword, dated 19 April 1947, to an album of 12 home-made magazines entitled *Nor Iron Bars* (*NIB*) he paid tribute to the courage of his officers and the risks they had taken in creating and circulating the magazines in camp. Kept hidden and eventually brought home, they were presented to the regimental headquarters at Fulwood Barracks in Preston which is where they have remained for over 70 years.[1]

Elrington's words leave little doubt as to the consequences if discovered:

> "... *what* [the reader] *cannot comprehend is the enormity of the disciplinary offences committed by those responsible for 'N.I.B.', nor the grievous insults to the semi-divine Imperial Majesty of Japan which our innocently irreverent fun constituted in the slanting eyes of our primitive hosts. Offences such as these were, believe it or not, punishable by barbaric torture and death.*"

Why would men take such risks, especially considering that life under their Japanese captors was risky enough already? One answer is that keeping up morale in that way was worth the risk. It brought pleasure to men starved of stimulus. Life hung by a thread, and any way in which they could assert themselves, especially at the expense of their captors, was worth it. Another, more practical consideration is that there were very few cameras, or film that was usable, with which to record the realities of captivity. Cameras, watches, pens, anything of value, were either sold to buy food in the early months or stolen by the guards. Of course, there were exceptions, for example the teenage Australian POW, George Aspinall, whose extraordinary photographic record of life in camps in Singapore and Thailand was published in 1997.[2]

The family of one of the artists revealed by the enquiry came across previously unseen and unknown photographs kept by their father, William Norways (known as Bill). These had been taken by an unknown cameraman, when Bill's party arrived back to Singapore Island in spring 1944 after working on the Thai–Burma railway. He was sent to the large hospital camp at Kranji in the north of the island. The caption on the back of the photograph below (Figure 1) reads: *Planning a theatrical event in Kranji, 1944.* Bill Norways, a pre-war trained commercial artist, was heavily involved with all manner of theatrical productions putting his artistic skills to good use.

Figure 1. Photograph, *Planning a theatrical event in Kranji, 1944.* Bill Norways sitting drawing with Padre Wearne standing looking over his shoulder (© *courtesy the Norways family*)

Several secret photographs also exist, taken by officers of the 2nd Btn The Loyal Regiment. These appear in the previously mentioned *Nor Iron Bars* magazines, a rich compendium of articles and verse interspersed with artwork, including many skilful and amusing caricatures and cartoons, and these photographs. The photograph below (Figure 2), while slightly blurred, shows on the left one of the Other Ranks, Lance Bombardier Arthur Butler, 122nd Field Regiment from Louth in Lincolnshire, strutting his stuff as the incomparable, well-known and much-loved, 'Gloria d'Earie',[3] on stage performing in the 1943 Christmas festivities at Keijo camp in Korea. We shall return to Gloria and the artists of the 2nd Btn The Loyal Regiment and other Lancashire regiments in Chapter 3.

Figure 2.   Photograph of Gloria d'Earie
on stage, Christmas 1943, Keijo Korea
(© courtesy Lancashire Infantry Museum)

Such rare photographs are compelling evidence of not only the skill of the photographer but also the risks men took to capture such moments in captivity. While sometimes grainy, fuzzy, dark, or all three, they are captivating glimpses of the unending battle to survive. However, if a scene, an event or an item was to be recorded in camp, the only really reliable way was for an artist to do so. Most sketched quickly and with great discretion, especially when recording the medical work or examples of brutality. The documentary artist can show the viewer precisely what he wants them to see. Unlike a photographer he is not limited to timed exposure, light and shade, the condition of the film and how to safely store as well as conceal it. The artist reveals to the viewer what he can see in the moment, the smallest detail made clear.

Being forbidden to keep records was the general rule in Far East captivity. However, as with all rules there were at times exceptions; in some places and at different times artists were able to work more freely. For example, the well-known British FEPOW artist, Gunner Jack Chalker 118th Field Regiment, said in an interview with LSTM in 2007,

> *"I did quite a lot of drawing in Singapore, that was alright, we were not restricted there. Some of those sadly were lost but some survived ..."*[4]

The reason that Jack was not restricted in his artwork early on was because he was one of over 60,000 Allied prisoners of war herded into Changi POW camp on Singapore Island. In those early months the Japanese, initially overwhelmed by the sheer numbers of enemy personnel and civilians, largely left the POW to their own devices.

Gunner William Wilder 135th Field Regiment (known as Will), like Jack, had studied art pre-war. He was moved from Changi POW camp to Bukit Timah POW work camp (also referred to as Sime Road camp) in Singapore in May 1942 as part of the party sent to build the Japanese Shinto Shrine on the golf course. He was able to sketch quite openly, including painting a world map in what was called the 'reading room' in camp,[5] and was even commissioned by the Japanese Commandant to sketch the building work on the shrine during the summer of 1942. However, as Jack, Will and the other artists and diarists soon discovered, this particular 'freedom' was not to last long.

Unlike British captives in European captivity held by the Germans and Italians, FEPOW had no realistic chance of escape. Put simply, as Caucasians they could not hide among an Asian population and to have tried would have brought fearful retribution upon those hiding them. Neither were the camps subject to regular monitoring visits from the International Committee of the Red Cross (ICRC). FEPOW were not allowed access to ICRC representatives or newspaper correspondents. Apart from a handful of stage-managed ICRC propaganda visits to selected camps in the early part of captivity, FEPOW were effectively cut off from their families and the world. They were completely isolated. How were they to record the monumental struggle to survive? And why would they want to take the risk?

It is important to note that all LSTM's FEPOW medical, and medical history, research studies have focused on the British military experience in captivity and the post-release physical and psychological aftermath for these veterans. LSTM has not worked with former Far East civilian captives as a group. It also follows therefore, that the focus is on men, as women did not serve on the frontline in the Forces in the 1940s.

The names of camps and some places vary enormously in the literature. The authors have endeavoured to use one spelling in each case, while acknowledging that many other versions exist.

The authors

The three authors contributing to this book bring specific experience and expertise to the understanding of FEPOW history, as well as different perspectives on the documentary artwork. While all three have collaborated on the text throughout, to assist the reader the book has been divided into four sections: this enables each writer to speak from their perspective and in their own voice and style. The fourth section contains subsidiary information.

Meg Parkes has a personal connection as the daughter of a FEPOW, Captain Andrew Atholl Duncan, Argyll & Sutherland Highland Regiment. He survived captivity in Java and Japan. Her interest in his FEPOW experiences began in 1972 when in her late teens she asked to read his diary. As well as his detailed account written throughout captivity, filling nine pilfered school exercise books and homemade notebooks, he also showed her the pencil sketches and three detailed camp plans he had made in camps in Java and Japan.

It was these drawings that excited her interest. They depicted the ordinary things, such as the latrines (see Chapter 4, Figure 61) or the interior of his hut at Zentsuji in Japan (see Chapter 4, Figure 15). The sketches were created not by an artist but a capable draughtsman, using skills honed while studying engineering pre-war. Reading his diaries, it was clear how, during the winter months in Japan he had dreaded washing as it was so cold. The sketch of his hut gave a glimpse at what leaving bed to go for a wash, or to the toilet at night, would have been like.

Why was Meg not familiar with these drawings and why had he kept them out of sight for so long? What motivated him take such great personal risks to create and keep them? These and other questions are addressed in Section I, which also gives a brief outline of FEPOW history, how and why LSTM embarked on the FEPOW art enquiry and what it has revealed.

Geoff Gill worked in Liverpool as an NHS consultant physician and academic professor at the University of Liverpool and the School of Tropical Medicine. He first worked at LSTM in 1975 (prior to medical duties in Africa), where for the first time, he became involved with the care of former Far East POWs admitted for investigation (and if necessary treatment) of the long-term effects of their captivity. He joined a small but dedicated group of doctors, nurses and scientists (led by the charismatic Dr Dion Bell, Senior Lecturer and later Reader in Tropical Medicine, and Honorary Consultant Physician). At the time, the patients were cared for at Sefton General Hospital – at other times in Mossley Hill and the Royal Liverpool hospitals. LSTM had been involved in Far East POW health assessments since late1945, and this was to continue until 1999. Other tropical physicians were involved before and after Dion Bell, but he led the 'FEPOW Unit' during the especially busy years of the mid and late 1970s and the 1980s. Dr Bell became Geoff Gill's mentor and inspiration to lead the FEPOW medical research, with a number of clinical and scientific colleagues, over the ensuing 20 years or more.

Section II will introduce newly-uncovered artwork illustrating camp life and some of the extraordinary medical artwork that has come to light both from archives and private collections. FEPOW artist Jack Chalker, one of the best known of the British artists of captivity, was a patient at LSTM. He donated a photographic set of his artwork to LSTM's FEPOW archives in the 1980s.

Jenny Wood has a professional interest in the artworks of war having worked at the Imperial War Museums in London for over 38 years. She joined the Art Department of the IWM in 1976 with a French degree from Warwick University and a knowledge of stagecraft from a stint as Property Mistress in a rep theatre company. Her initial role as art technician used those practical display skills and, as her knowledge of the art collection grew, she also dealt with a steady stream of research visitors.

She was part of a cohort of young curators who began to research small exhibitions drawn from lesser-known parts of the IWM collections. One of these shows 'Captive' in 1978, was a display of Far East POW drawings, curated by Vivienne Crawford. This was Jenny's first introduction to the arresting quality and fragility of these drawings and led to an abiding curiosity about the motivation of artists to draw in such adverse and threatening circumstances.

As conservation manager she programmed the remedial care and mounting of Ronald Searle's gift of over 400 FEPOW drawings in the mid-1980s. Later, in 2005, she curated another, larger 'Captive' exhibition, putting the 'unofficial' FEPOW drawings into the context of the official war artists' Far East works.

In 2011–12 Jenny had the privilege of collaborating with Rod Suddaby, Keeper of the Documents Archive, on a joint review of the IWM FEPOW art holdings in the art and documents collections. Rod Suddaby was, according to his obituary in *The Times* newspaper on 1 July 2013,

> "… one of the outstanding museum curators of his generation. His entire career was spent in the Imperial War Museum and for 37 years he served as Keeper of the Department of Documents. In that role he personally assembled what is globally recognised as one of the largest and most important collections of private papers, ranging from those of ordinary citizens to the most senior soldiers."

It is impossible to calculate how many FEPOW veterans or their relatives, WWII historians, authors and journalists, Rod helped over the years, such was his encyclopaedic knowledge and attention to detail.

Rod had an irrepressible delight in connecting people, not only with the IWM's collections but also with each other. Jenny and Rod's collaboration on the joint review of IWM's FEPOW holdings resulted in a much broader understanding of the significance of these works as witness and as therapy. The combined collections of art and documents are now the largest and most comprehensive in the UK. Jenny and Rod were two of a kind: quietly-spoken, informed, curious, immensely knowledgeable and generous-spirited.

In Section III Jenny explores the newly-identified artwork in the context of her experience of other war art and that of official war artists. She will examine the discipline of art therapy and its role in the recovery of service men and women traumatised by war in modern times. To what extent did FEPOW artists utilise art therapy as a survival strategy?

Shortly before LSTM's FEPOW art enquiry got underway, in early 2012 Meg and Jenny were introduced and over the next year or two Meg spent time becoming acquainted with IWM's FEPOW art collection. The findings of the newly-completed and substantial audit report compiled by Jenny, charted newly-identified material. Her depth of knowledge and understanding of the artwork produced by FEPOW artists during captivity is immense and she has shared her time unstintingly from the start of the enquiry.

When Meg and Geoff decided to write this book to share all they had uncovered to date, they were keenly aware that as neither had any formal art training or knowledge they would need a collaborator; someone with specific expertise in, and a knowledge of, art, the history of war art and of war artists, as reflected in the IWM's and other national war art collections. They asked Jenny.

Section IV contains a tribute to Ashley George Old and the personal reflections written by relatives of many of the newly-identified artists. Endnotes have been used where necessary to aid further enquiry and the book is completed with a comprehensive index.

The exhibition

The **Secret Art of Survival: Creativity and ingenuity of British Far East POW 1942–1945**, was hosted by the University of Liverpool's Victoria Gallery & Museum (VG&M) from 25 October 2019 to 20 June 2020, closing just ahead of the 75th anniversary of the end of the Second World War and VJ Day, on 15 August.

The exhibition was the result of a partnership between LSTM and the University of Liverpool, supported by funding from the National Lottery Heritage Fund, a successful Crowdfunding appeal in 2018, and the vital early-stage support from the Researching FEPOW History Group (RFHG), Birmingham FEPOW Association, COFEPOW (Children and families of FEPOW) and the National FEPOW Fellowship Remembrance Association (NFFWRA). It was also supported by other FEPOW-related groups and clubs.

The VG&M is situated in the original University College building at the top of Brownlow Hill, now at the heart of what is known as Liverpool's Knowledge Quarter. It occupies the magnificent Victorian building, replete with an ornate clock tower rising over the university campus. Exquisitely tiled inside throughout, the VG&M provides both an impressive and yet intimate exhibition space over three floors.

Almost 100 items of FEPOW artwork were chosen from over 500 pieces revealed by the enquiry. They came mainly from private collections with some items from major museums and archives. The exhibition was grouped under four themes: camp life, survival, medical ingenuity, environment and included paintings, pencil sketches and pen and ink drawings, as well as creative artworks such as carvings. A single piece of embroidery created by one of the best-known of the British artists and only recently discovered, gave yet another fascinating insight into the need for those with artistic gifts to create beauty amid chaos, fear and despair.

Many of these tangible relics of Far East captivity have not been seen in public before. They are very personal items; lasting reminders of survival to the creator and now treasured heirlooms for their descendants. They hint at the need within some human beings to find a practical outlet to cope with adversity. The act of creating something from nothing may even have become a form of therapy to calm frayed nerves by the channelling of creative endeavour. At the very least, it would have helped occupy the mind, providing a distraction from the all-pervading realities of daily existence. For those responsible for medical care – doctors, orderlies and volunteers – this must have been, at times, life-saving; a counter-balance to the relentless tide of disease, despair and death in the 'hospital' huts of jungle camps.

Some of the drawings and paintings exhibited at VG&M feature in this book, along with many more examples from the reservoir of talent uncovered; others will be showcased on the website where, eventually, all the exhibits will be available, forming a lasting legacy of the enquiry.

Due to the nature of their captivity and the unpredictability of their captors, most FEPOW lived in a permanent state of fear that dominated waking hours and often also their sleep. Japanese and Korean guards had total control over their captives' lives; some were ignorant sadistic bullies. There were of course exceptions. One thing to come out of the oral history interviews was the number of veterans who made a point of stating for the record that they had witnessed or experienced occasional acts of kindness from guards.

A FEPOW's life changed at the whim of their captors. At times the only constant was the haunting sound of the Last Post heralding yet another young man's death. Life, and keeping it, became a relentless lottery. Not surprisingly then, that this was the reality that shaped many men's post-war years; lives often blighted by severe, undiagnosed and untreated psychological disturbance. This was one of the findings to come out of medical research studies carried out at LSTM by Geoff Gill and by Dr Kamaluddin Khan. Dr Khan, an NHS psychiatrist, conducted his own academic study with FEPOW patients referred from LSTM's FEPOW unit.[6]

LSTM–FEPOW studies

The Liverpool School of Tropical Medicine was founded in 1898 and is the oldest such institution in the world. In 2013 the School achieved higher education institution status and in 2017 was granted degree-awarding powers by the Privy Council, thereby creating Liverpool's fifth university.

LSTM's foundation had come just a few years after the creation of the University College of Liverpool in 1881 (which in 1903 became the University of Liverpool). In the 1880s as a collegiate institution it was linked to the University Colleges of Leeds and Manchester, three of the six original 'red brick' universities. Throughout the decades of the FEPOW collaboration, LSTM was affiliated to the university. Therefore, it is fitting that the FEPOW *Secret Art of Survival* exhibition should be hosted by the university's historic Victoria Museum & Gallery.

FEPOW healthcare, medical and scientific research, new diagnostic developments and latterly medical history research, are the basis of LSTM's FEPOW research studies. This is the longest-running project in LSTM's history, lasting to date over 74 years. The medical research papers and journal articles are available through the Captive Memories website.[7]

This book is a companion volume to two previous books co-authored by Geoff and Meg. While underpinned by rigorous academic research, both were written for general readership. *Captive Memories* (2015) was published by Palatine Books in the 70th anniversary year of VJ Day. It features Meg's FEPOW oral history interviews with 67 FEPOW and 10 wives and widows. Significantly, it also charts for the first time the unique collaboration between FEPOW patients and medical staff at LSTM which began in late 1945.

Burma Railway Medicine (2017) is the first in-depth analysis, from a British perspective, of the medical crisis to befall Allied POW doctors in camps along the Thai–Burma railway. This book is once again published by Palatine Books. Unlike the previous two which were based on individual academic studies, *Captive Artists* is of necessity a work in progress, the result of LSTM's investigation into the artwork. It gives a vivid visual insight into aspects of the social and medical history of the FEPOW experience.

In the first part of the Introduction it was stated that LSTM's FEPOW studies concerned the experiences of the military captives, i.e. it was ex-military patients who were seen in Liverpool and not civilians who had also been held in Far East captivity. The terminology around military and civilian captivity can cause some confusion: the term for military personnel held captive by the enemy is 'prisoners of war', or POW. There were also large numbers of British civilians (and other nationalities) caught up in the rapid capitulation of successive western colonial powers: the families who had made up the colonial administration and business communities for many generations. To distinguish between combatants and civilians, the latter are known as 'civilian internees' or CIs.

Naturally, British civilian internees also returned to Britain sick and damaged by their years of dreadful hardship and neglect, but in the early months and years post-war it was not they who appeared at LSTM. It was the veterans: the sick, newly-demobbed, former prisoners of war who from late 1945 onwards slowly began to seek medical advice and help. Despite their long incarceration in the tropics, no special provision had been made for their medical needs once they had left the Forces. Understandably, most of them wanted to get back to their families and try to pick up civilian lives. In hindsight it seems scandalous that in releasing them from service the authorities effectively cut them adrift, leaving them to manage on their own with no adequate medical supervision. This, despite the powers-that-be being in no doubt about the effects of prolonged ill-treatment and ill-health, both clearly visible in the men's physical condition upon repatriation. We should also bear in mind that visiting a doctor was expensive in pre-NHS Britain, and these men were suffering myriad and complex health problems.

So, FEPOW did what they had been conditioned to do to survive, they coped by using whatever means they could. At first just a few, and then over time gradually more sick men from across the north of England, started to be referred and to fill beds in Liverpool's hospitals.

FEPOW Art Enquiry

This book is about an art enquiry, a survey, an investigation. It is not a formal academic research study. No ethics approval or detailed methodology was sought or required. Researchers set out to locate and discover previously unseen artwork created by FEPOW during Far East captivity. (NB artworks created from memory in later life have not been included in this enquiry). Each artist's work was examined and interpreted and as much information about each man was sought. This enquiry is a work in progress.

In 2012 the Wellcome Trust, convinced of its value as a factfinding enquiry, awarded a travel grant enabling Meg to travel around the UK, and to visit Singapore and Jakarta. It was not possible to visit all the potential archives or regimental collections that may hold FEPOW artwork around the UK. There is undoubtedly still more artwork to be identified.

In publishing the investigation and exhibiting some of the art during 2019 and 2020, LSTM is marking the 75th anniversary of VJ Day and the repatriation of FEPOW. It is hoped that this may stimulate more personal archives to come to the surface; that the artwork so far uncovered will act as a catalyst for others to want to explore the Far East prisoner of war experience through its visual history. Perhaps this may lead to further academic research. We apologise if we have missed any artist from this enquiry and if you know of others please do get in touch via the website (www.captivememories.org.uk). We intend to add new discoveries of artwork created during captivity to the virtual archive being created to showcase this work long after the exhibition has closed.

Section I charts where the artwork was found and introduces the 69 newly uncovered artists. Section II will add context to the artwork related to camp life and medicine. Studying the pictures closely – the differing landscapes of captivity, portraits, greetings cards, cartoons, images of medical ingenuity and survival – makes the viewer question what was in the mind of the artist at the time he sketched or painted. Using a magnifying glass picks up the fine detail and raises yet more questions, not least of which, why and how did they do this? Having examined the literature, sometimes left by an artist or in other written accounts, we have learned what materials were used and where they came from.

Section III explores how FEPOW art fits into the history of war art at the Imperial War Museum, Britain's largest museum collection dedicated to the two world wars of the twentieth century. It references the role of art therapy as an effective tool in helping to repair and rebuild the shattered minds and bodies of Britain's military over the past hundred years. And it will endeavour to answer the question, Were FEPOW artists using art therapy unconsciously? Was it the instinct to create something of and for themselves, to be keepsakes and talismanic objects, or for others to enjoy, that made them take such great risks?

It is important to make brief mention of a few of the artists from other nationalities who are not represented by this enquiry: Australian official war artists Murray Griffin and Keith Neighbour; New Zealanders Lt William 'Bill' Bourke (Sumatra railway) and newspaper cartoonist Sid Scales (Java); Dutch artists like Otto van Kleef and Flip Relf; Americans such as US Navy officer Kenneth Schacht (universally known as 'Buck') and fellow US naval officer, Lt W. C. Johnson. There are many more. To reiterate, this enquiry has focused exclusively on British military artists and perspective.

We are also aware of the art and creative art made by many Britons held in civilian internment in the Far East. In Singapore, for example, Charles Haxworthy and Dr David Molesworth (Changi Gaol, Singapore). Molesworth did the watercolour illustrations for the first edition of the 'Birds of Malaya' by Guy Madoc.[8] This phenomenal work, typed from memory and richly illustrated, was bound into a hard-back book by two French bookbinders also held in Changi Gaol. The women artists include Iris Parfitt (Sime Road, Singapore) whose wonderfully vivid cameos of women surviving captivity were published by her post-war in 'Jail-Bird Jottings, the impressions of a Singapore Internee'; Margaret Dryburgh, the Scottish Presbyterian missionary who escaped Shanghai only to arrive in Singapore shortly before the Japanese. The evacuation ship was bombed by the Japanese off Sumatra. Margaret and other survivors were held initially at the women's camp at Palembang and later scattered elsewhere in the jungles of southern Sumatra. Her simple sketches and evocative music and poetry enrich all who know of them, both then and now.[9] Daphne Bird, wife of FEPOW artist Godfrey Bird who together with her son Derek, and her vivid artwork, survived internment camp in the Philippines. Mother and son were reunited with Godfrey soon after liberation.

There were of course many internee artists of other nationalities, such as Australian internee Leslie Greener who wrote *The Happiness Book* for the children interned in Changi Gaol in Singapore. These few and many others all left an indelible record of life in civilian captivity in the Far East for future generations to learn from.

This investigation has turned the spotlight on a fascinating and still little-known aspect of Second World War history, brought to life for a new generation by the skill and creativity of 69 previously unrecognised British military artists to whom this book is dedicated.

As well as the exhibition in Liverpool during 2019–20, there is also LSTM's dedicated FEPOW history website – www.captivememories.org.uk – which provides a legacy, rich in resources for future enquiry and study. Let us now find out what these artists did, how they did it and what their work can teach us over 75 years after it was secretly created, now that more of it has finally come out of hiding.

SECTION I

Meg Parkes

CHAPTER 1

Documenting Captivity

Curiosity about finding previously unknown or unseen art of Far East captivity was first sparked by FEPOW veterans, interviewed for LSTM's FEPOW oral history study, sharing what they had made or kept. These sketches, watercolours, cartoons, greetings cards and artefacts had been treasured for over 65 years.

What has been revealed by the enquiry is the creative artwork of 69 unrecognised British FEPOW artists. They are referred to as 'unrecognised' because their names and much of their work are not familiar to either FEPOW research or to the public. Much of this artwork remains in private hands, some is in archives and museum collections but little of it has been seen, studied and really understood.

There are eight 'recognised' and celebrated British Far East prisoner of war (FEPOW) artists well-known to researchers for the quality, range and quantity of their work. They are: Gunners Chalker, Meninsky, Old and Rawlings, Sapper Searle, L/Bdr Mennie, Cpl Thrale and Lt Gimson. Perhaps the best known of these are Ronald Searle and Jack Chalker. The contribution made by these well-known artists to history's understanding of this subject is remarkable.

However, this book is concerned with highlighting the work of the many other men – the 'unrecognised' artists – whose work has come to light as a result of the enquiry. They too have contributed greatly to our knowledge and it is time that they too, are recognised. Among these artists several will be featured in greater detail, for example 'AKKI' Akhurst, Leslie Audus and Richard Philps. And the spotlight will also be turned on the work of George Old which is not well-known despite being recognised as one of the most accomplished of the medical artists.

A few of the 69 men exhibited their wartime art, or published their memoirs in later life, for example Stephen Alexander's *Sweet Kwai Run Softly* and Will Wilder's biography, *PoW Sketchbook, A story of Survival*, both published in 1995. Leslie Audus' *Spice Island Slaves* was published in 1996.

Other memoirs have been published posthumously, including Richard Philps' *Prisoner Doctor*, Robert Hardie's *The Burma-Siam Railway* and Atholl Duncan's *'Notify Alec Rattray ...'* Others were printed for private publication, like Thomas Wilson's *War Diary*, a slim paperback that the family made in the mid-1980s, around the time that his original diaries were donated to the Imperial War Museums (IWM) in 1984 (following an appeal by the museum for Second World War memorabilia). Several artists, including Will Wilder, AKKI and Old, have artwork held in major museum archives such as the IWM, the Wellcome Collection and the National Army Museum (NAM).

There is much more artwork and many more artists than at first imagined. Inevitably, most of these men were no longer alive when the investigation began in 2012 (except Jack Chalker). Most of the unrecognised artwork was found in private family collections; artwork is also held by the families of FEPOW to whom it was given during captivity. It is revered and treasured by these new custodians who have become the artworks' unofficial curators.

As there are so many artists to introduce, for the sake of clarity when revealing each artist, his name when first mentioned in conjunction an example of his artwork will appear in larger, bold text at the start of the paragraph, followed by a colon. Alongside this first example of his artwork a text box will give the artist's brief biographical details. If reference is made to same artist later in relation to other examples of his artwork, his name will again be in bold (but not enlarged and without the colon).

A personal perspective

I make no apology for writing this section from my personal perspective. My father was a FEPOW. He survived. This history, for me as for many thousands of other FEPOW descendants, is personal. Dad was a proud Scot, born and raised in St Andrews, Fife. In October 1939 he took a commission with the Highland Light Infantry (Figure 1) and was drafted to France in January 1940.

Shortly after arriving in France his transfer came through and he joined the machine gun unit of the 6th Btn Argyll & Sutherland Highlanders. Evading capture in Normandy in June 1940, by January 1941 he had been drafted to join the Argyll's 2nd Btn, serving as part of Singapore's garrison forces. A year later, he was senior cipher officer on British Headquarters (HQ) staff when HQ was hurriedly transferred to Java just a month before Singapore fell to the Japanese on 15 February 1942. He spent the first eight months of captivity in Tandjong Priok camp north of Batavia (now Jakarta) before being shipped to a coalmining camp in Japan in late 1942 where the identification photograph (Figure 2) was taken.

Figure 1.   2nd Lt A. A. Duncan,
Highland Light Infantry (HLI) 1939
(© courtesy the Duncan family)

Figure 2. Japanese ID photograph at Motoyama POW camp, Japan, January 1943 (© courtesy the Duncan family)

Captain A.A. Duncan

Figure 3. Capt. Duncan, left, with friend Lt Bill Balfour RE, Miyata, Japan, late August 1945 while awaiting liberation (© courtesy the Duncan family)

The Japanese camp ID photograph above reveals how the fresh-faced young man has been transformed after nearly two years in the tropics and 10 months in captivity. Now compare the images above with this one.

This photograph (Figure 3) was taken in late August 1945. Duncan is on the left (by now aged 27). He is painfully thin, his sunken eyes staring unwaveringly into the lens. There is the barest hint of a smile. By that time, according to the weight chart in his diary, he weighed just six and a half stone (he was 5' 10" tall). He is seated next to fellow officer, Lieutenant Bill Balfour RE. At last free to move around, they had left Miyata coalmine (his third camp in Japan) to go into the nearby village of the same name, where they visited a Korean dentist (standing with his family in the background).

Dad kept a diary. Reading it at the age of 19 was what had sparked my need to understand more about his war. He was not a diarist, before the war or after. I find myself still asking the same questions now as I did then, *"How did he survive? How do you do that?"* He used to say he was one of the lucky ones, *"I didn't have it so bad, not compared to others*" being his usual response to questions about being a POW. He was referring to those in Thailand, Sumatra and North Borneo building railways through jungles and also the many victims of forced marches.

However, he had endured two dreadful and dangerous sea voyages, battened down in the holds of small tramp steamers and his final camp, at the Miyata coalmines, was just 60 miles due north of Nagasaki. There he heard the long, low rubble of the exploding atomic bomb, though had no idea what it meant at the time. His retrospective notes, written in camp as they waited to be evacuated, make clear things at Miyata had been very bad at the end. The POW, like the population of Japan, were starving. The guards had waged a terrifying psychological war against the POW in the months to mid-August.

I grew up, like many others, knowing that my father hated the Japanese. He could never forgive them and that never changed. He was not a military man at heart; like millions of men he did his duty, served his country. He was captured, but mercifully survived.

I came to learn just how lucky I was to have his diary as my source material. In 1997 following my parents' deaths, I became the family custodian, having spent the preceding twenty years transcribing the diary (for myself and my sisters). Five years later I self-published it, feeling an instinctive need to share what he had documented. It was publishing that indirectly led to me working at LSTM five years later, where I have immersed myself in FEPOW history, honing skills in researching, writing and presenting in order to share what I have learned as widely as possible.

The reason I have started this section with family history is because my father drew sketches and camp plans, which he showed me when I first read the diary. He was not an artist but had learned technical drawing at university. We will return to his artwork shortly.

What follows is a background to the war in the Far East and an outline of captivity for the 50,000 British servicemen who account for almost a third of the 140,000 Allied Forces taken captive by the Japanese, between Christmas Day 1941 and 7 April 1942.

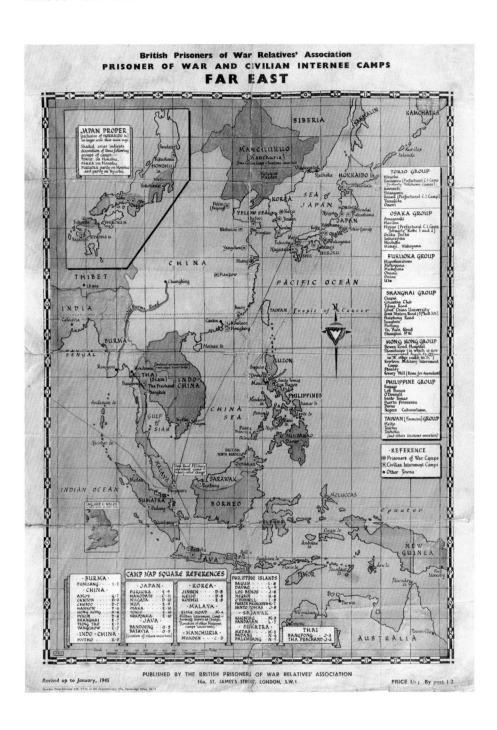

Figure 4. 1945 map of POW camps in the Far East, produced for
British relatives of Far East captives

The Imperial Japanese Forces entered the Second World War in December 1941 with their surprise assault on the American Fleet at Pearl Harbour on 7 December 1941. Within hours of this Japanese forces were also making simultaneous landings on the eastern shores of British Malaya, Thailand and the Philippine Islands and had initiated their attack on Hong Kong. This was their 'lightening war', which saw the eradication of almost 500 years of western colonial rule in the Far East, within five months.

Hong Kong was the first British colony to surrender, on Christmas Day 1941, after a brief and ferocious battle with approximately 8,000 Allied forces captured. Seven weeks later, on 15 February 1942, the strategically vital British garrison at Singapore was also forced to into a humiliating capitulation. Tens of thousands of Allied servicemen laid down their weapons (around 30,000 of whom were British). On 8 March the whole of the Dutch East Indies surrendered, including several thousand British servicemen diverted from Singapore in the final desperate weeks. Then finally, a month later, on 7 April, the Americans lost the Philippines.

Allied prisoners of war were largely made up of the British and their colonial forces from Australia, New Zealand, Canada and India, and of course the Dutch and Americans as well. The Japanese declared a new Eastern empire – the so-called Greater East Asia Co-Prosperity Sphere – under their rule. Japan had needed control of the vast and resource-rich colonies primarily for the raw materials – tin, rubber and oil – essential to wage industrial warfare. Their goal was to take India and Australia from the British, but to achieve that they needed not only the raw materials but also endless supplies of manpower to build the airfields and ships and to create and maintain vital supply lines to the battlefront.

Initially the Japanese were overwhelmed by the sheer numbers of POW, as well as many thousands of civilians. Despite Japan being a signatory to the 1929 Geneva Conventions they had refused to ratify the treaty in 1931. They therefore felt under no obligation to care for captives. Besides this, they had no concept of the act of surrender. To the ancient Japanese military code of Bushido which, from the early 1920s, had underpinned the aggressive, expansionist policies of their military-led government, this was anathema, unthinkable. Bushido is the Samurai code of honour requiring obedience and absolute loyalty, life meant nothing; warriors were either victorious or they died on the battlefield. It was inconceivable to a Japanese fighter to be captured by the enemy, to retreat or surrender as this would bring lasting shame not only to the individual but also his family and ancestors.

Initially, with no provision for prisoners of war, the Japanese herded large numbers of enemy personnel into holding camps wherever they were gathered – airfields, barrack blocks, schools – leaving Allied senior officers to organise and discipline their men. In large camps like Changi POW camp in Singapore or Bandoeng POW camp in central Java, with thousands of demoralised, isolated and depressed men crammed into overcrowded buildings with inadequate sanitation or food, Allied medical officers quickly realised that the potential for medical crisis was huge. The lack of clean water, attention to personal hygiene, overcrowding and meaningful medical provision, combined with the loss of self-discipline, would inevitably lead to unstoppable outbreaks of dysentery and other infectious diseases. With the understanding and co-operation of Allied senior officers Army discipline was soon imposed and the immediate risk to health reduced.

In addition to the fighting forces captured there were also tens of thousands of civilian men, women and children, who were trapped in the colonies when the war started. They too endured years of captivity, hardship and gross neglect in overcrowded multinational internment camps, mostly in the tropics but also in Hong Kong and China in the north.

Within a couple of months, the Japanese had organised the POWs into working parties needed to restore transport and supply systems, clear bomb damage and in the ports to get the docks functioning so that men and goods could be sent where they were needed. Work regimes were tough, treatment meted out by guards at times brutal. FEPOW learned quickly that their captors were irascible and unpredictable; punishment for minor infringements were both swift and painful. Before long, large numbers of FEPOW were being transported from holding camps to areas where major construction projects were being planned.

In Southeast Asia large drafts of POW left Changi POW camp for Thailand and later Sumatra, to build railways through raw jungle, creating supply routes to Japan's front lines; drafts were also sent from Java to Thailand, Singapore, Borneo and Japan. The first parties to arrive in Japan came from Hong Kong, providing slave labourers to replace young Japanese workers drafted into the defence of Japan's new empire and the battles raging in Burma and the Pacific. Airfields were built on coral islands in the Celebes (the Spice Islands) in readiness for Japan's planned assault on Australia. The losses among FEPOW there were appalling.

This is the backdrop to Far East captivity. The ensuing three and a half years took an enormous toll on FEPOW, due mainly to slavery and gross physical and mental neglect. Living with a permanent sense of fear and anxiety, watching young men in their prime die needless and dreadful deaths, left scars that for some would never heal. Of the 50,000 British FEPOW, approximately 25% per cent died during captivity. In contrast, during European captivity fewer than 5% of British POW died.

After the sudden end of the war following the dropping of two atomic bombs in early August 1945, the process of liberating the camps took a few weeks. Some FEPOW were too sick to embark on the long journey home and were hospitalised in the care of repatriation medical staff in hospitals in Singapore, Rangoon, the Philippines, Australia and New Zealand, depending on where captives were located, and which nation liberated the camps. The sickest men evacuated from the camps in Burma and Thailand remained in hospital in Rangoon and Bangkok, later stopping at Colombo or being hospitalised again in India, before being deemed fit enough to embark on the long sea journey home. The two-month-long voyage home was believed to be beneficial, allowing time to recover physically and mentally and to begin the long process of adjustment necessary for building future lives.

FEPOW and Liverpool

From 7 October 1945 onwards, repatriation ships sailed into Southampton and Liverpool, the latter being the port many thousands of servicemen had left from four years earlier. After a cursory medical consultation in transit camps set up on Southampton Common or in the towns of Maghull and Huyton on the outskirts of Liverpool, FEPOW medical papers were stamped A1 Fit and men given train warrants, taken to the nearest railway station for the next train to home towns and cities up and down the country. Among them was Lance Bombardier Desmond

Figure 5. *Lancashire Evening Gazette,* 9 October 1945 front page. Des Bettany second left *(© courtesy T. Lightbown)*

BACK from Far East prison camps, these men, after landing from the Monowai at Liverpool, call at the N.A.A.F.I. canteen at their transit camp. It was their happiest day for nearly four years. Left to right (front): L/Bdr. D. Betney and Gnr. T. Smith, of Lancaster; L/Bdr. G. Haworth, Preston; Gnr. E. Munn, Fordway-avenue, Blackpool; Gnr. F. Munktelelow (Blackpool Regiment), Devon, and Bdr. J. Stanworth (Blackpool Regiment), Nelson. Inset: Cpl. G. W. Smith, Glen Eldon-road, St. Annes. (See story on Page Six.)

Bettany 88th Field Regiment from Burnley in Lancashire, seen far left in this *Lancashire Evening Gazette* photograph on 9 October 1945 (Figure 5), with the NAAFI tea lady on his right (the caption has his name misspelt as Betney). These men had just landed in Liverpool on the *Monowai* to a heroes' welcome.

Bettany had trained as an analytical chemist in an artificial silk factory in Burnley pre-war. A prolific and accomplished cartoonist, he was one of the notable artists in Singapore camps. He remained on the island throughout and was heavily involved in theatricals, designing and painting sets and scenery and producing programmes for all manner of entertainments. This seems to have influenced his post-war decision to change careers, as he studied art at Leeds before becoming a tertiary art teacher at a college in South Shields. In 1958 the family emigrated to Australia. We shall learn more about Bettany's art work in Chapter 2.

Though many men were still suffering the after-effects of malnutrition and tropical diseases they wanted to get home as quickly as possible. By Christmas that year the majority had been back at home for a few weeks. Over half of all repatriated British FEPOW landed at Liverpool between 8 October and mid-December 1945. The MV *Monowai* (Figure 6) arrived in Liverpool the day after the first repatriation ship to make British shores, the SS *Corfu* (Figure 7) arrived

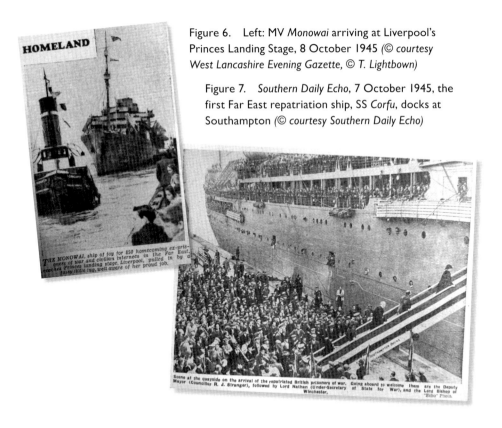

Figure 6.   Left: MV *Monowai* arriving at Liverpool's Princes Landing Stage, 8 October 1945 *(© courtesy West Lancashire Evening Gazette, © T. Lightbown)*

Figure 7.   *Southern Daily Echo*, 7 October 1945, the first Far East repatriation ship, SS *Corfu*, docks at Southampton *(© courtesy Southern Daily Echo)*

in Southampton. These two press cuttings capture the moment as both ships docked just a few hours apart.

In 2010 the Researching FEPOW History Group (RFHG https://fepowhistory.com/) began a nationwide fundraising campaign to create lasting memorials marking the repatriation of all Far East captives (both military and civilian). The first memorial was placed near the waterfront in Liverpool and two years

Figure 8.   Liverpool Pier Head 15 October 2011, Remembrance Service at Liverpool's Repatriation Memorial dedicated to the memory of all Far East captives *(© courtesy RFHG)*

29

later the second in Southampton. The Liverpool Repatriation Memorial was unveiled by FEPOW veterans on the Pier Head, on Saturday 15 October 2011 (Figure 8). Over 650 people attended the Service of Remembrance, including 300 invited veterans and their relatives from across the UK, local schoolchildren, Air Training, Army and Naval cadets, and civic dignitaries. The rest were members of the public who had wanted to pay their respects.

On the Pier Head the granite plaque faces the river, mounted on a low stone edifice just up river from the old Princes Landing Stage where the ships had moored. Both plaques list the ships that docked in each port during a two-month period from early October to mid-December 1945, either side of the same central dedication. Both memorials also pay tribute to the many thousands who did not return.

In Figure 9 FEPOW veteran Steve Cairns, centre, former FEPOW National Welfare Adviser (and an early post-war patient at LSTM) accompanied by Mrs Peggy Cooke, widow of FEPOW Bill Cooke RN, lead the walk past the memorial.

In Southampton, on Sunday 27 October 2013, a similar granite memorial plaque was unveiled by FEPOW veterans in Town Quay Park, after a Remembrance Service at St Michael's Church. The plaque is fixed to a remnant of Victorian

Figure 9. FEPOW lead walk past the newly-unveiled Liverpool Repatriation Memorial, 15 October 2011 *(© courtesy RFHG)*

Figure 10. November 2018 – former Royal Engineers Sapper, Bob Hucklesby, centre, aged 98, flanked by standard bearers remembering Far East captives who returned to Southampton in the autumn of 1945 *(© courtesy Friends of Town Quay Park)*

house wall at the heart of this small community park and is surrounded by bamboo and grasses reflecting the history of captivity. The park lies on the edge of Southampton's historic network of medieval streets, adjacent to Huguenot Gardens and next door to St John's primary school. Opposite the wall the RFHG team planted an American oak tree which will provide shade in the years to come.

The Southampton Repatriation Memorial faces the Isle of Wight Ferry Terminal and overlooks the quayside where another 28 repatriation ships docked during the same two-month period in the autumn of 1945. Although more ships landed in Southampton than Liverpool, they carried fewer repatriates. Each November since 2014, local FEPOW Bob Hucklesby from Poole in Dorset has led a Remembrance Service at the memorial on a school day closest to 18 November (see Figure 10). This was the date that Bob, on board the Italian hospital ship *Principessa Giovanna* docked at Southampton. Pupils from St John's primary school, along with volunteers who look after the park and the memorial, join Bob other veterans and relatives and Southampton's civic leaders to remember all the captives who came home from the Far East through Southampton.

These memorials also serve to remind those who read them that these two port cities played a vital part in the history of Far East prisoners of war and civilian internee captives. However, it is Liverpool that holds a special place in the memory of many FEPOW repatriates. It was from there throughout 1941 that many tens of thousands of Allied troops, initially bound for the Middle East but later diverted across the Indian Ocean to shore up the defences of Singapore and the Dutch East Indies. Several veterans interviewed for LSTM's FEPOW oral history project recalled both their departure from Liverpool and their return four years later, sailing back up the Mersey to the Pier Head. As with Bettany's photograph (p. 28), newspaper reports of the day give fascinating detail about their homecoming, including specific numbers of repatriated POW on board.

As outlined in the Introduction, it was during the latter weeks of 1945 that the first FEPOW patients began presenting at hospitals in Liverpool, seeking medical advice and coming under the care of LSTM's tropical medicine specialists. The complexity and severity of their problems often necessitated long stays in hospital sometimes lasting years. There were 'FEPOW' beds in the large Smithdown Road (later renamed Sefton General) and Mossley Hill hospitals, and at Liverpool Royal Infirmary situated next door to LSTM on Pembroke Place. This was the beginning of LSTM's involvement with former servicemen and initially the priority was to nurse these sick men back to health.

In the south of England, the centre for treating FEPOW was Queen Mary's Hospital Roehampton (QMR), a highly-respected military hospital since the First World War. This was also the centre for pension tribunal medicals on behalf of invalided FEPOW which continued at QMR until 1966 when responsibility was transferred to LSTM.

This slightly fuzzy photograph, from the Lancashire Infantry Museum's collection, shows FEPOW patients in one of several wards at QMR, taken at Christmas 1946 (Figure 11). In the bed at the far end, barely visible, is according to the caption, another FEPOW artist and Lancashire Territorial, Harold Kingsley formerly of the 88th Field Regiment.

Figure 11. Roehampton Hospital, 1946. Christmas in bed, friends together. Harry Kingsley in the bed at far end (© courtesy Lancashire Infantry Museum, Preston)

Kingsley, from Manchester, was a trained artist captured in Singapore and sent to Korea where much of his artwork was done. We will discuss his extraordinary and extensive art collection, held both at the museum and at the Harris Museum in Preston, later (in Chapter 3).

In the mid-1960s when LSTM took over the medical assessments for the DHSS in relation to pension tribunals, Dr Bell and colleagues began a screening programme – Tropical Disease Investigations or TDI's – to identify previously undiagnosed or untreated persistent tropical disease, as well as the physical and psychological aftermath of years of deprivation and mental cruelty during captivity. LSTM identified, prescribed and oversaw effective treatments and the development of new diagnostic methods which cut the time FEPOW spent in Liverpool from five days initially for in-patient care, to just one day as an outpatient. This became a unique medical and scientific collaboration between patient, clinician and scientists lasting until the late 1990s when the last of the FEPOW patients were seen in LSTM's outpatient clinic.

FEPOW Oral History Study

The FEPOW art enquiry grew out of LSTM's FEPOW medical history research. The latter began in the late 1990s when the numbers of veterans attending LSTM's clinics diminished as these men reached the end of life. Dr Geoff Gill now turned his attention to setting the research carried out in partnership with FEPOW patients into a medical history context. At about the same time he also commenced a Ph.D. study to examine the medical aspects of captivity in the Thai–Burma railway camps. It was during this research that he commissioned the FEPOW oral history study.

When I first met Geoff, in 2002 at a book launch for the first part of my father's diaries, he mentioned that his family had been patients of my father's GP practice, in Moreton, Wirral. In 2006 we met again at a FEPOW history conference in London at which Geoff was one of the speakers. A few months later he asked me if I would be interested in undertaking an oral history project for LSTM, to find and interview up to 50 FEPOW in one year and to record their experiences, unique long-term perspective and what effect, if any, captivity had had on post-war lives.

The School of Tropical Medicine collaborated with the IWM's Sound Archive where the interviews were to be made available, LSTM's remit being broad: to find veterans representing all ranks and services, and from as many different regions of captivity as possible. The majority, over 30,000, of British FEPOW spent some time working on the Thai–Burma railway. However, there were nearly 20,000 who did not, for example many of those held in Sumatra, Java, Borneo, Indo-China, Hong Kong, Korea, Japan and New Guinea. I started out with the names of several FEPOW, former patients at LSTM, and the few I had met when I was researching and publishing my father's diary. Once interviewing had started word soon got around and the list of potential interviewees grew. In all 67 men took part, nearly half of whom had not spent time in Thailand or Burma. I also interviewed a handful of wives and widows to record their own unique perspective on FEPOW post-war lives.

A couple of months after starting the interviews in the spring of 2007, I was offered the opportunity to do a Master of Philosophy (M.Phil.) study based on the interviews. Having chosen to train as a State Registered Nurse after leaving school, and with no higher education qualifications, I decided to accept and became a researcher and the interviews a research study. This led me to undertake a special project funded by the Thackray Medical Research Trust, exploring medical ingenuity and inventiveness in Far East captivity. This had personal resonance, as it was the medical miracles performed by overworked Allied medical officers in captivity that had ensured the survival of so many FEPOW, including my father. When I had asked him years earlier why he had chosen not to complete his engineering degree but to start medicine immediately after the war had ended, he said, "*I saw the doctors in camp work miracles, working with nothing.*"

Now I had the chance to understand what he meant. During my research I came across some extraordinary material, specifically medical artwork. This had been created by artists prepared to take even greater risks than others, given the subjects they were recording: young men dying from beriberi with swollen bellies and scrotums; recovering from a back injury bedridden on traction; minus a leg due to grotesque tropical ulcers; or perhaps with a small water bottle strapped over a colostomy. This and much more was recorded with stark clarity, in watercolours, pen and ink, pencil, charcoal and powdered clay. Medical artists worked tirelessly alongside Allied doctors, often when they too were very sick, thus giving them legitimate reason to take up a bed space in hospital huts. Here, their skills were required to chart the monumental struggle to survive. The guards tended to keep their distance, not only because of the risk of infection but also one suspects due to the overwhelming smell of disease and its various exudates.

George Old: At his interview in 2008, Jack Chalker revealed this miniature watercolour below, framed and on the wall of his studio. He treasured it. It is the work of George Old, a fellow trained artist that he respected and whose work he greatly admired. What Old depicted is the aftermath of an ugly incident at Tarsao camp, Thailand, in late 1943 (Figure 12). Gunner Chalker, who was himself ill and in the sick hut, was spotted with drawings by a passing Korean guard. The guard raced in, tore the drawings to pieces and dragged Chalker from the hut back to the guard house where he endured a prolonged beating that left him barely alive.

The painting measures approximately five by eight centimetres and was painted hurriedly by Old as Jack lay semi-conscious recovering from surgery to his face. The ferocious beating had left him with a hole at the top of his nose and covered in bruises and he was extremely lucky to survive this vicious incident. This is the

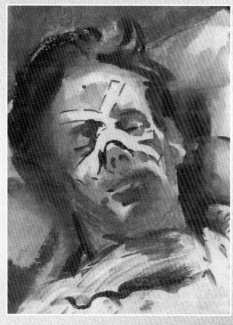

Gunner Ashley George Old

1st/5th Sherwood Foresters

Captured:	Singapore 15.2.42
Camps:	Singapore – Changi POW camp;
	Thailand – Chungkai hospital camp, Tamuang
From:	Northampton
DoB:	3.11.18
Died:	2001

Figure 12.   Injured FEPOW Jack Chalker, painted by George Old, Thailand (© courtesy T. Mercer)

only known portrait in captivity of Jack Chalker, by a friend prepared to take precisely the same risks as Jack had done to record the realities of FEPOW life.

During the oral history study, which ran from 2007 to 2010, men often shared items of artwork – birthday cards, cartoons, portraits of loved ones, posters advertising a play or concert – or, small handmade boxes, carvings, chess sets, etc. These had been created either by the FEPOW being interviewed or, in the case of the artwork, more often by a fellow prisoner of war, a close friend, or perhaps one of the well-known artists. Each small and precious item was treasured, imbued with special status; survivors, like their owners, of a dark and terrible period in the life of a young man now grown old, but who still held clear and painful memories. Well-known artists like Searle and Chalker were revered by many FEPOW veterans. They had created the visual record and were respected for their skill, their courage and the invaluable contribution to a greater understanding of what it had meant to have survived Far East captivity.

This was when we started to realise what a disparate and unrecognised personal archive may exist – visual and visceral reminders of the realities of Far East captivity – held privately in homes around the country. In 2011, towards the completion of the M.Phil., LSTM committed to explore the artwork of FEPOW captivity with a grant from the Wellcome Trust, to see what could be found. Both Geoff's and my curiosity had been sparked during our respective academic studies, with a growing awareness of the value of this artwork in providing the only visual documentary evidence of so many aspects of life, death and survival in captivity.

The hunt begins … with AKKI

It started on 9 April 2010, with a request to find out about a FEPOW artist who signed himself 'AKKI'. There were no clues as to his actual name in a manila file containing some letters and a numbered series of pencil drawings – A5-sized, black and white photocopies of 22 cartoon sketches some of which were humorous – together with typed captions, and a passing remark about AKKI having been a cartoonist for a Blackpool newspaper.

The subjects of the sketches were everyday things like latrines, bedbug hunts, a church service, bath time etc., with each clearly signed AKKI in the bottom right corner. The one below (Figure 13) is entitled 'Sick Parade' and dated 1942/43. It shows a medical officer (later confirmed as Captain A. M. Tomlinson RAMC, 137th Field Regiment RA) conducting a sick parade in the Medical Inspection, or MI, hut at Nong Pladuk camp in Thailand.

These photocopies were given to Dr Bell at LSTM by a patient in 1977, at around the same time as the originals were also donated to IWM.[1] However, that patient was not AKKI, but a Jack Sutter. That is, former Gunner in the 137th Field Regiment, Jack Toner Sutter, from Blackpool. A letter in the file, referring to the photocopies and dated 28 September 1983, was written by former Captain Charles Ewart Escritt 54th Infantry Brigade Company (RASC). An Oxford classics scholar, Escritt had worked pre-war as a freelance commercial artist for Tootal in Manchester. During an illustrious career post-war in university education he became a Fellow of Keble College, Oxford. In his brief summation of the cartoons he stated:

> *"… I judged the draughtsman was probably in 137 Army Fd Regt … His style is crude, relying for effect on a series of 'stock' comic characters, none of whom could be positively identified."*

Escritt was not able to put a name to the artist. Interestingly, the men in this picture were not 'comic' characters but caricatures. But Escritt's comment about anonymising characters struck a chord some while later when another medical cartoon sketch by AKKI came to light. However, significantly, the comment also gave a valuable clue as to where AKKI was from, placing him in Lancashire, or at least as a member of 137th Field, one of Lancashire's Territorial units, otherwise known as the 'Blackpool' regiment.

Figure 13.   'Sick Parade' at Nong Pladuk camp, Thailand 1943/43, by AKKI (© *courtesy IWM.IWM ART.7342 10)*

37

Next, in view of the reference to AKKI having been a Blackpool newspaper cartoonist, I rang the Blackpool Gazette and was put through to the librarian, Carole Davies. Initially she was not hopeful as AKKI's name was not familiar, but she kindly said she would have a look and get back to me. An hour later she rang to say that not only had she tracked down some of AKKI's cartoons, but also his former daughter-in-law! As she had put down the telephone suddenly the penny had dropped. AKKI's real name was Akhurst, Basil Parry Akhurst to be exact, and Denise Akhurst was Carol's best friend. Denise rang later that day and introduced us to AKKI's son David.

He could not have been more helpful or surprised to know that someone was interested in his father. During a long telephone call, I learned that his father was known to all as 'AKKI', had been a Bombardier in the 137th Field Regiment, was 22 years old when captured in Singapore in 1942, and in one of the early work parties sent to Thailand where he had remained for the duration. The family apparently had a large amount of his artwork, though none done during captivity. David knew about some pictures in the IWM but did not have copies of them. He said his father had always loved art, especially caricature and cartoons, and that after school had trained as a draughtsman.

Post-war AKKI worked hard to establish himself as a surveyor. As well as having cartoons in the paper two or three times a week in the early days post-war, his father also developed a nice side-line, supplying artwork to a postcard manufacturer specialising in the saucy seaside variety, an essential commodity in Blackpool in post-war decades.

We contacted IWM's Art Department to see what they knew about a FEPOW artist named AKKI and a collection of 22 pencil sketches drawn at Nong Pladuk camp in Thailand. They had no record of the name AKKI but asked if we meant the J. T. Sutter collection? LSTM's records showed that this was the same collection, and we shared what we had found out so AKKI's work could be properly attributed. The IWM informed us that the original sketches are coloured using crayons. We also exchanged information revealed in the Escritt letters to LSTM and the Art Department at IWM.

Escritt had been asked by the IWM sometime after Sutter's donation, to comment on the pictures and in this letter, handwritten in exquisite italic style, he noted that, "*before the war,* [AKKI] *was a cartoonist for Blackpool Evening Gazette*". Sutter had apparently supplied topics and captions for AKKI's sketches which had been exhibited at FEPOW reunions around the UK post-war. Escritt gave IWM a detailed explanation of the subject matter in each cartoon, as well as a critique.

We invited David Akhurst to visit LSTM where he showed us an album of politically-inspired cartoons by AKKI (and given to his fiancée Mary before he was drafted out east). It was a treasure trove, full of skilfully executed and humorous cartoons, like these two below (Figures 14 & 15).

We gave David black and white copies of the 22 sketches held at LSTM and IWM. David said his father had been a comedian, always looking on the bright side. He was renowned for impersonating Oliver Hardy, of Laurel and Hardy

Figures 14 & 15. Above, Churchill, Roosevelt and Hitler; right, 'Our very own Popeye!' 1940–41, by AKKI (© *courtesy the Akhurst family*)

fame, as this photograph (Figure 16) testifies, taken at an annual FEPOW reunion in the 1960s with AKKI, far right, in character!

This annual FEPOW reunion programme, dated 1956, also boasts AKKI's handiwork (Figure 17)[2] on the front cover and in the seven cartoons inside.

David showed us a letter that his father had treasured, from a former senior POW officer in Thailand, Major R. A. N. Davidson 4th Prince of Wales Own Gurkha

Figure 16. FEPOW reunion entertainers 1960s, AKKI, aka Ollie, second row far right
(© courtesy the Akhurst family)

Figure 17. AKKI's handiwork, dated 1956
(© courtesy R. Jackson)

Bombardier Basil Parry 'AKKI' Akhurst

137th Field Regiment Royal Artillery

Captured:	Singapore 15.2.42
Camps:	Singapore – Changi POW camp
	Thailand – Nong Pladuk and Nakom Paton hospital camps
From:	Blackpool
Born:	8.7.20
Died:	8.12.89

Rifles Regiment. He one of the older officers in captivity who served as adjutant to Lieutenant Colonel Toosey at Kanburi and Nakon Nyok camps in Thailand. In a long letter to AKKI, handwritten and dated Boxing day 1945, he says:

"... delighted to receive your letter a few days ago ... [and] *that you had taken the trouble to write ... some things we shall never forget ... one of those was your action with regard to the typewriter* [producing and copiously illustrating the daily newssheet, The Corfu Courier, on board *SS Corfu* en route to Southampton] *... I shall be delighted to hear from you at any time Akki* [sic] *... Tell me what you are doing and how life is treating you. The address over will always find me ..."*

Randolph Alan Noel Davidson, born 1902 and from Fleet in Hampshire, was first held at Pudu Gaol, Kuala Lumpur before being sent to Nong Pladuk in Thailand, in October 1942. This is where he would have first encountered AKKI, a volunteer in the hospital huts. The heartfelt sentiment expressed in his letter indicates the respect and admiration felt for a young man who had proved his worth during the most testing of times.

Jack Chalker: Another item David shared was this humorous birthday card given to AKKI on his 25th birthday, 8 July 1945 by Jack Chalker (Figures 18 & 19). The card is roughly 13 x 10cms, has an outer dark blue paper cover with a four-page white paper insert, the two stitched together. Watercolour sketches adorn each page of the insert, and it is signed by three men – Jack Chalker, Nigel Wright and Len Adams.

Jack obviously knew AKKI well enough to make fun of his physique, depicting him as the chubby comic character on the front of the card. AKKI's normal weight as a young man was around 16 stone, as evidenced by the photograph taken *circa* 1939–40, soon after he had enlisted in the 137th Field Regiment (Figure 20).

By the end of his captivity AKKI's weight had dropped by half to just eight stone. It is clear though that, thanks to the improved diet his portly physique was recovering by the time he got home (Figure 21), as seen with his father shortly after his ship SS *Corfu* arrived in Southampton on 7 October 1945. However, his face shows dark-rimmed sunken eyes.

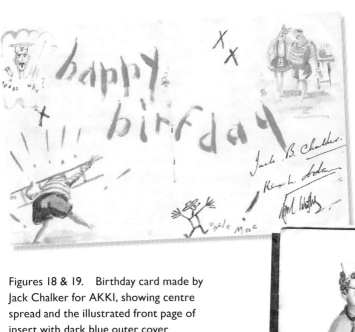

Figures 18 & 19. Birthday card made by Jack Chalker for AKKI, showing centre spread and the illustrated front page of insert with dark blue outer cover
(© *courtesy the Akhurst family*)

Gunner Jack Bridger Chalker

118th Field Regiment, Royal Artillery

Captured:	Singapore 15.2.42
Camps:	Singapore – Changi POW and Havelock Road, River Valley Road work camps
	Thailand – Kanyu River camp, Tarsao camp, Chungkai, Nakom Paton hospital camps
From:	London
Born:	10.10.18
Died:	15.11.14

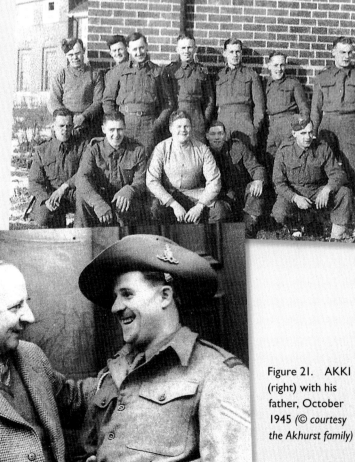

Figure 20. Bombardier Akhurst with fellow members of the 137th Field Regiment, 1940 (© courtesy the Akhurst family)

Figure 21. AKKI (right) with his father, October 1945 (© courtesy the Akhurst family)

No doubt Jack Chalker would have appreciated AKKI's artistic and comedic worth, as both men, together with Chalker's good friend, Nigel Wright,[3] spent much time working together on shows and concert parties at Nakom Paton Hospital camp in Thailand, in what turned out to be with hindsight the final months of captivity.

'AKKI' Akhurst: In November 2012 during a visit to the IWM I was shown this watercolour (Figure 22) signed by AKKI, of Captain Tomlinson which was discovered among the private papers of FEPOW W. L. Davis.[4]

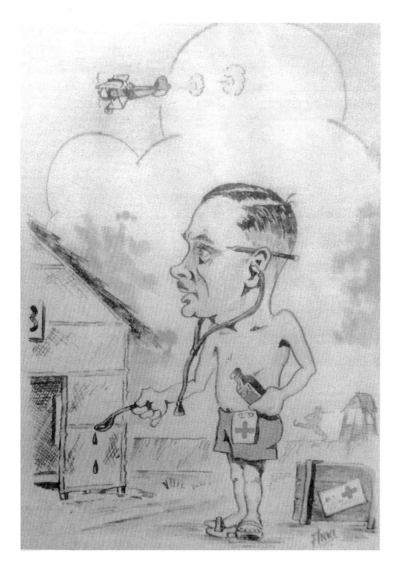

Figure 22. Captain Tomlinson, by AKKI (© *courtesy* *IWM.IWM* *DOC.8728)*

It is an accomplished caricature and compares well with the image of the same medical officer seen in 'Sick Parade' (Figure 13). It is easily recognised as AKKI's distinctive and humorous style: exaggerated detail in the head and face atop a smaller body; red crosses and stethoscope identifying the man's calling; a small, biplane backfiring its way across the sky (an allusion to old Japanese aircraft having to be brought into service, or maybe Tomlinson was a keen aviator?), the dripping medicine spoon in his hand, a pencil behind the ear, while in the distance the comedic figure of a guard struts about shouldering his rifle. The artist shows us what he wants the viewer to see.

In this case, however, the comedy evaporates when it is realised that the guard is goose-stepping along the top of a high bund. A bund in this context refers to a raised earth embankment with a deep trench on the camp side (from where the earth for the bund came from), built by FEPOW around the perimeter of camps in Thailand and elsewhere. This detail helps to date AKKI's caricature as bunds were not built until later in captivity. AKKI, Captain Tomlinson and Jack Chalker were all at Nakom Paton in the final year or so of captivity. In his acclaimed memoir, Jack Chalker describes the bund at Nakom Paton, in June 1945:

> "Our camp perimeter consisted of a wide, deep trench beyond which rose a
> huge bund, nearly 15 feet high patrolled day and night by armed sentries.
> Disturbingly, machine-gun posts were now being set into all corners of the
> bund commanding the trench, which could obviously be used as a mass
> grave."[5]

The veracity of their fears was later confirmed by documents seized after the Japanese surrender, ordering the annihilation in mid-September 1945 of all POW in their camps.

Back in 1983 Escritt had described AKKI's art work as 'crude', which we interpreted as meaning simplistic, immature perhaps, naïve. At that time the 22 pencil sketches were the only evidence of his FEPOW art and both the sketches and AKKI remained largely unrecognised. In 2005, the Museum of Lancashire staged an exhibition entitled, *Nor Iron Bars, Lancashire Artists in Captivity 1942–1945*, as part of the 60th anniversary commemorations marking the end of the war in Europe and the Far East. It featured the work of FEPOW artists Desmond Bettany, Leo Rawlings, Harry Kingsley.[6] Regrettably, neither AKKI nor any of his artwork featured in the exhibition.

We had started the search for AKKI five years after that exhibition ended, and two years before the official start of this art enquiry. As we gradually identified more of AKKI's work, most of it was in private ownership like these examples below. This wealth of material of different styles reveals AKKI to be a more skilful artist than was previously thought and he deserves to be acknowledged. We know that he brought laughter and much-needed distraction to many men throughout captivity, not only with his art but also his theatrical endeavours. And he went on doing so at FEPOW reunions through the post-war years. In history as in life, there are always questions left unanswered. In the case of AKKI one in particular remains a mystery: why was it Sutter and not AKKI, who was still alive in the 1970s, that made the donation of the 22 sketches to the IWM?

In May 2010, at the 3rd Researching FEPOW History conference held at the National Memorial Arboretum (NMA) at Alrewas, Staffordshire, delegate Richard Brown shared with us a theatrical poster by AKKI which he had inherited from his father. He had brought it in response to an appeal LSTM circulated to FEPOW clubs and groups to find more of AKKI's artwork. Richard's father, Band Sergeant William Brown 2nd Btn The East Surrey Regiment, was known as 'Nosher'. A musician, he had also been a producer of theatricals and concert parties in camps in Singapore and Thailand. The last one he produced was 'The Rajah of Coconut', (Figures 23 & 24) heralded by this glorious poster created by AKKI.

This was the first musical comedy performed at Nakom Paton after the Japanese surrender. On the reverse (Figure 24) is an inscription by AKKI, finished in a flourish with, "They will never be forgotten!" Jack Chalker's hilarious description of the production of 'The Rajah of Coconut' can be heard in his first interview with LSTM, recorded in 2007.[7]

Below is another concert party poster by AKKI that Nosher Brown had also kept (Figure 25). It advertised a concert party at Nakom Paton, planned for

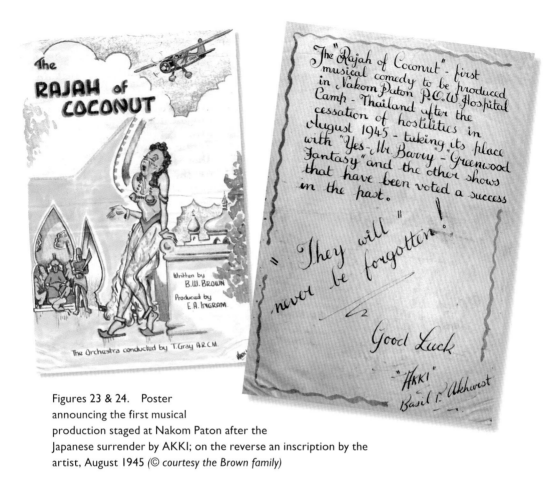

Figures 23 & 24. Poster announcing the first musical production staged at Nakom Paton after the Japanese surrender by AKKI; on the reverse an inscription by the artist, August 1945 (© *courtesy the Brown family*)

18 July. Although the year is not shown, we know that it was 1945.[8] However, it seems that the show was postponed, the 18 crossed out and 20 written underneath.

Professor Sears Eldredge, Emeritus Professor of Dance and Performance at Macalester College, St Paul, Minneapolis USA, has spent over two decades researching the concert parties and theatricals in Singapore and Thailand. In his fascinating study, now published as a free-to-view ebook, *Captive Audiences/ Captive Performers*, he said this about the show:

> "On 20 July, a variety show starring Eddie Monkhouse appeared. Band
> Sergeant Bernard Brown, who played a cornet in 'The Untirables,' preserved

Figure 25. Variety show featuring Bernard 'Nosher' Brown and The Boys of St. Noshers!, 20 July 1945, drawn by AKKI
(© courtesy the Brown family)

this poster of the show embellished with cartoons by 'Akki' (Basil Akhurst). In the contrary way of British humor, the extremely slim Brown had been given the nickname, 'Nosher', by his comrades. So 'The Boys of St. Noshers!' act on the bill was probably performed by men from Brown's own hut, as they would later present him with a specially commissioned cartoon by 'AKKI' in 'appreciation for [his] "fatherly" care'."

Here is that card Eldredge references, given to Nosher by the men of Hut 16 at Nakom Paton. It is a beautifully-crafted AKKI classic, the watercolours still vibrant, the animation superb. Nosher, blowing his cornet, sits atop of a pile of possessions ready to go home, with at least two guards squashed under the weight of it all (Figure 26). Visible in the background on the right is the golden-domed Chedi, the renowned landmark near to Nakom Paton POW camp.

Yet another AKKI work is this collection of caricatures under the heading: 'Crookery Nook Nacom [sic] Paton. P.O.W. camp. Thailand. November 1944' (Figure 27). These are members of the Nakom Paton canteen led by Lieutenant Walter Pollock, depicted in the bottom right corner, frying pan in hand.

Figure 26. AKKI cartoon of
Nosher Brown packed up and
ready to leave Nakom Paton
(© courtesy the Brown family)

According to Pollock's son John, this is a good likeness to his father. As all
(except Pollock) autographed their images it appears it may have been a tribute
to his stewardship.

John and his family now live in Australia. Some years ago, he was introduced
to an Australian FEPOW, John Holman, who told him he had worked with
his father in camp. Holman gave John copies of some comical posters done by
AKKI (Figure 28) and told John that:

Figure 27.
'Crookery Nook
Nacom Paton
canteen', by AKKI,
November 1944
(© courtesy the
Pollock family)

"On the Japs surrender these posters were rescued from the canteen notice board at Nakon Paton, Thailand where 'Heavy Sick' personnel were evacuated to, after the railway was finished. The drawings, on cheap paper and [using] homemade colours, were made by a Dutchman under the pen name 'Akki' who let his imagination run riot. Anyone consuming these 'Delicacies' also had to use a lot of imagination."

It is interesting to note that Holman thought that AKKI was Dutch!

Figure 28. Copies of three of seven small posters by AKKI, Ginger Tart, Banana Fritters and Sambal, from the noticeboard at Nakom Paton canteen, 1945 (© courtesy the Pollock family)

Most of AKKI's artwork is humorous though often with a serious message. In Chapter 5 (Figure 7) there is another of his cartoons which was shown to us by Jackie Sutherland in 2013. Jackie is the daughter of FEPOW medical officer and pathologist, Captain Jack Ennis RAMC who remained in Singapore throughout captivity.[9] The drawing has both cartoon figures and a caricature of the medical officer. The setting is the MI hut. AKKI depicts a queue of anxious patients observing the man being examined. In this work AKKI shows the skill, intelligence and discretion that typifies his work. He recorded what was a highly problematic aspect of medical life during the first months of captivity at Changi POW camp.

The 'recognised' and 'unrecognised' FEPOW artists

Over the years FEPOW researchers at LSTM have become familiar with the artwork created by the few recognised British artists of Far East captivity namely, Ronald Searle, Jack Chalker, Stanley Gimson, Philip Meninsky, John Mennie, Charles Thrale, Leo Rawlings and George Old. Most had had formal art training pre-war, either in fine art, anatomical, commercial and graphic art, or all three. Gimson was the exception and interestingly, he was also the only officer among them, the others were all from the ranks.

Both Thrale and Rawlings had toured exhibitions of their artwork for years during the first two decades post-war – perhaps it was a way for both men to deal with the legacy of their wartime experiences? In later life Searle, Chalker and Rawlings published memoirs and Searle, Chalker and Meninsky exhibited their FEPOW artwork both in the UK and abroad.

Jack Chalker had been a patient of LSTM in the early 1980s. In 1983 he donated a photographic set of some of his best-known works to Dr Bell for reference; in later years he contributed to both the oral history project and to a study into inventive medicine and ingenuity in FEPOW camps. He remained in touch with LSTM researchers and supportive of their work up until his death in 2014. There are examples of his work at IWM but by far the largest collection is in the Australian War Memorial in Canberra. A considerable amount of his personal collection of original FEPOW artwork, including copies made after the war, was auctioned in 2002 by Bonham's in London.

Among the 69 'unrecognised' artists discussed in this book, several, despite being less well-known, were capable amateur or trained artists. Examples of their art are also to be found in IWM's art collection, for example Basil 'AKKI' Akhurst, Desmond Bettany, Geoffrey Coxhead, Kenneth Elwell, Geoffrey Gee, Robert Hardie, Stanley Strange and Alan Toze. All, except Coxhead, Strange and Toze, remained in the tropics; Coxhead was captured in Hong Kong and later shipped to Japan, Strange and Toze were both captured in Singapore and shipped to Korea, with Strange later being moved again, to Japan. All except Kenneth Elwell survived captivity and returned with their artwork; Elwell was drowned when being transported to Japan in September 1944.

It is also worth noting that some of the medical artists had their artwork published in the early post-war years, such was the skill, clarity and anatomical accuracy of their work. For example, some of Chalker's sketches featured in a paper by Captain Jacob Markowitz RAMC, published in the Journal of the Royal Army Medical Corps in 1946.[10] Some of Gimson's drawings of medical and utilitarian ingenuity featured in an article in the *London Illustrated News*, 27 March 1946, entitled, 'The Ingenuity of Prisoners-of-War: Mechanical Gadgets Made of Junk'. The brief article opened with the following comment:

> *Allied prisoners of war returning from the Far East have brought with them not only tales of hardships and atrocities, but also accounts of the resource and ingenuity displayed in making life bearable in the Japanese prison camps.*

The article states that the six drawings reproduced had all been done by Lieutenant Stanley Gimson Royal Artillery (RA) at Chungkai early in 1944. Jenny Wood examines Gimson's artwork and that of the other recognised artists in Section III (Chapter 7), how they worked, some of the materials they sourced and how they preserved their art work.

Desmond Bettany's artwork is now online – www.changipowart.com – as is Jack Spittle's in a blog – https://bspittle.wordpress.com/2009/05/02/ronald-john-jack-spittle/. Both were created by the artists' families.

In recent years, many previously unseen items of FEPOW artwork have been discovered in the IWM's Private Papers collection, created by men like Charles Holdsworth, medical officer Harry Silman, Cecil Pickersgill and many more. The enquiry has explored this rich seam of FEPOW art.[11]

Another trained artist, William Carthew 'Will' Wilder, who had been a teacher of art at Culham College of Education in Oxfordshire pre-war, recorded various aspects of camp life in Singapore and a number of medical subjects at Chungkai hospital camp in Thailand, some of which features in Section II. An example of his work can be found in the archives of the National Army Museum, along with art created by George Old, Jack Chalker and Kenneth Elwell. However, most of Wilder's original sketches remain with his son at home in Oxfordshire.

As mentioned in the Introduction, in 2012 a Wellcome Trust grant facilitated travel to archives and museums in this country and abroad, to seek artists and their artwork. A wealth of material depicting many aspects of camp life, disease and death in captivity came to light, as did the names of many more amateur and trained artists. In between trips and exploring the online archives and catalogues, in November 2012 I made the first of several visits to IWM's Art Department to meet senior art curator, Jenny Wood. It was Jenny who introduced me to their extensive FEPOW art collection, including significant collections comprising several hundred items each, donated by Ronald Searle and Philip Meninsky.

The enquiry

Initially the focus was on FEPOW art representing the medical aspects of survival, in view of the material that had emerged during the study into inventive medicine. However, very quickly we realised that much of the new material we were finding represented the psychological aspects of survival as much as the physical: the theatricals and concert parties, education, faith, and the beauty of the tropical landscapes. None of it could be ignored and a revised and broader remit included all aspects of life in captivity – working, resting, escaping mentally if not physically, dying – represented in art and the creative arts. Carvings, gadgets, chess sets, toothbrushes, items created that brought pleasure, practical benefit, a sense of achievement and even perhaps moments of contentment were also included in the enquiry.

The timing of LSTM's enquiry was fortuitous as during the previous year the IWM's then Keeper of the Department of Documents, the late Roderick Suddaby together with Jenny Wood, had undertaken a comprehensive review of the FEPOW Private Papers in the Documents' collection. The purpose was to uncover any FEPOW artwork among the journals, papers, letters and photographs held in this part of the collection. This artwork may have been itemised during the cataloguing process years earlier but often without specific detail and much of it unattributed. With knowledge accrued over time, some obscure signatures had acquired meaning and could now be correctly attributed. The audit brought a marvellous array of visual documentary artwork to light and in Section III Jenny will expand further on it and IWM's FEPOW art collections.

Research visits continued, to museums and archives in the UK, including three major archives in London, namely the Wellcome Collection, the National Army Museum and the Clavell Library at the Royal Arsenal, Woolwich (although the latter revealed little artwork). Further afield, a significant collection related to captivity in Korea was found at the Lancashire Infantry Museum (formerly the Museum of the Queen's Lancashire Regiment) based at the Fulwood Barracks in Preston. Visits to both the Second World War Experience Centre near Wakefield and the regimental archives of the 9th Royal Northumberland Fusiliers at Alnwick Castle in Northumberland also proved worthwhile. North of the border, the National Library of Scotland in Edinburgh provided new insights as did the archives and museum of the Gordon Highlanders Regiment in Aberdeen and the Mitchell Library and the City Archives in Glasgow.

A discovery

In September 2013 I visited FEPOW archives in Singapore and two rather special windows in Jakarta, Java. At Singapore's Changi Museum, in the section 'Art of Captivity', in the front left-hand corner of a display case I noticed a small, thick, homemade, illustrated sketchbook. The top page was battered and stained but the illustration, a pencil cartoon sketch of the head and shoulders of an angry-looking military figure (perhaps a Sergeant Major barking orders?) was clearly visible. The caption alongside the sketchbook read: 'Artist Unknown. An original sketchbook of drawings depicting scenes of life in prison'.

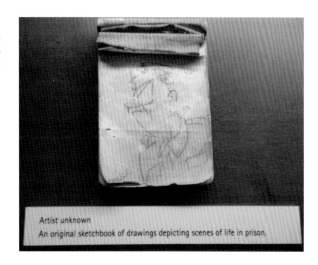

Artist unknown
An original sketchbook of drawings depicting scenes of life in prison.

On closer inspection it still had remnants of the cover, a piece of canvas or perhaps cut from an Army issue, olive-coloured gas cape. Then I saw it. There, clear as day, in the bottom left-hand corner. It was AKKI's unmistakable signature.

To my knowledge at that time, and now, this is the only known AKKI sketchpad to have survived captivity (Figure 29). It was thrilling to make the discovery. A member of the museum staff took the sketchpad to a quiet research area in the museum where it could be inspected more closely.

The sketchbook comprises a series of booklets, cut from a larger pad, hand-stitched and bound together at the top. It was approximately 9cms wide by 13cms long and almost 2 cms thick and looked and felt quite robust. AKKI's moniker appeared on most of the 60 or more facing pages beneath, on cartoon after caricature, after cartoon. A couple are shown below (Figures 30 & 31) but many more can be seen on LSTM's FEPOW art pages.[12]

His signature, being mostly in the bottom right-hand corner, is now very faint on some pages, the corners smudged having taken the brunt of page-turning. On the verso pages there are drawings, sketches, doggerel verse, poems, mostly written by others, some signed and dated, many not. It seemed as if AKKI had used this pad like an autograph book, collecting the thoughts and work of others over time.

Several of the cartoons seem to refer to his earlier days in the regiment, the one on the left (Figure 30) with the gas mask for example. It seems unlikely that

Figures 30 & 31.   Two examples from AKKI's sketchpad, with verso page visible, left
(© courtesy The Changi Museum Pte Ltd. Singapore MAY)

they were paraded in the tropics wearing gas masks! Regrettably, when they consulted the museum's documentation the only information concerning the sketchpad was that it had come from the original museum collection when it was transferred to the purpose-built museum in 2001. Frustratingly, there was no information about who had presented the sketchpad to the museum, when, or where it had come from. That was the only disappointment on what is still remembered as a very exciting day. What comes over very clearly is that this sketchpad was meant to be shared, and was intended to raise a laugh.

Back in the UK, between these archive visits families of FEPOW artists were responding to online appeals posted on FEPOW research networks and in the FEPOW club newsletters[13] and at talks and lectures given at public meetings, history workshops and conferences. Visits were made to descendants, who held varying quantities of unpublished and, in most cases, unseen artwork (outside of immediate family circles, that is). It was important to clarify from the outset that our interest lay in what had been created secretly and kept hidden throughout captivity, and not artwork created by FEPOW post-war from memory. The importance of the latter, and of art used as therapy more widely, will be discussed in more detail in Section III.

This book brings together for the first time many of these unsung artists showcasing the range, scope and skill of their work. Artwork was sometimes anonymous or signed by an unrecognised, and often unrecognisable, name meaning regrettably that some FEPOW artists are lost to history. The subject matter revealed is wide-ranging, everything from landscapes and camp scenes to medical conditions and treatments; the psychological escape afforded by theatricals is evidenced by sketches of elaborately-painted scenery, concert programmes and billboard posters; birthday, anniversary and Christmas cards remind us of the need to keep loved ones close; the longing for home, freedom and normality.

Jack Kemp: Portraits of a wife, mother or sweetheart were especially treasured, created from tattered photographs by artists like Jack Kemp, often in exchange for cigarettes or whatever the prevailing currency was in camp at the time. Kemp did the sketch below of his wife, while at Chungkai camp in 1943.

Not surprisingly though, it is the portraits of FEPOW done during captivity that are among the most treasured items by descendants, affording a permanent, sometimes shocking, reminder of lost years in captivity. Trained artist, George

Sergeant Jack Ernest Kemp
Royal Army Ordnance Corps (RAOC)

Captured:	Singapore 15.2.42
Camps:	Singapore: Changi
	Thailand: Ban Pong, Chungkai, Tarsao, Takanun, Chungkai, Tamarkan, Chungkai, Tamuan
From:	Lowestoft, Suffolk
DoB:	22.11.12
Died:	not known

Figure 32. Portrait of Hilda Kemp, sketched in 1943 at Chungkai POW camp, Thailand, by husband Sgt J. E. Kemp (© courtesy J. Upcraft)

Old, did over a thousand (in his own estimation later in life) in camps in Singapore and Thailand, for the price of a fill of tobacco. Old's artwork will be discussed further in Section III and Section IV.

Atholl Duncan: Figure 35 shows the camp plan of a large Allied transit camp, Uniekampong Tandjong Priok, which was in a derelict former dockside 'coolie' labour camp on the coast north of Batavia in Java. Drawn by Captain Duncan on the inside cover of a school exercise book he had acquired, it is full of interesting detail and includes a compass bearing. At its height this camp held over 4,500 POW, British, Dutch, Australian and a few Americans, and it was from here they were drafted to all points across Japan's new empire.

The camp was sub-divided into numerous sub-camps, barbed-wired off from each other as indicated by the dotted lines. Duncan's hut was in sub-camp No.1, top left, which had a stage at one end. To the right of centre is a chapel. There is also a football field, where Wilf Wooller and members of the pre-war Welsh international rugby team (all members of the 77th Heavy Anti-Aircraft Regiment) took on all-comers early on, before disease and death decimated their numbers.

Captain Andrew Atholl Duncan

2nd Btn Argyll & Sutherland Highlanders
Intelligence Corps, HQ Staff

Captured:	Garoet, Java
Camps:	Java – Tandjong Priok Uniekampong, Batavia;
	Japan – Motoyama, Zentsuji, Miyata
From:	St Andrews, Scotland
DoB:	4.3.18
Died:	15.2.97

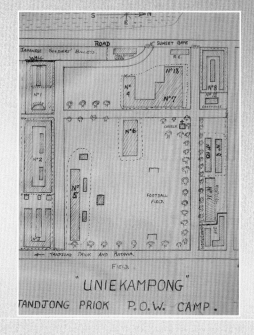

Figure 33. Plan of Tandjong Priok transit camp, by Capt. A. A. Duncan (© courtesy the Duncan family)

Top right is a building marked R.E. – the Royal Engineers' workshop. The Japanese had brought in RE prisoners of war immediately after the capitulation to prepare the derelict site as a transit camp. They erected the barbed wire fencing and put in rudimentary water supply and sanitation. Once the camp was occupied the engineers continued working for the Japanese, but also clandestinely supplied utensils for the camp kitchens and much-needed equipment to the hospital hut.

Early on in Java, Duncan had swapped his British issue kit bag, which had rotted in the tropical climate of Southeast Asia, for a Dutch one. This was not only more robust but was formed from two layers of material, an outer cover with an inner lining. The latter he split to create pockets along its length and across the base to store his diary and notebooks.

Ronald Spittle: There are several other men revealed by the enquiry who also did camp plans and maps, for example Sergeant Ronald 'Jack' Spittle, an experienced member of an RAMC anti-mosquito squad sent to Singapore to try to minimise the risk of malaria. A pre-war sanitation officer for Slough Council, Spittle filled several notebooks with his designs for improved latrines and urinals. As previously mentioned, his son Brian created a fascinating blog to share his father's diary, copious notes and sketches (he is currently writing a biography about his father).[14] Brian noted that while

> *"some POW drew scenes from the camps, others sketched portraits of fellow POW. Dad drew urinals. What can I say?"*

Spittle was also an avid ornithologist who filled a notebook with detailed observations. He filled others with intricate pencil sketches of latrines, Otway pits, soakaways and urinals (see Chapter 2, Figures 41 & 42). Spittle remained in Singapore for the duration and his detailed plan with key of the Changi peninsula and his 'bird's-eye view' are ones to savour (Figure 34). The former was drawn on a large piece of flimsy paper which is now fragile, the latter inside one of his notebooks.

A subaltern in 135th Field Regiment (which was led by Colonel Toosey) Stephen Alexander did two detailed, intriguing and imaginative sketches. Drawn from

Private Ronald John 'Jack' Spittle

32 Coy Royal Army Medical Corps (RAMC), anti-mosquito squad

Captured:	Pulau Tekong (Island off Singapore) March 1942
Camps:	Changi POW camp, Selerang Hospital and Kranji Hospital camps
From:	Slough, Buckinghamshire
DoB:	30.3.14
Died:	28.9.04

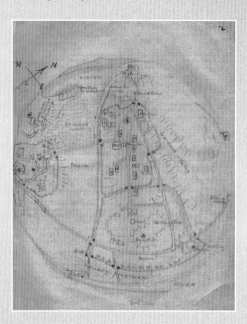

Figure 34. Changi peninsula, Singapore. Spittle's Bird's eye view of Changi camp with compass bearings and the Japanese flag indicating the direction that Japan lay, both drawn by Sgt R. J. Spittle RAMC (© courtesy the Spittle family)

memory, his town plan of Cambridge where Alexander had studied English pre-war, is extraordinary. It was published in his memoir *Sweet Kwai, Run Softly*.

His other 'plan', of the large POW camp at Tamarkan in Thailand, is in Chapter 6 (Figure 16). Alexander was also a poet and a founder member of a small group of like-minded officers in Thailand. Chapter 18 of his 1995 memoir is entitled, 'Little Bloomsbury on Kwai'. Through their shared love of poetry, Alexander and fellow poet friends John Durnford and Terence Charley, found an escape route back to the people they had once been, and with luck would one day be again.

The artwork uncovered in the enquiry provides a vivid window on an aspect of Second World War history that has all but slipped into obscurity. With each new discovery, more questions arise about captivity and how it was endured. Why would men take such risks when life was so precarious? How did they find the materials to create their art? What might it be able to tell us about survival in

Far East captivity? We shall endeavour to answer these and other questions in this book.

This is not a definitive collection. There are undoubtedly more artists, and artwork, to uncover. But this is the start of what is a significant, and until now largely overlooked, canon of artwork, created by British servicemen with a gift for sketching, painting, cartooning and caricaturing, who inadvertently have become the unofficial documentary war artists of British Far East captivity during the Second World War. They give us a vivid insight into their world at a moment when their urge to sketch, paint or capture a caricature, overcame their fear of being caught with pencil and paper by a guard.

CHAPTER 2

The 'Unrecognised' Artists – Part I

The purpose of the FEPOW art enquiry was to see how much more artwork, created by British military artists during captivity, could be found. So far, LSTM has uncovered the work of 69 artists, much of it is still in private family ownership. Among that number we have also included several FEPOW artists who are also known to researchers and whose artwork has been published or can be found in archives and museum collections, men like Will Wilder and Des Bettany.[1] To distinguish from the handful of celebrated British FEPOW artists, the group of 69 is referred to as the 'unrecognised' FEPOW artists.

As mentioned before, a larger, bold font is used when a new artist and his work is being introduced. Most of the unrecognised artists are unknown to the public or to the wider FEPOW research community. We will share what we have been able to find out about these men, which regrettably in some cases is very little. We are aware that we will have missed out others and as more artists and artwork are made known to LSTM they will be added to the list featured on the online gallery that we have created to showcase this work.[2]

Over the next two chapters these men and examples of their artwork will be introduced. Due to the numbers involved the 'unrecognised' artists have been split into two parts. Some of them will feature again in Sections II and III. This is the list of the unrecognised artists, in alphabetical order:

Basil 'AKKI' Akhurst, Stephen Alexander, Leslie Audus, Stanley Bagnall, Ronald Barnes, John Beckerley, Desmond Bettany, Archie Bevan, Godfrey Bird, Robert Brazil, Edward Burch, Hamish Cameron-Smith, Derek Clarke, Donovan Clarke, John Clement, Geoffrey Coxhead, Walter Cullen, Atholl Duncan, Herbert Elsey, Kenneth Elwell, John Excell, Basil Ferron, Wyndham Forbes, John Gale, Robert Gamble, Geoffrey Gee, Maurice Green, Robert Hardie, Mike Hardy, John Harris, George Harrison, Charles Holdsworth, Noel James, Jack Kemp, Harry Kingsley, Maurice Kinmonth, Frederick Margarson, Claude McLaren Reid, Robert Milner-Moore, Alfred Mitchell, Geoffrey Munton, Reginald Newman, William Norways, Nowell Peach, Richard Philps, Cecil Pickersgill, Norman Power, Norman Pritchard, Desmond Pyment, Frederick Ransome-Smith, Malcolm Rivron, Robert Rogers, Stanley Russell, Mervyn Scott-Lindsley, Harry Silman, Rex Spencer, Jack Spittle, Eric Stacy, Frederick Stallard, Stanley Strange, Donald Teale, Alan Toze, Herbert Upton, Tom Henling Wade, Stanley Warren, Jack White, William 'Will' Wilder, Thomas Wilson, Alexander Young.

Several of the 69 were medical officers or scientists, namely Leslie Audus (botanist) and medical doctors Robert Hardie, Maurice Kinmonth, Nowell Peach, Richard Philps and Harry Silman. Channelling their artistic ability would undoubtedly have been a welcome, if brief, distraction from the appalling reality of their daily existence. Doctors and orderlies woke each day to face the impossible, bearing witness to an endless sea of pain, suffering and despair, doing what they could with what they had, which was very little. Was art a way of helping to keep them sane?

Another group of professionals with artistic flair who appear in this list were architects: Godfrey Bird, Desmond Pyment (architecture student), Cecil Pickersgill, Eric Stacy and Herbert Upton. All but Pickersgill survived captivity. These men used their training to assist in building projects or, in the more organised camps, by giving lectures to educate or relieve the tedium of camp life. Godfrey Bird's collection contains dozens of sketches of architectural styles illustrating the history of architecture, as well as detailed plans of previous projects recreated from memory. Upton and Pyment used their knowledge to help design and construct a concrete chapel at Tandjong Priok transit camp in Java.

Several were trained artists but by far the majority were amateurs with a flair and a need to record, document and inform. Regrettably, a few of the artists listed do not have an example of their work in the book. The enquiry has examined the materials they used, how they improvised and the ways they found to keep art work hidden and safe.

Some artists feature again in Sections II and III. This chapter and the next reveal the artists according to the different regions of captivity. Starting with those in camps in what was the Netherlands (or Dutch) East Indies (NEI or DEI) and is now Indonesia. A vast archipelago, it is spread across the largest and most southerly area of Southeast Asia, encompassing thousands of islands, the largest of which are Sumatra and Java.

Dutch East Indies: Java

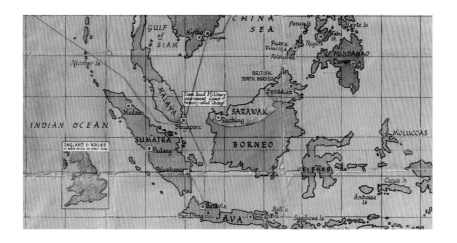

Nowell Peach, Maurice Kinmonth and Leslie Audus were captured in Java. Both Peach and Kinmonth were working with Australian surgeon, Edward 'Weary' Dunlop at No.1 Allied General Hospital in Bandoeng in the central

Highlands of Java when the Japanese invaded. After six weeks the hospital was closed and the staff and patients sent into captivity. Following a brief time in camps in Bandoeng, Kinmonth and Peach were transferred to Batavia (now Jakarta) in the west of the island where they remained for the duration. Leslie Audus was captured on an airfield in the west and moved to Soerabaya in the east, prior to being drafted to the Moluccas.

Maurice Kinmonth: The young surgeon whittled away much of his spare time during the early months of captivity making a beautiful wooden box (Figure 1). Carved out of a small piece of wood over many months, the box is roughly five inches by four and a half inches by an inch and a half deep. It has beautifully rounded ends with the opening on the underside, closed with a wooden slider.

It is the top of the box which draws the eye – a piece of inlaid engraved aluminium features a skilfully-crafted caricature of the young moustachioed surgeon, with a wide grin and menacing glint in the eye as he wields his sharpened knife, ready for action. Barbed wire encompasses the central figure, which looks for all the world like the genie in the lamp, except that he is standing in a jug, beneath which is written, There I Was!

Flight Lieutenant Maurice Henry Kinmonth
Medical Officer RAF Medical Service, 242 Squadron

Captured:	Java 9 March 1942
Camps:	Java: No.1 Allied General Hospital, Bandung;
	Mater Dolorosa hospital camp, Batavia
From:	Lisdoonvarna, County Clare, Ireland
DoB:	14.5.17
Died:	30.1.09

Figure 1. Small wooden inlaid box made by Fl/Lt M. Kinmonth (© courtesy the Kinmonth family)

Both the artistry and engraving were done by New Zealand newspaper cartoonist, Sid Scales. The inlaid work was then skilfully applied to the wooden box. It is difficult to see in this photograph, but the top and bottom of the metal has been shaped to fit perfectly into the curvature of the wooden box. How the aluminium was affixed is not known. There is no evidence of nails and so some sort of adhesive must have been used; whatever it was, it remains effective.

Kinmonth kept this small memento with him throughout captivity. At interview, 67 years later, it was clear that it remained a source of great pride, tangible evidence of both the box's and his own survival. Post-war Kinmonth went on to train as a plastic surgeon and established the first plastic surgery units in Leicestershire and Lincolnshire. In retirement he took up wood engraving, commenting that, *"wood doesn't bleed!"*[3]

Nowell Peach: Being a keen ornithologist, an interest nurtured as a young boy, helped Peach during captivity. He filled a pilfered school exercise book with observations of plumage and the nesting habits of Javanese birds and, after finding a school text book on the subject, he reproduced numerous sketches, like the ones in Figure 2 over the page.

The caption at the bottom of the sketch on the right states: 'Scarlett headed flower pecker. Drawn from observations of a pair nesting in garden. Mater Dolorosa POW Hospital Batavia. 29.5.43'.

While at Tandjong Priok transit camp, Peach spent any spare time he had when not recording bird life, whittling. He made an elegant teak handle for a patella hammer (a medical instrument made by Royal Engineers in the camp). He needed the hammer to test reflexes, required for the secret neurological investigations he conducted on 58 patients suffering from peripheral nerve damage caused by lack of vitamin B in the diet.[4] He also used his surgical skills to carve a small and exquisite Balinese woman's head which, like Kinmonth's wooden box, remained with him throughout captivity (Figure 3). Post-war he added the tiny ear rings to complete his memento of Java.

Leslie Audus: In 1941 Audus led a small specialist team of RAF technicians sent out to Johor in Malaya to set up the first secret radar installation in

Figure 2.   Pages from Peach's bird notebook,
1943 Batavia, by Fl/Lt A. N. H. Peach
(*© courtesy E. Hatton-Smith*)

Flight Lieutenant Alfred Nowell Hamilton Peach

Medical Officer RAF Medical Service

Captured:	Java 9 March 1942
Camps:	Java: Bandung, Landsop camp, Batavia: Tjimahi, Cycle camp, Tandjong Priok transit camp, Mater Dolorosa and St Vincentius Hospital camps, Bandung POW camp
From:	Bristol
DoB:	30.6.13
Died:	13.1.12

Figure 3. Balinese woman's head
carved by Fl/Lt N. Peach, Java 1942
(© courtesy C. Bean)

Southeast Asia. In early 1942 with the Japanese invasion imminent, this highly
specialised unit was hurriedly evacuated via Sumatra en route to India. From
Sumatra they fled south to Java but were eventually captured.

Pre-war Audus (a plant physiologist) had been a senior lecturer in botany at
University College, Cardiff. Post-war he was to become Professor of Botany at
the University of London and a world authority on the hormones that control
plant growth. As well as being a scientist, Audus was a gifted amateur artist –
encompassing watercolours, detailed cartoons and caricatures and botanical
studies. He also had a passion for classical music and mah-jong. Incredibly, he
not only brought back home over 150 separate pieces of artwork, including 99
caricatures of fellow officers and men and pen and ink cartoons of his medical
work in Java and the Moluccas, but also a homemade mah-jong set and his
gramophone together with his prized collection of 78rpm classical records! He
had used the latter to give talks and lectures in camp. It is also interesting to
note that, unlike other caricaturists Audus did not give away his sketches to the
subject but kept them all together. In retirement he had the originals bound into
a volume with accompanying detailed captions.

In captivity in Java and later the Moluccas, his specialist knowledge was
invaluable in helping POW doctors. This work is described more fully in chapter
5. His watercolours in Java include scenes around the large Jaarmarkt camp in
Soerabaya (Figure 4) done in 1942, and two watercolours of the Gunong Lawu
volcano that he painted three times on the same day in May 1942 (Figure 5; also
Chapter 4, Figure 32).

Figure 4.   A scene at Soerabaya, watercolour by Fl/Lt L. J. Audus (© *courtesy H. Audus*)

Figure 5.   Two views of Gunong Lawu volcano, Maospati, Java at sunrise and noon, May 1942, by Fl/Lt L. J. Audus (© *courtesy H. Audus*)

Flight Lieutenant Leslie John Audus

Scientist, RAF 512 AMES (Air Ministry Experimental Station)

Captured:	Java 9 March 1942
Camps:	Java: airfield at Tjimahi, Maospati, Lyceum, Jaarmarkt in Soerabaya
	Moluccas: Haroekoe, Ambon: Liang and Wijami camps
	Java, Batavia: Kampong Macassar; Bandoeng: Depot and L.O.G. camps
From:	Soham, Cambridgeshire
DoB:	9.12.11
Died:	5.5.11

Figure 6.   Caricature of Fl/Lt Alex Gooding, by Fl/Lt L. J. Audus *(© courtesy H. Audus)*

Audus' caricature work is extraordinary. Almost all of the caricatures feature a heraldic shield tailored to the individual. Here are a couple of examples (in both cases the likeness is assumed): Audus' good friends, Fl/Lt Alex Gooding, RAFVR (Figure 6) and Bill 'Doc' Tierney (Figure 7). Gooding's accoutrements are self-explanatory, walking purposefully, fly swat in hand. With his heraldic shield depicting a fly shot with an arrow we can assume Gooding was a member of the fly swatting party.

Tierney was one of the young medical officers, an Irishman who had a passion for cigars and card games as the shield observes. In his caption, Audus commented:

"A bluff, outspoken graduate of University College Cork, unstinting and untiring in his care and concern for the 'erk' [RAF Other Ranks]*, resourceful and inventive when it came to improvisation. He enjoyed playing football and card games and smoking cigars ... He survived and on repatriation enthusiastically flung himself into the broadening of his medical horizon in specialist hospitals in the UK ..."*

Figure 7.   Caricature of Fl/Lt Bill 'Doc' Tierney, by Fl/Lt L. J. Audus *(© courtesy H. Audus)*

Audus worked closely with British and Dutch medical staff, using his knowledge and expertise to help counteract symptoms of vitamin B deficiency, one of which is blurred vision. Audus was suffering and knew the cause and what was required. Producing yeast he could make a rudimentary form of 'Marmite' which, if taken as a daily supplement, would relieve this and other symptoms. There is more about this work in Chapter 5 p. 234.

This sketch (Figure 8), signed by Leslie Audus and dated April 1943, with the location Jaarmarkt Soerabaya in the top righthand corner, has as its central caricature, Pilot Officer Bill Altson RAF. Bill, by that time aged 50, was a British scientist, a plant pathologist working in Malaya at the outbreak of war. Standing in the background to the right of the picture Leslie has drawn a self-portrait. The scene depicts the inside of a disused lean-to shack, appropriated and set up as a secret laboratory for the cultivation of yeast, situated behind the camp hospital of the vast Jaarmarkt transit camp. In the foreground, on the workbench to the left of Altson, is a Bunsen burner made from scrap metal by the camp handyman. The resulting extract, a greenish-coloured goo, was given as a daily dose to the affected men.

The two scientists eventually parted company in mid-1943 when Leslie was sent on the Moluccas draft to the island of Haroekoe, by which time he had perfected the manufacturing process for yeast (Chapter 5, Figure 15). Audus also indulged his passion for botany using the opportunity of such close proximity to tropical flora

Figure 8. Caricatures of Altson and Audus in the yeast hut, Jaarmarkt Camp, Soerabaya Java, April 1943, by Fl/Lt L. J. Audus (© courtesy H. Audus)

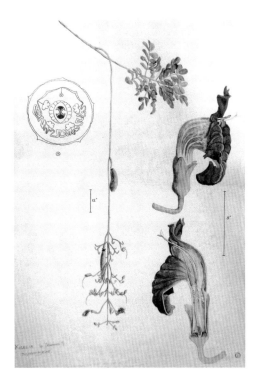

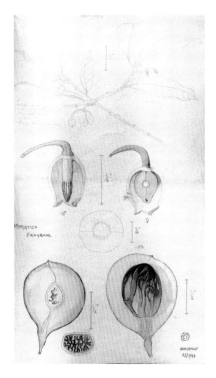

Figure 9. Kigelia Bignoniaciae, Lyceum,
Soerabaya, Sept 1942 by Fl/Lt L. J. Audus
(© courtesy H. Audus)

Figure 10. Nutmeg and mace,
Haroekoe, Spice Islands, 23 July 1943,
by Fl/Lt L. J. Audus
(© courtesy H. Audus)

to study and to record exquisitely detailed watercolour sketches of specimens found on both Java and Haroekoe (Figures 9 and 10; also Chapter 4, Figure 30).

Most of Audus' work features his distinctive moniker (Figure 11), using his initials 'L J A' to make a smiley face!

He also made delicate and detailed watercolours of the living conditions (see Chapter 4) as well as the marvellous 'Maurice the Mantis' (Figure 12). Whether the creature was painted in Java or on the island of Haroekoe is not known.

Also, in his kitbag on repatriation was a miniature mah-jong set (Figure 13) that Audus had made in the early weeks of captivity, cutting the tiles from a piece of thick Perspex rescued from a bombed airfield in Java. He not only made the numerous pieces including the miniature dice seen in the photograph, he

Figure 11.   Close up of smiley face moniker, by Fl/Lt L. Audus

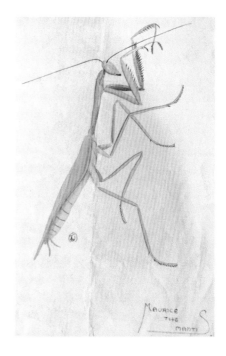

Figure 12.   'Maurice the Mantis', sketched during captivity, by Fl/Lt L. Audus
(© courtesy H. Audus)

engraved and coloured the symbols on each tile. He also made the aluminium tin and leather pouch to keep it in.

Audus' medical work, in which he collaborated with both British and Dutch scientists, is described in detail in his autobiography, *Spice Island Slaves*, published in 1995. At interview in 2009, following a stroke which had left him nearly blind, Audus, when prompted with the name and caption he had put with each of his caricatures, provided clear and insightful thumbnail sketches of each

Figure 13.   Photograph of the mahjong set made by Leslie Audus, Java 1942, by Fl/Lt L. J. Audus
(© courtesy H. Audus)

of the 99 men he had depicted. It was both hilarious and revealing to listen as his scientist's eye for detailed observation extended beyond his art into personal observations of human character.

Both scientist and doctor, Leslie Audus and Nowell Peach, had a special interest in the natural world. Both observed and made copious notes, sketches and watercolours of plant life and tropical birds. One can imagine the fleeting sense of peace each man found in recording the flora and fauna in their midst, for a brief while distracted from the realities of their existence.

In 2013 the enquiry moved briefly to Indonesia in pursuit of British FEPOW artwork known to be there. In Jakarta, hanging on a wall either side of the font inside the Anglican Church of All Saints (Figure 14) in the centre of the city, are two precious artefacts from the Second World War.

Held by the church for safekeeping for over 75 years, are two, small, painted faux-stained glass windows in their original frames (Figure 15). They were given sanctuary there in autumn 1943, when Tandjong Priok transit camp, on the dockside north of Batavia, was finally evacuated of all its FEPOW inhabitants. Left behind was the tiny St George's Chapel. Designed by British and Australian POW architects and built from reinforced concrete in the first four months of captivity, the chapel was completed by the British after the Australians at Tandjong Priok were transferred to another camp in May.[5]

Figure 14. Anglican Church of All Saints, Jakarta, October 2013 *(photograph M. Parkes)*

It is only thanks to the quick thinking and courage of the members of a small Christian community living near the camp that the painted windows survive today. Set into the wall behind the altar, they removed them for fear that the chapel would be destroyed by the local Muslim community. The chapel did not survive.

Herbert Upton: The creator of the chapel windows in spring 1942 was British naval officer, Lieutenant Commander Herbert Upton RNVR. Pre-war he had been working in Malaya as an architect with Cable and Wireless. According to his report, written in 1946 for the Royal Navy, the windows are predominantly painted in red and yellow gloss house paints pilfered from nearby abandoned Dutch houses. He tried to give the work a more translucent effect by smearing the paint using the ball of his thumb.

The full story of the discovery of the two original windows (and the subsequent creation in 2005 of replica windows to form the Java Memorial windows in the FEPOW Memorial Building at the National Memorial Arboretum (NMA) in Staffordshire) has been already been told in *Captive Memories*.[6] Interestingly,

Lieutenant Commander Herbert Cooper Upton RNVR
HMS Rahman

Captured:	2 March 1942, Java
Camps:	Singapore: Batam Island
	Java: Cycle Camp, Boie Glodok, Tandjong Priok
	Sumatra: Pakenbaroe No.1 and No.5 camps
From:	West Sussex
DoB:	2.6.10
Died:	1978

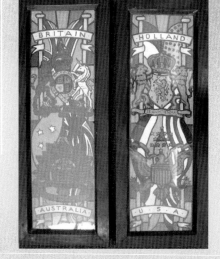

Figure 15.   Photograph of both the original windows, side by side (© courtesy M. Parkes)

Figure 16. Photograph showing the detail in British section, with the Lion Rampant smoking a large red cigar (© *courtesy M. Parkes*)

the windows contain no Christian symbolism but instead are split into four sections, one window bearing the national flags and insignia of Britain and Australia and the other those of the USA and Holland. Wirral artist, the late David Hillhouse, was commissioned to make replicas of the originals, and on close examination of photographs discovered something rather unusual in one of them. The British section, with the Royal Coat of Arms in its centre, has the Lion Rampant with Churchil's face, smoking a large red cigar (Figure 16)! Several FEPOW artists recorded the chapel during captivity, as did a few of the men who kept diaries, but none had revealed this secret.

Gunner Charles Holdsworth did a pencil sketch of the chapel which looked like an archetypal English parish church. It was designed by British and Australian architects. Holdsworth's sketch is in the IWM's collection.

Gunner Holdsworth was from Porthcawl in South Wales. A capable illustrator, also provided several front cover designs and sketches for a POW camp journal edited by Lt Ron Williams, entitled, *The Jungle Journal.*[7] These were produced in various POW camps in west Java. Holdsworth eventually ended up in Thailand, sent with H Force to work on the Burma–Thailand railway. He survived the war.

Desmond Pyment: A third year architecture student, Desmond Pyment drew these visualisations for St George's Chapel and its exterior pulpit at Tandjong Priok POW camp, Batavia, on flimsy paper. He worked on it with Captain Ray Watts. The chapel building was designed to shelter just the altar with the congregation standing under the shade of the surrounding trees (Figure 17). It was built at one end of the football pitch as is clearly shown in Duncan's camp plan (Figure 18).

During 1943, at Motoyama camp in Japan, Duncan wrote a narrative of his captivity in Java entitled, *Java, Jeopardy and Jail,* in which he described St George's chapel:

Staff Sergeant Desmond Arthur Pyment
Royal Engineers

Captured:	Java 9 March 1942
Camps:	Java: Tandjong Priok; Singapore; Borneo: Kuching POW camp
From:	Chipping Camden, Gloucestershire
DoB:	22.8.20
Died:	25.1.99

CHURCH OF ST. GEORGE   TANDJONG PRIOK. JAVA.

Figure 17. The grove of locust trees surrounding the chapel, by Staff Sgt D. A. Pyment (© courtesy M. Pyment)

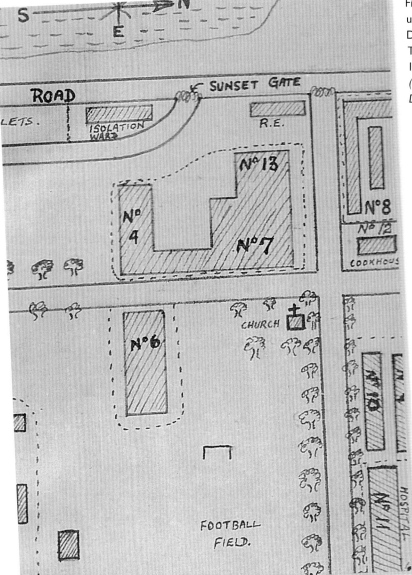

"Not long after we arrived at Priok, it was suggested that a small chapel should be built as there was plenty wood in the camp as well as cement, the skilled labour and architects were all there too … The site that was chosen was at one end of the football pitch where locust trees with their scarlet blossom and overhanging shady foliage provided shelter from the blazing heat of the tropical sun, and work was begun early in April 1942.

The walls of the chapel were made of reinforced concrete with the north side left open in the shape of a gothic arch whilst the south wall had two windows let into it which were later to contain stained glass designs incorporating the figure of St. George of England and the flags of all the nationalities of the prisoners in Priok; inside the chapel itself there was an altar covered with sarong cloth and carved wood candlesticks on each side of a crucifix, teak wood polished with talcum powder and brown boot polish being used for the altar and its fittings ... Every Sunday, weather permitting, a service was held at 10A.M. and the congregation led by a choir sang popular psalms and hymns and then listened to a short sermon ... communion was held every Sunday at 8A.M. and 11A.M. and a Toc H group held meetings in the evening.

There was a serene charm about the whole of the chapel area which was not to be found anywhere else in the camp and I used to look forward to the service each week as a great source of spiritual comfort ..."

But here there is some confusion as Duncan relates that

"the south wall had two windows let into it which were later to contain stained glass designs incorporating the figure of St. George of England and the flags of all the nationalities of the prisoners in Priok."

A competition was held in Tandjong Priok camp for the design of a third window and one of the submissions was St George slaying the dragon, coloured in crayon by Lieutenant Noel James, 77th Heavy Anti-Aircraft Royal Artillery, the same unit as Charles Holdsworth.[8]

Also, among Ron Williams' private papers in the IWM is an anonymous design for six window panels in the chapel. It is another detailed layout clearly showing three small square windows above three longer narrower ones described earlier, set into the south wall of the chapel.

This is the only known photograph of the chapel, taken on that day by a Japanese propaganda photographer (Figure 19). The large congregation stood behind the photographer, including Capt. Duncan. A year later,

Figure 19.   Japanese propaganda photograph of the consecration of St George's Chapel, Tandjong Priok POW transit camp Java, July 1942 led by Padre Harper-Holdcroft, centre, with Padre Phillips at the organ. *(original cutting © courtesy the Duncan family)*

Duncan recognised the location of the photograph when he saw this newspaper article, published in an English language version of the *Nippon Times* on 23 June 1943, which was circulated in his camp in Japan. He tore it out and kept it.

This photograph was first seen in public when the story of the creation of St George's chapel Tandjong Priok was first published in 1946 by Revd Lewis Bryan's *Churches of The Captivity in Malaya*, despite the chapel not being in Malaya!

A lieutenant in the Royal Artillery, Stanley Bagnall was an inmate of the notorious Boie Glodok civilian gaol in Batavia, where he painted several watercolours of the camp.

One moody scene, with grey overcast sky, the small windows and proximity of the concrete walls, gives the viewer an impression of the heat and oppressive atmosphere experienced by the POW held within overcrowded cells of the gaol.

Bagnall was in a draft that left Java in September 1942 destined for Borneo. However, we know more about some of the POW occupants of Boie Glodok civilian gaol, thanks to the work of an RAF officer held there at the same time as Bagnall. In 2017 a visit to the COFEPOW archives at the FEPOW Memorial building at the NMA revealed an intricately carved teak table top (Figure 20) that had recently been donated.[9]

Claude McLaren Reid: One of the older RAF officers, born in Scotland at the beginning of the twentieth century, Claude Reid was brought up in Argentina and later became a pre-war resident of Sydney, Australia. Before being captured in Java he was working as a customs officer in Malaya. Reid was part of a large group of RAF men held for a while at Boie Glodok gaol. Needing a table, he found a large panel from an old door but soon his table was to provide a different purpose.

Reid listed the names of the 60 RAF officers and warrant officers held in the gaol with him early in captivity. The names are either side of a central carving depicting the gaol's solitary confinement cells which face an open courtyard and so perhaps despite the concrete construction may not have been as oppressive as first imagined? In three of the four corners of the carving, the small oblong boxes contain his name 'Reid-o' in three different forms of Japanese characters; bottom right are the artist's initials followed by the year, '42.

In 1947, when back working as a Custom's Officer in Kuala Lumpur, Reid wrote *The Tale of a Table*, a history of the table top. The idea for the carving had been inspired by the Japanese Commandant of the gaol, a regular who had actively

Flying Officer Claude McLaren Reid
SHQ RAF

Captured:	Waranadjah, Java 21 March 1942
Camps:	Boie Glodok, Tandjong Priok, Cycle camp, Depot Bandoeng, L.O.G., Cycle camp
From:	Sydney, Australia
DoB:	26.7.02
Died:	not known

Figure 20.   Carved teak table top, made by F/O C. Reid
(© *courtesy COFEPOW archives*)

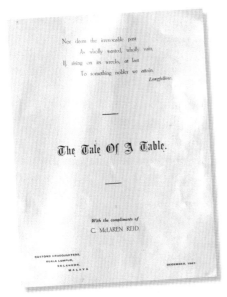

Nor deem the irrevocable past
As wholly wasted, wholly vain,
If, rising on its wrecks, at last
To something nobler we attain.
Longfellow.

𝕿𝖍𝖊 𝕿𝖆𝖑𝖊 𝕺𝖋 𝕬 𝕿𝖆𝖇𝖑𝖊.

With the compliments of
C. McLAREN REID.

CUSTOMS HEADQUARTERS,
KUALA LUMPUR,
SELANGOR,
MALAYA   DECEMBER, 1947.

encouraged arts and crafts and had held an exhibition of work made by the POW. This then, was not created secretly, but with the knowledge and encouragement of the Japanese.

The table top, like its creator, survived the following three years of captivity despite being separated for much of the time. *The Tale of a Table* (Figure 21) details what happened to the table top after Reid was drafted from Java and it was left in the care of a Dutch officer and friend, Lieutenant G. Vischer who remained in the gaol briefly. The history is reproduced on the website.[10]

It took Reid four months to create the table top and it is remarkable that he managed to finish it before being drafted. For the painstaking task of carving out of the heavy, dense timber the 60 names of RAF officers and warrant officers, the central picture and around the edge the beautifully symmetrical chain links, he used a sharpened penknife, a file and nails. One can only imagine his worry of the blade slipping and making a mistake as the work slowly grew and took shape.

When one looks at Reid's craftsmanship one cannot help wondering who watched him at work? What did they gain from such an endeavour? Reid had the determination and tenacity to focus on something creative, a positive endeavour. He created something to admire, and to be admired. On page 3 of *The Tale of a Table* he describes the pride he felt in the achievement (Figure 22). How important that sense of achievement must have been to him.

The perspective of the row of cell doors leading up to the palm tree draws the viewer in to the centre of the piece. This scene is flanked by the names of 60 officers, his own name appearing on the left-hand side, right-hand column,

THE TALE OF A TABLE.

Java 1942.

THE R.A.F. orderly room in Boei Glodok, the civil gaol in Batavia for long-term prisoners, in half of which some 1200 R.A.F. personnel were crowded, was a cell-like room in the administration block some twelve feet by six. The furniture consisted of one small table, a chair and a couple of empty boxes, and the table did duty for the C.O., myself and the clerk, as necessity demanded. After cajoling, threatening and imploring the officer in charge of the workshops for a month or more an extra table was made for myself. The table was made from old sleeping boards used by the civil prisoners in peace time, but found to be so hopelessly bug-ridden as to be unusable by our men. The top was a single piece of teak, approximately thirty-four inches by twenty inches.

As Adjutant and interpreter, my time was more than fully occupied for the first three months, but after that things got easier, and I occasionally found myself with nothing to do, there being very few books available. The then Japanese Commandant, a regular officer, had encouraged arts and crafts, and a successful exhibition had been held, many of the exhibits being made by expert hands. One day it crossed my mind to do something of the sort myself, and the idea of carving the names of the Officers and Warrant Officers on my table occured to me. I found that I had more space than was needed, so included a view of the solitary confinement cells. I finished up by placing a symbolic chain round the outside, the links being copied from the chains used on the civilian prisoners.

I managed to borrow an extremely blunt and jagged-edged gouge for a short while to remove the wood to give depth to the picture, but, apart from that, had only one blade of a "Dewars" advertisement penknife, a bone handled nail-file and a sharpened nail or two to work with. It took nearly four months to complete and looked a pretty amateurish job when it was finished, but it kept me occupied and I was quite pleased with, not to say proud of, it. In October, the night before our first draft left, I got everyone available to autograph the back of it, but one man would never be there to sign. He had been captured one night early in April with two Sergeant pilots while making a gallant and very

Figure 22.   Page 3 of *Tale of a Table* (© courtesy COFEPOW archives)

third from the top. As a point of interest, the man listed above Reid is J. (John) Fletcher-Cooke. He left Java on the draft to Japan in October 1942 and was later to become camp interpreter at Miyata camp on Kyushu.[11]

The carved chain link was modelled on the chains used on the civilian inmates of the gaol. The centre bottom link however was made one inch longer than the rest in preparation for the day of liberation would one day dawn. He describes how, once reunited with the table top in December 1946, he cut that link to denote their freedom. Into the broken link he would later insert an inscribed, engraved silver plate. The silver plate came from the melted fork and spoon he had kept and used throughout captivity which a local silversmith created for him. He sent the small silver plate to Lord Mountbatten explaining the purpose and asking if he would sign it (Figure 23). This was returned, duly signed, and Reid had the signature engraved and the silver set into the broken link.

At the end of his booklet, Reid states: 'To the relatives of those who have gone, I offer it as my humble tribute to the memory of the dead'. His table top is a tour de force. A list of the names Reid carved is at www.captivememories.org.uk

Figure 23. The engraved silver plate on teak tabletop signed Mountbatten of Burma, by Lord Mountbatten 1946 (© courtesy the Booth family and COFEPOW archives)

Dutch East Indies: The Spice Islands

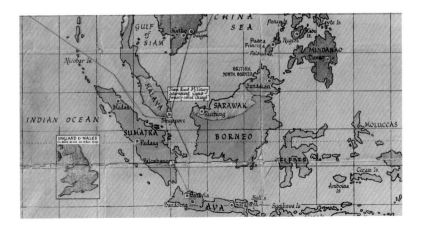

RAF Medical Officer Richard Philps was one of several doctors drafted to the Moluccas, the eastern most part of the NEI, along with 2000 mainly RAF men, including Leslie Audus. They were sent to the islands of Ambon and Haroekoe (also spelt Haruku), more commonly known as the Spice Islands, to build airfields for Japan's planned assault on Australia. Over 1200 of the 2000 sent with Philps died.

Richard Philps: Known to his friends as 'Dickie', Richard was another lifelong amateur ornithologist and naturalist. He was also a talented artist and used watercolours he had acquired to record the scenes around him (Figure 23), like this view from the shoreline close to Haroekoe camp.

Stretching away into the distance is what appears to be a tropical idyll. He painted seven watercolours, all just a little larger than A5 in size. These watercolours were reproduced in his 1995 memoir, *Prisoner Doctor*, based on his diary notes written up in early 1946 but were regrettably black and white photographs of the originals. When seen in colour they are mesmerising.

This depiction of what looks like a clean, orderly camp (Figure 25) belies the truth of the nightmare squalor inside the hut far right, marked with the large red cross. We know this because trained RAF medical orderly, Arthur Turbutt, worked with Philps in Haroekoe. In his strong north London brogue, Turbutt revealed at interview the following realities of looking after dysentery patients at Haroekoe:

"The biggest killer of course was dysentery, amoebic dysentery ... our main job seemed to be, trying to lift these poor fellows off the bamboo and, as weak as we were, trying to carry them along to an old cabin trunk ... the lid had been taken off and the cabin trunk was lying in the centre of the floor and those that needed had to ... put their bottoms over the side and do what they had to do ... Now that was swimming with filth and slime and blood and, of course, you've got to remember, that the place was full of flies, millions upon millions ... we had nothing we could give them. All we could give them was physical, mental and perhaps I don't know, spiritual comfort. You couldn't do any more for them; they were crying ... They knew they were dying, and they were dying in agony a lot of them, terrible agony of dysentery. And, all we could do is try and comfort them and make their passing as easy as we could."[12]

Figure 24. View from shoreline, Haroekoe, 1943, Fl/Lt F. R. Philps *(© courtesy the Philps family)*

Flight Lieutenant Frank Richard 'Dickie' Philps

Medical Officer RAF Medical Service

Captured:	Java 9 March 1942
Camps:	Java: Tasik Malaya, Lyceum Soerabaya, Semarang, Jaarmarkt
	Moluccas: Haroekoe POW camp, Ambon, Macassar
	Singapore: Morse Road, Keppel Harbour, Changi
From:	Radlett, Herts
DoB:	9.3.14
Died:	16.10.95

Figure 25. Scene across Haroekoe POW camp, 1944, Fl/Lt F. R. Philps
(© courtesy the Philps family)

In addition to his beautiful watercolours of the island, Philps documented the dental surgery of another colleague and friend, RAF dental officer, Fl/Lt Clifford Beales. This sketch below (Figure 26) was discovered by Beale's daughter Carol Friend in 2011 when she was going through documents from her parents' home. It was thrilling to watch as she opened a box full of documents and took out a plain manila folder, inside which was this sketch. She had not seen it before.

Figure 26. Dental surgery on Haroekoe, sketch by Fl/Lt F. R. Philps
(© courtesy C. Friend)

Until that point we were unaware of the existence of a dental surgery on Haroekoe. The sketch is signed, F R Philps 1943, in the bottom righthand corner. There is also another small inscription to the left of the signature which reads:

CMB from FRP
Christmas 1948. Haroekoe.

What a fitting memento for the dentist, from his doctor friend. The detail in this sketch is most interesting. The surgery is most likely at one end of a larger bamboo and atap hut, perhaps the hospital hut. Facing the open window shutter sits a robust looking, homemade dental chair with adjustable headrest and tilting backrest, constructed not from bamboo but from wooden planks. On the seat there appears to be a folded blanket, perhaps some small comfort for the patient! There is an instrument tray fixed to a bamboo upright facing the chair.

On closer inspection it appears it may have been a preliminary sketch to be worked up later (like another painting by Philps, the 'Doctors' Hut' – Chapter 4, Figure 14) in watercolour. This is evidenced by the two framed pictures on the far wall; when closely examined (Figure 27) the one on the left is clearly entitled 'Picture', while the one on the right bears a rough sketch of a boat at sea with what appears to be an airplane diving, and underneath is written 'By Nip'.

Figure 27.   A close-up of dental surgery on Haroekoe, by Fl/Lt F. R.Philps
(© *courtesy C. Friend*)

The cloth-covered bamboo table under the pictures holds what looks like a tincture bottle with applicator. There are more bottles on the bamboo shelving to the righthand side of the picture and beside the chair there is a kidney dish, perhaps for swabs. Looking out of the window, to the left of the dental chair, there appears to be a homemade treadle drill constructed like the chair from wooden planks. A wheel is visible in the background, though not attached to the apparatus, so perhaps an indication of the mechanism for a later, more detailed, study. Arthur Turbutt remembered the dentist and his surgery:

> "The [sketch of the] *dental surgery is marvellous, all that Heath-Robinson*
> *stuff! I wasn't a patient, because of my work I had restricted movement*
> *around camp as it* [dysentery] *was highly contagious. I worked in Ward 3.*
> *Beales' character? I remember him with his nose in the air, head held back.*
> *This gives the wrong impression though, he was completely not the snooty*
> *type, a very efficient dentist, wonderful man"*.

In this caricature (Figure 28) by **Leslie Audus** he depicts three medical officers. On the left is Scotsman, Flight Lieutenant Alistair Forbes, from Aberdeen. He wrote a detailed report for the Air Ministry in 1946 in which he paid special tribute to Turbutt and five other medical orderlies he had worked with on Haroekoe, stating that

> "... [they] *did*
> *particularly good work*
> *during the dysentery*
> *epidemic and at all times*
> *maintained the traditions*
> *of the Service."*

Figure 28. Caricatures of three medical officers on Haroekoe, 1944, by Fl/Lt L. Audus
(© courtesy H. Audus)

The central, seated figure is Dickie Philps and on his right is Dutch medical officer, Dr Tromp. Philps is holding in his hand a small painted kingfisher, that he carved from teak during the early months of captivity. In his memoir *Prisoner Doctor*, he describes the bird as his talisman:

> *"The other remarkable thing that happened at this camp was that I carved my kingfisher. The wood burned in Javanese railway engines at that time – and in our cookhouse – was so called bastard teak, a knotty, curly-grained, very hard teak, useless for any other purpose. I managed to get hold of a piece, found myself a hacksaw-blade, ground it into a knife-blade on a building stone and spent many a happy and emblistered hour whittling out the effigy of an ordinary European kingfisher to keep me company. I painted it with some of the watercolours I had bought at Tasikmalaya [Java], gave myself a sharp attack of lead poisoning through licking my brush, and managed to keep it, finally bringing it home. It became one of my talisman possessions ... and I think I owe my life to it."*

Philps painted his kingfisher with great care, using brushes and paints that he managed to buy at the start of his captivity (Figure 29). At Tasikmalaya airfield in central Java early in 1942, where hundreds of RAF men were rounded up by the Japanese, Philps was sent to acquire essential medical

Figure 29. Carved wooden kingfisher, Fl/Lt R. Philps, 1942
(© courtesy the Philps family)

and general supplies locally. He used the opportunity to also purchase paper, pencils, brushes and a few paint boxes. These turned out to be of Japanese origin and, as he explained in the extract above, he later discovered they were highly toxic. Philps kept his little kingfisher with him throughout captivity.

The kingfisher features again in Philps' watercolour of the Doctors' Hut painted in 1943 after his transfer to the island of Haroekoe (see Chapter 4, Figure 14).

In later life, both Philps and Peach became noted and highly-respected ornithological and wildlife photographers. On his retirement to Devon in 1973 Philps devoted himself to his passion for wildlife and bird photography making wildlife films for the BBC.[13] Later he returned to painting, having work exhibited at the Royal Institute for Watercolour Painters and the Federation of British Artists.

When Leslie Audus was interviewed, he remembered Dickie Philps as

"… a gifted and skilled surgeon. A naturalist, well-known bird photographer, splendid water-colourist, a skilled craftsman in the construction of makeshift artificial limbs for prisoners. He was the overworked doctor on one of the returning ships which took over two months to make the normally five-day journey back to Java on which 300 out of the 600 prisoners died from starvation and disease."

Dutch East Indies: Borneo

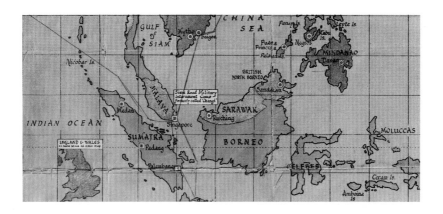

Returning to Stanley Bagnall, in September 1942 he was on a draft that left Java, going first to Changi POW camp in Singapore for a few weeks before moving on again to Jesselton camp in Sarawak, British North Borneo. Soon after he was transferred again, south to Batu Lintang camp at Kuching which had been, until the Japanese invasion, in part of Borneo governed by the DEI.

At Kuching Bagnall joined the secret 'Kuching University' which had been set up by FEPOW Frank Bell, a Cambridge graduate and linguist. His detailed and beautifully bound teaching notebooks are held by the IWM and his memoir, 'Undercover University', first published in 1990 and based on Bell's diary, is illustrated with many of Bagnall's lovely watercolours and sketches. Some of these are held in the IWM.[14]

As well as watercolours, Bagnall also did pencil sketches and portraits. One, a study of fellow repatriates was sketched on board the SS *Cilicia*, bound for Liverpool in late October 1945. Fellow passengers included Leslie Audus, Nowell Peach, Richard Philps and Maurice Kinmonth.

Reg Newman: Another student of the Kuching University was Reg Newman. He also features in 'Undercover University', as a signatory to a card presented to Bell on his birthday in 1944.[15] Newman dreamed of building a caravan after the war. In a small home-made notebook (the pages a mixture of lined paper and envelopes in which he had received mail, censor marks clearly visible and bound together) he had made detailed plans and copious notes for the design and construction of the caravan (Figure 30).

In August 2014 BBC's television's 'Antiques Roadshow' featured Newman's daughter, Janet Fursier, showing the military expert her father's small notebook from his captivity in Borneo. It contained page after page of sketches of his dream caravan, down to the finest detail including the bedside lights made from old bottles, the water pump for the sink and door and drawer handle designs. Contacting Janet afterwards she readily agreed to having his drawings included in the enquiry.

Captain Reginald Newman

48th LAA (49th Bty) Royal Artillery

Captured:	Java
Camps:	Java: Tandjong Priok; Singapore: Changi POW camp (2 weeks);
	Borneo: Jesselton briefly, then Kuching
From:	Newport, Monmouthshire
DoB:	15.07.18
Died:	6.1.72

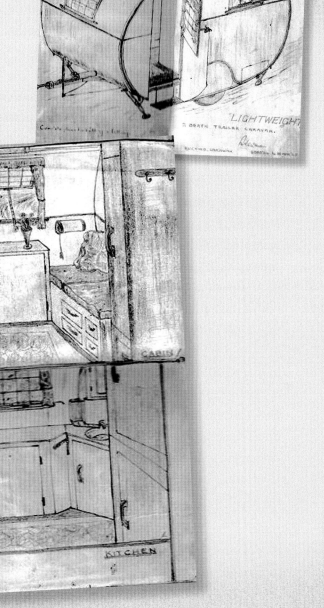

Figure 30. Two drawings of the
exterior and interior of his dream
caravan, by Capt. R. Newman
(© courtesy J. Fursier)

Figure 31.   The finished caravan
(© courtesy J. Fursier)

In 2016 the team from Channel 4's 'George Clark's Amazing Spaces' programme took on the challenge to recreate the caravan right down to the smallest detail (Figure 31). The programme was aired in December 2016.[16]

Dutch East Indies: Sumatra

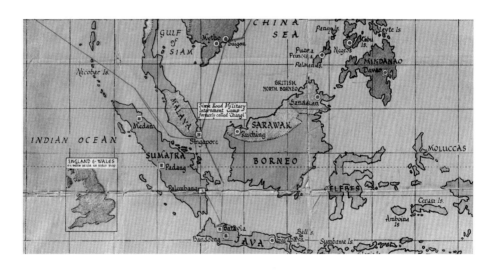

By comparison with Java and the Moluccas, comparatively little British artwork has emerged from camps across Sumatra during the art enquiry. POW camps were spread across this huge island in some of the wildest and most remote jungle areas. Petty Officer writer Bill Bolitho RN, who was interviewed for LSTM's FEPOW oral history interview, mentioned a British artist, Leading Aircraftsman Rex Spencer.

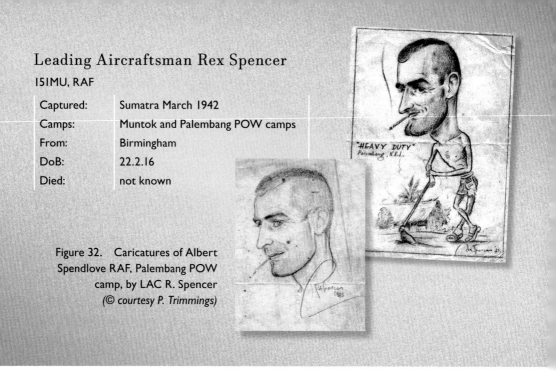

Leading Aircraftsman Rex Spencer
151MU, RAF

Captured:	Sumatra March 1942
Camps:	Muntok and Palembang POW camps
From:	Birmingham
DoB:	22.2.16
Died:	not known

"HEAVY DUTY"
Palembang, N.E.I.

Figure 32.   Caricatures of Albert
Spendlove RAF, Palembang POW
camp, by LAC R. Spencer
(© courtesy P. Trimmings)

Rex Spencer: On Spencer's Liberation Questionnaire he has written under Unit: Air Sea Rescue Service. His artwork first came to light back in May 2010 when Pauline Trimmings emailed the enquiry. She is the daughter of Albert Spendlove who was a friend of Spencer's. She had attached two caricatures (Figure 32) of her father done at different times by Spencer at Palembang POW camp in the south of Sumatra.

BACON & EGGS,
SUNGEI RON.
SUMATRA

Figure 33.   'Bacon & Eggs, Sungei
Ron, Sumatra', two Australians
of 2/20 Btn, late August 1945,
by LAC R. Spencer
(© courtesy P. Winstanley)

In the one of the left, Spendlove is nonchalantly leaning on the ubiquitous chunkol, the favoured earth moving tool used throughout captivity to dig holes, build roads and railways through jungles, and airfields on tropical islands. More recently another of Spencer's excellent caricatures (Figure 33) came to light on the website of Australian military historian, Peter Winstanley.[17]

Wally Cullen: Captured in Java, Cullen remained there until May 1944 when he was sent to Sumatra to work on the Pakenbaroe railway. His pen and ink sketches conceived during that final stage of captivity are both vivid and interesting. This sketch below (Figure 34) is captioned 'Yasoomi' (sic) – yasume is the Japanese word for 'rest' – is on flimsy paper with evidence of foxing (brownish coloured spots on paper indicating the aging process) across the top, and with just the title, bottom right. In it he depicts a group of FEPOW sitting around, leaning against tree stumps. It gives a sense of the men having to cut through forest to create the space for the track. In the centre, the railway trace is seen, bridging a small stream running out of the jungle beyond.

Alongside, is what looks like a copy of the original sketch which the family found. This has additional annotations in different handwriting – his signature bottom left, and in the centre the words 'Sumatra Railway'. It seems likely this sketch was done post-war. In captivity Cullen also drew a few cartoons, like this one (Figure 36) again done on flimsy paper. The title is 'Oliver asks for leggi', the word *leggi* being Malay meaning 'more', hence the Dickens reference.

Cullen was a self-taught watercolourist, an illustrator and later in life a glass engraver. Interestingly, in 1988 he gained the distinction of being one of only handful of artists to have illustrated the works of Charles Dickens. Published in 1989, *The Tugg's at Ramsgate* is one of Dickens' short stories.[18]

Stanley Russell was 27 when he was captured at Padang on the west coast of Sumatra in March 1942. A Lance Corporal in the Royal Corps of Signals, he was sent in a draft to the northernmost province of Atjeh (or Aceh), to Gloegoer Medan on the east coast of Sumatra. There he began sketching

Lance Bombardier Walter Sidney Charles 'Wally" Cullen

46th LAA Battery, Royal Artillery

Captured:	Garoet, Java
	Java: Tandjong Priok, Boie Glodok, Cycle camp
	Sumatra: May 1944 onwards Padang, Medan, northern Aceh and Pakenbaroe
From:	Ramsgate
DoB:	19.10.19
Died:	30.4.01

Figure 34.   Original sketch of 'Yasoomi' done in Sumatra, by L/Bdr W. Cullen (© *courtesy the Cullen family*)

Figure 35.   'Yasoomi', by L/Bdr. W. Cullen (© *courtesy the Cullen family*)

Figure 36.   'Oliver asks for leggi' by Wally Cullen (© *courtesy the Cullen family*)

including two studies of Judy, the only dog officially registered as a prisoner of war during the Second World War. He recorded various aspects of life in camp, sometimes humorous but always informative. Russell was later sent in a party to Pakenbaroe to work on the construction of the Sumatra railway.

Singapore

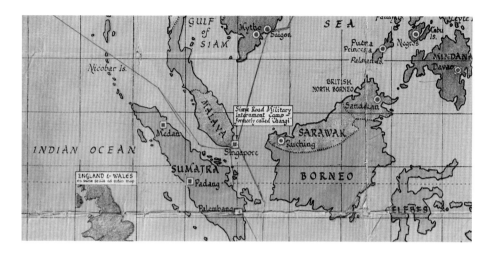

Over 30,000 British forces were captured by the Japanese at the Fall of Singapore on 15 February 1942, among them 37 of the unrecognised artists in this enquiry. They started recording daily life and their surroundings early on in captivity when there were few, if any, restrictions on the making of any sort of records. Some of them may have thought that they would soon be free and wanted to note the circumstances of their captivity. We know from the literature that some of the celebrated artists had with them paper, pencils, pens and ink, but it is doubtful that many others did. However, in the early months at the vast Changi POW camp, opportunities arose to pilfer such items when out on working parties.

Officers and men alike documented their surroundings and aspects of life in Changi POW camp, among them Des Bettany, Don Clarke, John Excell, Geoffrey Gee, Maurice Green, Mike Hardy, Jack Kemp, Cecil Pickersgill, Robert Rogers, Harry Silman, Ronald Spittle, Eric Stacy, Fred Stallard, Stanley Warren, Jack White, Will Wilder and Toss Wilson.

Don Clarke: Brought up in the village of Islip outside Oxford, Don was keen on art at school, encouraged by his teacher. On leaving school he was unable to study art further but in his late teens Don undertook a correspondence course. Clarke's only sketch from Changi, done early in captivity, depicts his tented camp (Chapter 4, Figure 1). Remarkably, he managed to send this small pencil sketch back home to his sister while he was in Changi. On the reverse there are three small pencil portraits, lightly enhanced with crayon, of Don's sister and her two children, done from photographs (Figure 37). According to Mike Clarke (Don's son) this small piece of paper arrived at his parents' home in Islip sometime during 1942. No envelope exists and how he was able to get it posted out of Singapore remains a mystery.

Known to his friends as 'Nobby', Don's other pencil sketches were done while in Thailand when he was working on the railway and then latterly at Ubon camp where they were building an airstrip. During captivity he became a close friend of fellow Oxfordshire artist and teacher, Will Wilder, who sketched Nobby's portrait in 1944 in Thailand. We will return to Wilder's work later.

Gunner Donovan Clarke

135th Field Regiment, RA

Captured:	Singapore 15.2.42
Camps:	Singapore: Changi, Bukit Timah
	Thailand: Tamarkan, Kanburi, Kanu, Kinsaiyok, Chungkai,
	Nong Pladuk, Nakom Paton, Bangkok, Ubon
From:	Islip, Oxfordshire
DoB:	9.11.07
Died:	13.2.00

Figure 37.   Three portraits from photographs, on reverse of 'E Troop Lines' tented camp sketch, by Dvr D. Clarke (© courtesy C. Tuffrey)

Captain Harry Silman

MO, RAMC, attached to 9th Royal Northumberland Fusiliers

Captured:	Singapore 15.2.42
Camps:	Singapore: Changi; returned from Thailand, Changi Gaol POW camp
	Drafted with F Force to Thailand and Burma camps
From:	Leeds
DoB:	21.12.10
Died:	9.5.05

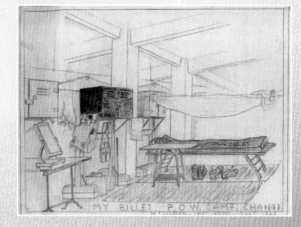

Figure 38. 'My Billet Changi POW camp July 1942', by Capt. H. Silman (© courtesy IWM)

Harry Silman: Yorkshireman and Medical Officer, Captain Harry Silman, was an experienced doctor when he joined the RAMC. During his few months in Changi POW camp he did a few simple sketches of some of his fellow officers and of his immediate surroundings, like the one of his billet (Figure 38).

Silman also collected artwork from several FEPOW, including Robert Rogers, John Excell and Cecil Pickersgill, who all did at least one sketch each of buildings in Changi POW camp. Regrettably, we do not have these illustrations. In this extract from his diary he gives a vivid insight into life at Changi in the early weeks:

> *"Sunday 8th March Had to move the MI [Medical Inspection] room from the NAAFI to the small room beside the officers' mess – very useful for the duty officer who can lie in bed awaiting the call. The third compartment has been taken over by a dentist which will be very useful for us.*
> *Six members of the 198 FA [Field Ambulance] came along with authority*

and threw our orderlies out. This caused much discontent and argument and finally the mistake was discovered, and the FA blokes moved on. There is too much of this state of affairs – chaos and confusion. The RNF [Royal Northumberland Fusiliers] orderlies slept in the ambulance behind the MI room.

Monday 9th March Companies busily engaged in wiring us in our enclosure. Others were occupied in collecting coconuts outside the area – large opportunity. The minor industries that go on are legion. Simpson has his yeast factory, Sandy his vegetable gardens. I make fly covers, fly traps (that are not very successful)."

Another of his sketches, 'The Evening Meal' (not illustrated) is again simple and informative though regrettably, there is no mention of which of his fellow officers he drew.

In April 1943, Silman was drafted with F Force to Sonkurai, Thailand where he spent eight months, briefly crossing the border to camps in Burma, before returning to Singapore where he spent his final 20 months or so at Changi Gaol POW camp, working in the medical block there. Captain James Bradley, on page 56 of his memoir, *Towards the Setting Sun,* recalls Silman at work in Nikke camp, Thailand:

"The way the doctors worked under such appalling conditions was truly marvellous; the one I remember with particular affection was Dr Harry Silman, of 9th Battalion Northumberland Fusiliers who worked ceaselessly for the benefit of all. I had known him so well in Changi, as he was one of those with whom I had sat and talked on the roof of our barrack block at night. He was always cheerful, despite our circumstances, and he was to remain on the railway until he returned to Changi on 21 December 1943."

Maurice Green: In April 1942 Liverpudlian Maurice Green, a young Company Quartermaster Sergeant in 287th Field Coy Royal Engineers, made this pencil sketch on a sheet torn from what looks like a ledger (Figure 39). As he sketched he was looking out from his hut window, beneath the low atap roof and across at the hutted encampment he was in at Changi POW camp. He had married Doris Irene Rose in July 1940. Perhaps this view was captured to show her how they had lived?

Company Quartermaster Sergeant Maurice Charles Green

287th Field Coy, RE

Captured:	Singapore 15.2.42
Camps:	Singapore: Changi
	Thailand: Sonkurai
From:	Waterloo, Liverpool
DoB:	29.5.16
Died:	17.8.00

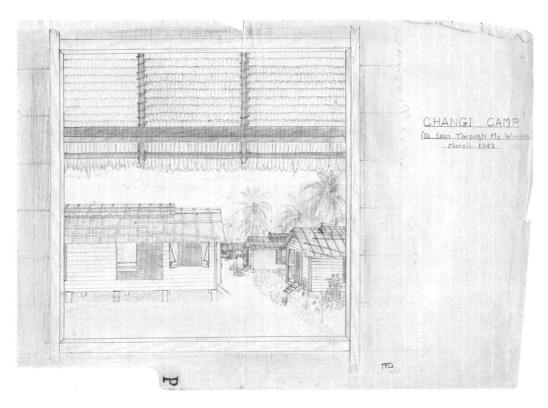

Figure 39. View from my window, Changi 1942, by CQMS M. Green
(© courtesy M. Green)

Figure 40. Photograph of Maurice with his wife
October 1945 *(Daily Despatch)*

Maurice Green's younger brother John, a Sapper in the same regiment, was also in Changi but only for about a month.[19] Maurice remained at Changi until October that year when he was sent with F Force to Thailand. On his Liberation questionnaire the only camp he names is Sonkurai, which was situated in the northern reaches of the Thailand end of the railway. The omission of other camps is perhaps understandable as he endured and survived five dreadful months at the Sonkurai camp, from 20 May to 20 October 1943 (along with medical officer Silman). There, during the appalling 'speedo' period, when the Japanese, desperate to get the railway finished ahead of schedule, the labour force worked night and day. Disease was rife, with cholera outbreaks making survival a lottery. It was a dreadful place and Green was lucky to survive it. He returned home on board the SS *Tegelberg* arriving in Liverpool on 12 October 1945, where this photograph (Figure 40) was taken by a press photographer.

In the 1980s Maurice was seen at LSTM where he was found to have had an undiagnosed intestinal worm infection, *Strongyloides Stercoralis*, nearly 40 years after first becoming infected.

Jack Spittle's artwork was introduced in Chapter 1. A former Local Authority sanitary inspector in the Home Counties, he was a member of a specialised RAMC anti-malarial mosquito squad sent to Singapore in November 1941 to help bring under control mosquito breeding grounds. His detailed maps of the Changi peninsula give an indication of his attention to detail.

Taken into captivity two weeks after the fall of Singapore Spittle and his team had continued working, unmolested by the Japanese, on the small island of Pulau Tekong to the north east of Singapore island in the Johor Straits, close

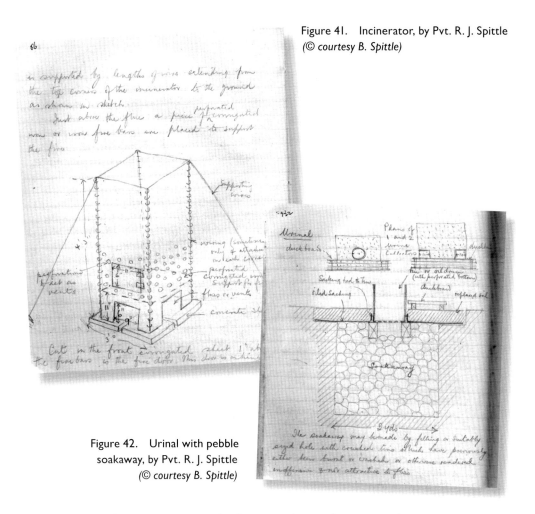

Figure 41. Incinerator, by Pvt. R. J. Spittle
(© courtesy B. Spittle)

Figure 42. Urinal with pebble
soakaway, by Pvt. R. J. Spittle
(© courtesy B. Spittle)

to the Malayan coast. From the first months in Changi, Spittle was a man on a mission to try and prevent the spread of dysentery.

During his captivity he filled several exercise books with detailed sketches of various ingenious devices, inventions and latrine designs, all intended to improve sanitation and the men's health. For example, Figure 41, this design for an incinerator was done in March 1942. A sketch of a urinal (Figure 42) in another exercise book gives detailed directions for how to make this effective, sanitary facility. His son Brian has shared his father's diaries and notes online in his excellent blog, 'Changi Notes'.[20]

It's fair to say that Spittle was obsessed with sanitation; perhaps the right man in the right place at the right time?

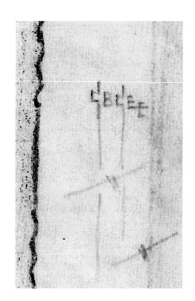

Figure 43.   Close-up of Geoffrey Gee's distinctive signature

This sketch by Geoffrey Gee is of Changi POW camp (Figure 45) was drawn from an elevated position looking out across Changi and showing accommodation in concrete buildings with tents in the distance. On the right of the drawing is a small mosque which was converted into St George's chapel early on.

Gee's distinctive signature (Figure 43) is barely visible in this portrait of FEPOW Wally Davis' wife. His signature is most often found in the lower right corner, like the one below enlarged from another of his sketches. The vertical lines running down from the two stylised 'G's' in his name appear to resemble posts, criss-crossed by two intersecting lines of barbed wire.

Sapper Geoffrey Barlow Gee

560 Field Company Royal Engineers (RE)

Captured:	Singapore 15.2.42
Camps:	Singapore – Changi POW camp;
	Thailand – Chungkai, Rin Tin, Tamarkan, Linson POW camps
From:	Renfrewshire
DoB:	21.10.14
Died:	not known

Figure 44.   Portrait of Wally Davis' wife from a photograph by Sapper G. Gee (© courtesy M. Parkes)

Figure 45. Looking across Changi POW camp, by Sapper G. B. Gee *(© courtesy the Cordingly family)*

Eric Stacy: Trained as an architect, like Gee, Eric Stacy did several sketches of the interior of the chapel and other scenes around camp before being sent up to Thailand. His fine watercolour and pencil sketches give a sense of the peace and tranquillity in and around St George' chapel (Figures 46 & 47).

Lt Eric Francis Stacy

560th Field Coy, RE

Captured:	Singapore 15.2.42
Camps:	Singapore: Changi, River Valley Road, returned to Changi, then Changi Gaol
	Thailand: Kanburi, Nikke,
	Burma: Tambaya
From:	London
DoB:	28.11.09
Died:	not known

Figure 46. Sketch of St George's chapel Changi POW camp, by Lt E. Stacy *(© courtesy the Cordingly family)*

Figure 47. View of interior of St George's chapel Changi POW camp, by Lt E. F. Stacy *(© courtesy the Reynolds family)*

Padre Frederick Hugh Stallard

5th Bedfordshire and Hertfordshire
Regiment, 55th Inf. Brigade

Captured:	Singapore 15.2.45
Camps:	Singapore: Changi
	Taiwan: Heito and Shirakawa
From:	Peterborough
DoB:	27.8.11
Died:	12.3.03

Figure 48. 'My tent, after van Gogh', by
Padre F. Stallard (© *courtesy BMH Stallard*)

Frederick Stallard: Padre Stallard made this glorious watercolour of the inside of his tent which he captioned 'My Tent, after van Gogh' (Figure 48). He had undertaken art training while still a curate pre-war and during captivity did several sketches, portraits and watercolours in the different camps he was in Singapore and Taiwan.

It was painted in the early months of captivity. However, for the first few weeks in camp he and six officers occupied a room above a Chinese laundry in Changi Village. In his private memoir, *entitled Mugshots* (so named due to the number of portraits he did in captivity) created for the family later in life, he recalled the first night there:

> "... [We] *were given a shed with Kwong Sun Chinese Laundry above the door. The first night there was just room for us to lie on the floor. It was very hot and there was little room to turn over. The floor was hard. At midnight you could hear that everyone was awake. Suddenly Hugh Hoppé (B Company Commander) started telling us a fairy story about goblins. We*

listened wrapt [sic] and at the end went to sleep. What inspired him to do it, is hard to say and even more surprising is that it was acceptable and why it worked. After that one of us used to prepare a story to tell every night while we slept in the laundry shed."

In August 1942 Stallard was drafted, along with the senior Allied Officers, to Taiwan, transported in the hold of a small coaling vessel, the *England Maru*. This and other coastal steamers were used for transporting human cargo around this vast region, wherever the Japanese needed a slave labour force. The ships were unmarked and became known to FEPOW as 'hellships'. Stallard's pencil sketch of conditions below decks is in Chapter 4, Figure 29.

Kenneth Elwell: One of the unrecognised artists who is known to have died in the sinking of a hellship was Kenneth Elwell, from Beverley in the East Riding of Yorkshire.[21] He survived battle, railway construction camps in Thailand and was in a draft en route to Japan when the ship he was on, the *Rakuyo Maru*, was attacked by an American submarine and sunk in September 1944. Several of his detailed pencil sketches were however, given to people before he left Thailand, like this one (Figure 49) dated 1944, of medical officer, Captain Ian MacIntosh RAMC working at his microscope.

Driver Francis Kenneth Elwell

Royal Corps of Signals, 18th Division

Captured:	Singapore 15.2.42
Camps:	Singapore: Changi
	Thailand: Chungkai hospital camp
From:	Beverley, East Yorkshire
DoB:	9.8.05
Died:	12.9.44 drowned in sinking of *Rakuyo Maru*

Figure 49. Sketch Captain MacIntosh at his microscope, Chungkai hospital camp Thailand, 1944 by Dvr F. K. Elwell (© courtesy ShellMex 44 Club News)

This pencil sketch was found illustrating the leading article on the front page of the ShellMex pension company newsletter, *44 Club News*, dated March 1992. MacIntosh was presumably a former employee.

Leaving Singapore for Thailand with O Party on 3 November 1942, Elwell joined Work Group 4. Although there is no Liberation Questionnaire to refer to for precise information, it is likely that he spent time in both Chungkai hospital camp, where several of his sketches were done, and later Tha Muang (also Tamuan(g)) camp before eventually being drafted back to Singapore in the spring of 1944. His likely destination would have been River Valley Road camp.

Elwell's carefully detailed pencil sketches are interesting. One depicts the Chungkai dental surgery used by Army Dental Officer David Arkush (Chapter 5, Figure 9). The other shows the start of an above knee amputation of the left leg (Chapter 5, Figure 23). Both sketches would have been done at the request of the dental or medical officers. Elwell was in a draft for Japan that left Singapore on 4 September. His convoy HI 72 sailed on 6th and was torpedoed off the Philippines and sunk by USS *Sealion II* on 12th. Elwell was among over 1,150 who lost their lives. These fine studies are his legacy.

John Clement: Like Padre Stallard, Gunner John Clement 5th Field Regiment, was another FEPOW artist who spent only a short time at Changi before being sent to Taiwan. A trainee accountant from Glasgow, Clement was also on board the *England Maru*. The sheer quantity of John Clement's artwork is staggering, running to 23 exercise books and home-made notebooks and diaries, all richly illustrated in the same style.

The collection is held at the Glasgow City Life archives based in the Mitchell Library. The photograph gives an idea of Clement's graphic style of design and art – simple illustrations in comic book style on the left of each page, with related notes on the right. These two pages (Figure 50) in an early notebook describe Clement's arrival at Changi where his unit were among the men herded into Changi Gaol initially. Interestingly, he notes the date of arrival there as 30 February! By March 10 they had been moved into Changi POW camp.

Gunner John Francis Clement

5th Battery, 5th Field Regiment, 11th Indian Division

Captured:	Singapore 15.2.42
Camps:	Singapore: Changi
	Taiwan: Taihoku, Taityu, Indun, Shirakawa and Taihoku
From:	Glasgow
DoB:	5.10.15
Died:	28.6.94

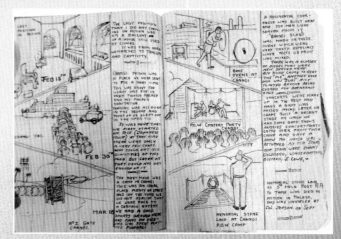

Figure 50. Notebook sketches of arrival at Changi, by Gnr J. Clement *(photograph M. Parkes; courtesy Glasgow Life: Glasgow City Archives and the Clement family)*

The pages are ruled paper, presumably cut down to make smaller booklets then turned so that the lines run vertically and not horizontally, folded and bound together in multiple pages to make each booklet. He used colour, red in this example, to demarcate his illustrations. The top left image depicts the veranda of a civilian house where and his pals cooked their final meals before being rounded up at Tanglin barracks. Moving down the page he goes on to describe, both visually and in writing, their move initially to Changi Gaol before entering, through No.2 gate, Changi POW camp itself.

On the top of the next page are the baking ovens at Changi, with a description of the food they produced; then the entertainments with a view of the theatre. In the notes to the right he mentions two other FEPOW, renowned entertainers John Lowe, a fellow Other Rank (OR) in 5th Field Regiment, an accomplished artist himself, Danny Goldberg and Jim Brennan. Lowe, also a pianist, and Brennan formed a singing double act while in Changi.[22] Clement's extraordinary collection relating to his captivity in Taiwan, where we believe the books were created, is detailed later in Chapter 3.

Figure 51. 'Padre's Room', dated 26 June 1942 by M. Hardy
(© courtesy the Cordingly family)

Figure 52. Congregation inside St George's Chapel, Changi POW camp, by M. Hardy
(© courtesy the Cordingly family)

Mike Hardy: This name cropped up several times during the enquiry, first in Padre Cordingly's archive relating to Changi POW camp and later in Lt Col. Johnson's from the camps on the Thai–Burma railway. He produced several works but regrettably we have been unable to find any information about him from either source, nor from documents such as a Japanese record card or Liberation Questionnaire (the lack of the latter on file indicating that perhaps he did not survive?). In Singapore, Hardy sketched Padre Cordingly's room (Figure 51) which was next to St George's Chapel, as well as the interior (Figure 52) and exterior of the chapel.

These two sketches must have been given to the Padre at some point as they form part of his collection.

Soon after settling at Changi POW camp, men were moved out to work camps on the docks, becoming stevedores or clearing bomb damage and restoring vital services across the island.

Stanley Warren: A commercial artist pre-war, Stanley Warren worked in the film promotion business, making film posters for Granada Cinemas in England. In the Army his artistic abilities were again utilised once in Malaya, working as an observation post assistant drawing the panoramas used to plot targets. He was to make a vivid and vital contribution to the life of many POW in Changi.[23]

Warren was one of those drafted early on from Changi to Bukit Timah work camp in the centre of the island, where the POW were to build an access road for the large Japanese Shinto shrine on the Royal Singapore golf course. One of the padres at Bukit Timah asked Warren if he would decorate the altar areas of the makeshift atap-roofed, chapel in the camp. Warren used charcoal to create these, his first two murals on panels in the chapel: one depicted the nativity and the other Christ's descent from the cross. He modelled some of the biblical characters on his FEPOW friends. These panels were later moved to the Sime Road camp to adorn St David's church there.

In mid-May, having contracted amoebic dysentery and renal disease, Warren was desperately ill at Robert's Barracks Hospital back in Changi POW camp. By August he was recovered enough to be transferred to Robert's dysentery block

Bombardier Charles Stanley Warren

135th Field Regiment, RA

Captured:	Singapore 15.2.42
Camps:	Singapore: Changi, Bukit Timah, Roberts Hospital, Selarang, Kranji
From:	Tottenham, London
DoB:	9.4.17
Died:	20.2.92

Figure 53. One of five murals made for St Luke's Chapel, Robert's Hospital Changi, by Bdr C. S. Warren (© courtesy Changi Museum)

– called W Block then, now known as Block 151. While slowly recuperating, he was asked by two of the padres, Chambers and Payne, if he could help them. Aware of his work on the chapel at Bukit Timah camp they asked if he would paint murals of biblical scenes to decorate the newly-created St Luke's Chapel at the hospital (Figure 53). The chapel was situated in a small room on the ground floor of W Block, directly underneath the dysentery wards.

It was a long, slow, labour of faith and love, the finished works measuring roughly three metres wide and two metres high. The story of the Changi Murals is available online from the National Library of Singapore and also in a small booklet, published by Changi Museum in 2003.[24]

William Wilder: Known to friends as Will, Wilder had a degree in art from the University of Reading. He, like Warren, was also at Bukit Timah camp and on the working party constructing the road across the golf course. In September 1942 Wilder, who was known to the Japanese as an artist, was taken off the working party and commissioned by the Commandant as his official artist. His job was to document all stages of the building work (Figures 54 & 55) and he was given an official pass (Figure 56) and was no doubt grateful for the respite from heavy work. Nonetheless he had his problems. The 2014 edition of his biography, *PoW Sketchbook, a story of survival,*[25] published by Wallingford Museum, described what happened to some of his artwork:

> "... Will had been on working parties constructing the approach roads. Hashimoto [Japanese Commandant] wanted to see some of Will's pictures with a view to using him as an official artist to paint pictures of the shrine. The interview did not altogether please will. 'My drawings were shown to Captain Hashimoto. Unfortunately, he wanted three of my best ones and I was obliged to let them go ... Am very upset at losing these pen and ink sketches which I was most anxious to take home ... However, I have the pleasure of making official drawings of the shrine and bridge ... Am to be taken into Singapore tomorrow by the Japs to get the materials I require. Shall take advantage of this and shall keep some of the work I do. Hope to get oil paints ...*"

Will Wilder's medical work is detailed in Section II.

Driver William Carthew 'Will' Wilder

135th Field Regiment, RA

Captured:	Singapore 15.2.42
Camps:	Singapore: Changi, Bukit Timah/Sime Road
	Thailand: Chungkai, Nong Pladuk, Ubon
From:	Wallingford, Oxfordshire
DoB:	16.6.15
Died:	18.7.98

Figures 54 & 55. Right: bridge to the (above) shrine, Singapore, by Dvr W. C. Wilder from his biography (© courtesy Anthony Wilder [not to be reproduced without permission])

Figure 56. Wilder's official Japanese pass with his name in centre (© courtesy Anthony Wilder [not to be reproduced without permission])

Jack White: In early April 1942 Jack White was sent in a draft to Towner Road work camp. While there he did several pen and ink sketches which provide us with the only graphic record of the camp to date (Figures 57 & 58). By April 1943 he was at Sonkurai camp in Thailand and from there went across the Burmese border to two camps, before returning to Singapore in December that year.

Lt John Wilbye Benson 'Jack' White

88th Field Regiment (Lancashire Gunners)

Captured:	Singapore 15.2.42
Camps:	Singapore: Towner Road and Serangoon Road camps, Changi POW camp; returned to Changi Gaol
	Thailand: Sonkurai
	Burma: Chaungayya, Tanbaya
From:	Surrey
DoB:	1.4.19
Died:	10.12.01

Figures 57 & 58. Top: Singapore, POW Home, Towner Road camp. Above: Towner Road Cookhouse, both by Lt J. W. B. White (© courtesy J. Aldridge)

Towner Road camp was one of 35 similar small work camps in and around Singapore town (as it was then known) housing working parties assigned to specific tasks, for example Golf Club Sime Road camp housed some of the POW building the Japanese shrine at the golf club. In Section II we shall look at more of these camp life illustrations from across captivity.

Geoffrey Munton: Born in Lincolnshire, Sapper Geoffrey Munton remained in Singapore throughout captivity and used his artistic talents to distract, inform and teach. Munton's archive, comprising dozens of drawings, sketches and portraits (Figure 59), was donated to the IWM in 2016 by his daughter Sally.[26]

It contains numerous architectural drawings sketched from memory which he used to illustrate talks, plans for his dream house, a sketch of the Changi lych gate and the burial ground at the camp, a map of Singapore done in 1942, which would have been difficult to explain had it been discovered. There are also several excellent pencil and crayon portraits of film stars, presumably providing a helpful distraction from daily existence. In Section III Jenny explores more of his work.

Sapper Geoffrey Charles Munton

560 Coy, RE, 18th Division

Captured:	Singapore 15.2.42
Camps:	Singapore: Changi, Blakang Mati
From:	Digby, Lincolnshire
DoB:	3.11.18
Died:	19.8.93

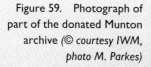

Figure 59. Photograph of part of the donated Munton archive (© courtesy IWM, photo M. Parkes)

Back to Singapore from the railway

Hamish Cameron-Smith: In December 1943, Hamish returning to Singapore from Kanburi camp in Thailand was sent to River Valley Road camp. There, before the year was out, he drew this interesting sketch of the dental surgery (Figure 60).

The dentist is using what appears to be a treadle drill and there is an extended electric lamp, fixed to the bamboo hut support on the left of the drawing. By spring 1944, many more men were returning to Singapore from the railway camps in Thailand and Burma. They were sent to either Changi Gaol (in May 1944 it became the main POW camp after the civilian internees were moved out), to River Valley Road or Kranji Hospital camp (Woodlands) where part of Changi's Roberts Hospital had been relocated.

A member of 84 Squadron, Welshman and Leading Aircraftsman **William John Beckerley** from Tredegar in Monmouthshire, was captured in Java. He arrived at Changi POW camp in October 1942 (in a party destined for Thailand) and

Hamish Ninian Cameron-Smith

RE, Bombay Sappers (rank unknown)

Captured:	Singapore 15.2.42
Camps:	Singapore: Changi, River Valley Road (from Dec 1943)
	Thailand: Kanburi (for 3 months Aug – Nov 1943)
From:	Dunlop, Ayrshire
DoB:	7.3.18
Died:	not known

Figure 60.   Dental surgery at River Valley Road camp, Singapore December 1943, by H. Cameron-Smith
(© courtesy Museum of Military Medicine)

spent some time in Roberts Hospital before being sent with H Force on 5 May 1943. There he spent time at Hintok camp before returning to Singapore in late 1943. He was sent to Sime Road camp where he got involved in the theatricals, understudying female roles and working alongside Ronald Searle on stage scenery. He later moved into Changi Gaol POW camp.

> "Sime Road and Changi [Gaol] were heaven on earth to all who survived the railway. At five feet nine I had weighed 10 stone; back from the railway I was under six." [27]

He said this about Ronald Searle:

> "Sime Road concert parties used a large barn-like shed, The Barn Theatre. Ron Searle designed the sets, sometimes a large 'backdrop' with plain side flats. Guess who was detailed to paint those? Ron would draw outlines on his cartoonlike backdrop with precise directives re- block colour with shading and fading in and out to produce 'our now' finished background. He understood my limitations, was always considerate and encouraged rather than criticized. I learned fast."

Beckerley did a series of sketches (coloured with crayon) including one entitled, 'The Flies, Changi'. It shows how the scenery backdrops were stored above the stage at Coconut Grove, the theatre in Changi Gaol POW camp. In this sketch the viewer looks down to the stage and wings below, with the props and stage sets acting as a counterbalance to the weights on ropes and the lighting rig.

His sketches are held in the Victoria & Albert Museum collections in London. In his post-war correspondence with Professor Sears Eldredge, Beckerley recalled scenery painting at Changi Gaol's theatre:

> "Searle and I produced scenery there which would pass muster in any theatre anywhere; from rocky mountains to village inns, English and continental: luxury bedrooms and poor working class living rooms, palace foyers and

actor's dressing rooms: all grist to the mill to Ron Searle and his dedicated assistant.

Luckily, I liked him as well as admiring him … I owe him a great deal, not least because he taught me to paint …"

Jenny will explore more of Searle's work in Section III.

Thomas 'Toss' Wilson: Born and raised in Belfast where he trained in medicine, Toss Wilson started captivity working at Roberts Hospital. In late April 1943 he was in one of the last parties of F Force to go to Thailand. After arriving at Ban Pong his group marched north for over a month until they reached their destination Sonkurai on 8 June. He stayed there until late November that year before being drafted back to Singapore, arriving on 21 December. He went first to the hospital at Selarang Barracks before making the move to Changi Gaol in May 1944 where he spent the rest of his captivity working in the newly-erected hospital huts and laboratory within the gaol precincts. There he created 14 ink and wash sketches which vividly record what he saw, where he worked and rested. In mid-1944 another small church, The Chapel of the Good Shepherd (Figure 61) was created inside Changi Gaol and the following year Wilson sketched it.

Captain Thomas 'Toss' Wilson
RAMC

Captured:	Singapore 15.2.42
Camps:	Singapore: Changi Roberts Hospital
	Thailand: Sonkurai
	Singapore: Changi Gaol POW camp
From:	Portstewart, Northern Ireland
DoB:	5.11.05
Died:	3.8.88

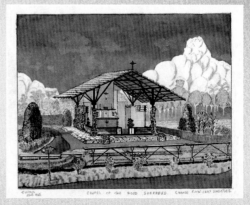

Figure 61.   The Chapel, Changi Gaol POW camp, 1945, by Capt. T. Wilson
(© courtesy the Wilson family)

There are more of Wilson's ink and wash sketches in Section II. The sequel to Wilson's story is that after liberation, and a brief sojourn back in Northern Ireland, he resumed his career as a District Health Officer for the Malayan Medical Service. He later worked at the Institute for Medical Research (IMR) in Kuala Lumpur and in 1959 returned to the UK, taking a senior lectureship at the Liverpool School of Tropical Medicine. In 1962 he was appointed Professor, taking the Middlemass Hunt Chair of Tropical Hygiene and working there until his retirement in 1971.

William 'Bill' Norways: Another man to arrive back in Singapore from Thailand was trained commercial artist (Chelsea School of Art 1935–6), theatre producer and actor, Bill Norways. At Changi early on, Bill lectured on Advertising and Art at the 'university' and edited the POW magazine. In Thailand he was very involved with theatricals but when he arrived back on the island in early 1944 he was sent to Selarang Hospital camp and began working with the doctors there, recording the ravages of disease and malnutrition.

His sketch of the inside of the dysentery hut at Kranji Hospital camp (Section II, Figure 1) is one of two illustrations that he did of this large hospital camp established in 1944 on Singapore Island. They are the only known sketches of

Cpl William 'Bill' George Norways
2nd Cambridgeshire Regiment

Captured:	15.2.42
Camps:	Singapore: Changi, Havelock Road, Tandjong Rhu, Pasir Panjang
	Thailand: Kanu, Kanburi Hospital camp
	Singapore: Selarang & Kranji Hospital camps
From:	Hackney, East London
DoB:	10.2.18
Died:	25.9.86

Figure 62. 'Light Classical Concert' programme, Kranji POW Hospital camp, Singapore, January 1945, by Cpl W. Norways (© courtesy the Norways family)

Figure 63.
'View from
my bed, Changi
Gaol' 1945, by Lt
J. W. B. White
(© courtesy
J. Aldridge)

this hospital camp to have come to late as yet (his other sketch, of an operation in progress, is in Chapter 5, Figure 8). He was also a prolific graphic artist and spent what spare time he had doing cartoons, posters for camp concerts (Figure 62; also Chapter 3, Figure 30) and creating numerous designs for business cards, posters and stationery for his entrepreneurial FEPOW comrades.

Jack White, having returned from Thailand and eventually ended up in Changi Gaol, White drew this descriptive view of the occupants of his hut, lying on their camp beds while he sketched the scene from his (Figure 63). One can almost feel the heat, lethargy, boredom even, pervading the page. These officers are in the new hutted camp buildings, constructed around the prison buildings, and not in the cells.

Desmond Bettany: Another prolific artist who had also spent time at Towner Road camp before later moving into Changi POW camp and then Changi Gaol, was Lancastrian Des Bettany. He is notable for the range and quality of his cartoon and caricature work (see example Figure 64). His humorous take on the absurdities and the realities of captivity must have cheered many who saw his work; it provides history with vivid insights into the extraordinary resilience and resourcefulness of FEPOW as this illustration shows.

Lance Bombardier Desmond Bettany

88th Field Regiment, RA

Captured:	Singapore 15.2.42
Camps:	Singapore: Towner Road, Changi POW camp, Changi Gaol POW camp
From:	Burnley, Lancashire
DoB:	11.10.19
Died:	14.12.00

Figure 64. 'Repairing Shoes', p. 21, Changi Rubber Factory 1942–5, by L/Bdr D. Bettany (© courtesy Bettany family)

This cartoon is one of 17 featured in a book published by Changi University Press in 2005 entitled, *The Story of Changi Industries Inc.* by Captain John G. Clemetson.[28] This small, richly-illustrated, soft back book is based on a manuscript written post-war by Clemetson. It details a fascinating history of ingenuity and enterprise in Changi, illustrated throughout by Bettany's sketches, given to Clemetson later. Changi Industries Inc was set up initially to keep men in footwear by repairing, remaking and in time making all manner of shoes and boots. Over time it diversified into spectacle and denture repairs, boot polish, soap and cork manufacturing.

The two sketches below (Figures 65 & 66) are of Captain Ronnie Horner. In Horner's diary, dated 18 October 2019, he notes:

"... An OR named Bettany has presented me with an excellent caricature of myself feeding a biscuit to a shaggy dog! Very hot these days, even for Singapore, sweat simply pours off you without any effort."

The other references Horner's propensity for singing in the bath!

In 1991 Bettany, by then retired and living in Australia (where he and the family had settled in the late 1950s) was invited by the Singapore Tourism Promotion Board in 1991 to contribute to the preparations to mark the 50th anniversary of the Battle for Singapore. He wrote a summary of his captivity, entitled 'Life in

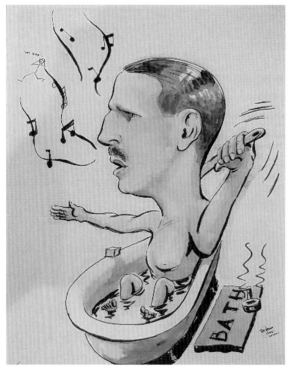

Figures 65 & 66.
Two examples of Bettany's cartoon and caricature work, featuring Captain Ronnie Horner, by L/Bdr D. Bettany
(© courtesy S.McQuaid)

Singapore at a P.O.W. February 1942 – September 1945' with these interesting insights into the POW rumour mill and the risky business of being a captive artist:

> "… Rumours abounded but I particularly remember the night of the 'D-Day' landings in Normandy. When the report reached us, the whole camp within and without the Jail began to stir and murmur, to the consternation of the Japanese. This was accepted as fact, but the stories of the bombing of Hiroshima and Nagasaki with atomic bombs, were met with disbelief …
>
> My personal worst moments came when I had to appear before the Japanese Commandant and an assortment of interpreters, to try and explain away to humourless Japanese officers a book of political cartoons I had drawn. I had lent the book to a careless person who allowed it to fall into the hands of Japanese guards. This was at a time when the war was going badly for Germany and Japan and this was reflected in the cartoons. I was extremely lucky to get away with a whole skin. The Japanese did not approve. I never saw the book again …"

Much of Bettany's artwork was apparently lost before he and the family emigrated to Australia. Unbeknown to him it was all eventually given to the Harris Museum in Preston for safekeeping. Decades later the museum traced Bettany and returned all his artwork to him; he in turn donated much of it later on to Changi Museum in Singapore. In recent years his family have created a website – www.changipowart.com – to share as widely as possible their father's extraordinary, vast collection of humorous cartoons and portraits.

Having a sense of humour as a FEPOW was not a prerequisite for survival, but for those blessed with one, it certainly helped.

CHAPTER 3

The 'Unrecognised' Artists – Part II

Thailand and Burma

The building of the 415km Thai–Burma railway through raw jungle is the majority British experience. Over 32,000 of the total 50,000+ British forces captured were sent to Thailand or Burma. Most were transported by train from Singapore with drafts arriving at Ban Pong from as early as June 1942. Working parties continued to be sent north until early summer 1943. FEPOW also came from overseas, with men drafted from camps in Java.

Consequently, many British FEPOW artists spent some part of their captivity in Thailand or Burma – all eight of the celebrated artists were sent there from Singapore, as were over 20 of the 69 unrecognised artists – all recording different aspects of captivity in the tropics.

One artist stands out above the rest for the quality and quantity of portraiture that he did – George Old, whose work was introduced in Chapter 1 with his graphic miniature watercolour of the injured Jack Chalker. Old's work features throughout the book, reflecting the influence it exerts over our understanding of FEPOW captivity in the tropics.

The artwork of George Old

Medical Artist: George Old's art is well-known to FEPOW researchers and yet he remains perhaps the least celebrated of the eight 'recognised' artists. He was certainly one of the most accomplished, standing alongside Searle, Chalker and Meninsky for the quality and quantity of his medical and anatomical artwork. Known to all but close family as George (the family called him Ashley), Old had trained at the Northampton School of Art after leaving school, which included completing a course on anatomical drawing. From art school he entered the world of commercial art in the mid-1930s, working for the Carlton Studios advertising agency in London creating posters and marketing materials for use in the men's fashion industry.

The largest collection of his artwork is held at the State Library of Victoria in Australia, forming part of Australian FEPOW surgeon, Major Arthur Moon's, wide-ranging collection of medical art from captivity. In Changi and in Thailand Moon had asked both Old and Philip Meninsky to work closely with him, recording the detail of life and death in the operating theatre hut as well as in the vast sick huts. This work had to be done clandestinely as they were recording numerous medical and surgical challenges faced particularly in the railway camps in Thailand.

Immediately after the end of the war all three met again in Rangoon where Moon was working with the sick repatriated from the railway and evacuated to Burma from Bangkok. There will be more discussion about Old's medical work in Section II.

The Portraitist: Old's work is also known to an indeterminate number of FEPOW descendants for the striking and sensitive watercolour portraits he did of countless FEPOW during captivity. It is impossible to know precisely how many portraits he painted (and sketched in pencil) but at his own admission post-war, potentially there could be hundreds still in existence known only to families of FEPOW veterans. The authors know of the whereabouts of 17 portraits (four were shown to Meg Parkes during the oral history interviews and two others are in the Liverpool exhibition). How many more are yet to be found? LSTM would like to hear of the whereabouts of other portraits signed by Old (with his distinctive forward sloping *OLD*, usually in the bottom right corner).

One portrait to survive is that of Private James Stinson 1/5 Sherwood Foresters, painted when both men were at River Valley Road camp in Singapore in early 1942 (Figure 1). Stinson, like Old, survived captivity and returned home. From his Liberation Questionnaire we learn that he was just 20 years old when captured in Singapore on 15 February 1942. Old later wrote that he was the youngest conscript in the 1st/5th Sherwood Foresters. Interestingly, Stinson was one of those FEPOW who refused to reveal anything about his captivity when asked to fill in a Liberation Questionnaire during the repatriation process in autumn 1945. He wrote an emphatic 'NIL' across each section dealing with camps. However, his Japanese camp record card states that, like Old, he was liberated from Thailand.

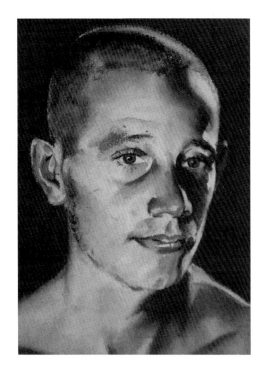

Unlike so many of his known portraits, Old employed a wide range of colours in working on Stinson's: red, pink, brown, yellow, green, black for the face and body, with a darker shade for the background. As a trained artist he would no doubt have carried a basic art kit comprising brushes, pencils, charcoal and paints. However, we

Figure 1.   Private James Stinson 1st/5th Sherwood Foresters, Singapore early in captivity 1942, by Gnr A. G. Old
(© *courtesy D. Bartholomew*)

know from fellow artist and friend, Corporal Philip Meninsky, that he shared materials with Old, such as paper and pencils given to him by friendly guards in camp.[1] Meninsky was also at River Valley Road camp with Old and Stinson. There, a Japanese Warrant Officer admired Meninsky's artwork and offered to trade it for supplies of tobacco and paper. In 1985 Old said of Stinson's portrait:

> "... it was painted in River Valley Road camp [Singapore] immediately after capture ... I painted him inside a small, very tiny area inside a long roughly assembled, raggedly tied together, bamboo and palm lead thatched hut ... I was painting him on a much larger piece of paper when through the many big spaces beneath the bamboo floor three Japanese officers slowly walked underneath. I could see 'em quite plain, and if they had looked up they would easily see me and for that reason I suddenly went wrong and got Stinson's left shoulder and deltoid all wrong and, being watercolour, you can't make alterations easily. So, because of unconscious Japanese interference I had to cut Little Stinson down to size ..."

Old's fee was a handful of cigarettes.

George Old's work is typified by his use of powdered laterite clay found across Southeast Asia. When dried, powdered and mixed with water it provided an earthy, reddish/umber pigment making his portraits, and much of his medical watercolour work, instantly recognisable. The pigment retains a depth of colour which in many cases has lasted for over 75 years. Another member of his regiment, Private Ernest Charles Proctor, known as Charlie, had his portrait done twice by Old (Figures 2 & 3). Proctor was the oldest man in the regiment in captivity. Old did the pencil sketch in mid-1942 while they were still at Changi then, 18 months later at Chungkai in Thailand, he painted a superb watercolour of a man, aged and weary. The difference in Charlie's expression says it all.

One officer (and fellow artist) who had his portrait painted by Old when in Thailand, was Lieutenant Stanley Gimson who, in later life donated it, along with the rest of his artwork from captivity and his diaries, to the IWM (see Section III, Chapter 7 for more information about both Gimson and Old).

Figures 2 & 3.   Left: pencil sketch of Charlie Proctor, Changi 1942. Right: watercolour portrait of Charlie again, Chungkai early 1944, both by A. G. Old *(© courtesy D. Bartholomew)*

Old's portraits help to bring many human stories of FEPOW captivity to life. Whether the subject is staring off into the distance or directing his gaze at the artist, Old's skill was in recording more than just the facial features. The viewer feels close to these men.

In a newspaper article in 1950, reporting that Old had been awarded a London County Council grant to study art at Camberwell School of Art,[2] the journalist wrote:

> *"... all that's left of the 1,000s portraits he drew* [in captivity] *... He is tall, blond, with wide powerful shoulders and clear blue eyes ... helped in medical work, paper was smuggled or stolen, pencils appeared from nowhere. A Japanese guard was persuaded to supply a child's paint box in return for unlimited hand-painted sentimental postcards to send home ... daily, hour after hour he painted dying men. Not their faces but their dreadful wounds. These he recorded in colour so that one day medical scientists would be able*

to study the tropical diseases which caused them or aggravated them … subjects were held up, semi-conscious … one case took six and a half hours' non-stop painting."

And in the same article Old said:

"The one great advantage of three-and-a-half years imprisonment was that it gave me time to meditate and observe humanity stripped of its reserve," he says, *"I knew men as they really are. I saw how a man's spirit can influence his face. You can't learn that at art schools."*

Some of the known portraits are in their original frames, treasured and tangible reminders of survival now inherited by the next generation. Others were discovered by families after the death of the veteran, often unaware of who the artist is. Researchers at LSTM would like to know of the whereabouts of any other portraits by George Old[3] as they are creating a digital resource in honour of an exceptionally-gifted artist who, during his lifetime, received little recognition for his extraordinary documentary artwork. These portraits will help introduce future generations to the history of Far East captivity during the Second World War.

Appendix I has a personal reflection on Old, by close family friend David Bartholomew.

More artists

So far very little information has come to light about Herbert Elsey, John Gale, John Excell and Robert Gamble. Each man is known to have survived as they filled in Liberation Questionnaires during repatriation, and to have sketched at least one piece of artwork.

Herbert Elsey A pencil portrait of FEPOW Peter Allen is the only known piece of artwork by Elsey (see Section IV, Personal Reflections).

John Gale This pencil sketch, (Figure 4), simply signed Gale, was done at Wampo camp and depicts a row of bamboo and attap huts.

Warrant Officer John Kendell Gale

SRA(V) SSVF

Captured:	Singapore 15.2.42
Camps:	Singapore: camps not known
	Thailand: Wampo (others not known)
From:	Birmingham
DoB:	1906
Died:	not known

Figure 4. 'Wampo', Thailand, by W/O J. Gale (© courtesy M. Nellis / A. Harpham)

WAMPO CAMP

Robert Gamble Captured in Java, Leading Aircraftsman Gamble was part of an RAF maintenance unit. He was sent from Java to Singapore then north to Thailand where he spent time at Hintok and Kanburi camps.[4] He later returned to Singapore from where he was liberated. His only known work to date is of the graveyard at Kanburi in Thailand which is in Padre Cordingly's collection, (Chapter 4, Figure 24).

RAF Flight Sergeant Fred Margarson was a plumber from Grimsby pre-war. During captivity he was renowned for having run the workshop at the large hospital camp at Chungkai camp in Thailand, producing medical instruments from cutlery, repairing broken equipment, making utensils and designing and making artificial limbs. In this he worked closely with RAMC medical orderly and former Post Office engineer, Private Gordon Vaughan from Wallasey in Merseyside. Margarson did a sketch of the exterior of the surgical hut at Chungkai (Chapter 5, Figure 21).

Don 'Nobby' Clarke, like so many others, moved north to Thailand during 1942 where he continued to record what he saw around him, like this fine pencil

Figure 5. 'Officers' Mess, Ubon', by Dvr D. Clarke (© courtesy the Clarke family)

sketch of the Officers' Mess at Ubon camp in Thailand (Figure 5). There are more of his sketches in Chapter 4.

Alexander Young: A Scot, Alexander was known as Alex or Alec. His father was the Rev. J. Young of the Dunollie Road Free Church in Oban. Captured in Singapore Young was sent to Thailand in June 1942. While there he did this fine pencil portrait, dated 22 October 1943, of fellow artist and friend Will Wilder at Nong Pladuk camp (Figure 6).

Figure 6. Portrait of Will Wilder, Nong Pladuk, Thailand, by Bdr A. Young (© courtesy Anthony Wilder [not to be reproduced without permission])

Bombardier Alexander McGowan Young

80th Anti-tank Regiment, RA, 11th Indian Division

Captured:	Singapore 15.2.42
Camps:	Singapore: Changi
	Thailand: Nong Pladuk, Tamarkan, Nakom Paton
From:	Oban
DoB:	12.8.19
Died:	not known

Stephen Alexander did a most engaging illustrative watercolour of the area around Tamarkan camp where the two large bridges built by POW crossed the River Kwai (Chapter 6, Figure 16). He worked there from October 1942 to May 1943 and in his LSTM interview in 2007 recalled that

> *"... we had several months in Tamarkan where the bridge was being built and that was extremely hard work but quite well-organised and the food was reasonable. Hours of work got longer and longer and 1943 was the 'speedo' year when the Japanese were prepared to do anything, didn't matter how many people they bumped off provided the railway got through to Burma in that year. And so, I was posted up river from Tamarkan when the main bridge – we built a wooden bridge, temporary bridge, first and then the metal bridge which had been shipped up from Java – and when that was well on the way to being finished, we were sent up to work on other bridges upriver and digging up the railway trace of course ..."[5]*

Lieutenant Alexander revealed in his diary as well as in skilfully in his artwork, his contempt for the absurdity of war, and especially for the situation British Forces faced in the Far East. He reflected on these matters in his interview:

"... I certainly finished up when we surrendered, by thinking that everything had been so totally chaotic and incompetent that I didn't believe that any of the other so-called great victories of history were not equally incompetent.

I just felt that this opened my eyes to what has been the absolute nonsense written about any war, and I think most people felt the same. Some were relieved that we surrendered, it was very nice not to be bombed and shot at; others, like me, were absolutely ashamed and felt that, when we saw these ragged scruffy little Japanese who had defeated us so roundly, coming in and shaking hands, we'd much rather have fought to the bitter end ..."

He identifies the deep-rooted sense of shame that many FEPOW veterans interviewed by LSTM also acknowledged. It was a feeling many carried throughout their captivity and long into post-war life.

As already seen, tropical flora and fauna held a fascination for many artists, enthralled as much by the colours as by the profusion of unfamiliar wildlife. Will Wilder sketched these two monkeys (Figure 7) – Satan the mother on the left and her daughter Nipper on the right – which according to the caption had been tamed by Fergus Anckorn the magician.[6]

Jack Chalker described his first impressions of jungle life:

Figure 7.
'Satan and Nipper', by Gnr W. Wilder
(© courtesy J.Dewey)

"... being an artist, it all started by just, I was fascinated by what I was seeing, it was lovely. There were the most beautiful birds, white ibis and these beautiful blue kingfishers. And there were some lovely butterflies and monkeys, gibbons flying about, and of course I was a young man, I'd never been in the Far East before ... And so I was, in the first instance, indulging myself although in fact we weren't supposed to. ... up country I did some little paintings of plants, hibiscus and passion flower and there is a beautiful little, a blue orchid that grew out of the ground, and lovely orchids in the trees. And anyway, I made some notes of these things just to entirely suit myself ..."

Lieutenant Colonel A. A. Johnson MC was CO of the 4 Suffolk Regiment and for a while the notable senior British officer (SBO) at 244 camp. He was not an artist but rather an avid collector of art. Johnson was wounded in the chest during the Battle of Malaya. Known to all as 'Ack Ack', thanks to both his initials and because he led an anti-aircraft unit, he was also affectionately referred to as 'Crackers Ackers'. This was in part at least due to his somewhat eccentric behaviour. However, behind the eccentricity lay a leader with a steely determination to get as many men as possible through captivity alive.

Faced with the enormity of the daily challenges – physical, mental and emotional – Johnson believed the best thing he could do was to keep the men active, occupied in positive ways and thereby distracted. Post-war, in a personal tribute to his former camp CO, FEPOW (and journalist) Ronald Hastain said of him:

"... this brisk, dapper British commander ... set the hallmark for appearance, bearing and conduct; and it was an example which we followed with pride."

And in a later quote, describing a particularly dreadful time upcountry, Hastain also noted:

"... On arrival we found that owing to sickness little had been done by way of preparation by the advance party. Rain hampered all activity and then cholera broke out which added to the horrors ... Colonel Johnson was everywhere, urging on the work of improvement and personally supervising the construction of huts ..."

Appointed by the Japanese as POW officer in charge of R Party, which left Changi on 31 October 1942, Johnson and his men moved from Chungkai base camp up the line to Ban Khao, then in stages on to several unnamed camps. These were numbered in kilometres from the base camp, the first 110Km, next 203Km and then, in late 1943, 227Km after the railway was completed. Just to add to the confusion, these initial numbers were later changed. As SBO, during his tenure at this last camp its number was changed to 244Km. It was also to become known as 'Johnson' camp.

Johnson was a keen lifelong amateur naturalist. Captivated by the abundance of wildlife around them, he contrived to indulge his growing passion for butterflies and orchids. He encouraged the men to capture and bring to him any butterfly that they could catch. He made a net using mosquito netting attached to a bamboo pole, and on his daily journey on foot through the jungle to check up on the working parties, he would distract himself catching specimens. Any passing artists who arrived in camp were asked to paint or sketch the butterflies. These, often anonymous, studies (Figure 8) were done from live specimens. Johnson kept the small watercolours in an old natural history book he had taken into captivity, removing the original illustrations and replacing them with sketches, so they appeared to belong to the book.[7] He also kept some inside tubes of bamboo to keep them hidden.

How Johnson killed the butterflies is not recorded but we do know from a press photograph taken in Rangoon and published in The Sphere magazine in September 1945 (Figure 9) that he kept them, wings folded together and wrapped in scraps of paper or leaves, stacked neatly into an old biscuit tin he had acquired.

Johnson had his portrait painted by George Old when the two were at Chungkai in 1944. The black and white copy of the portrait (Figure 10) comes from a catalogue produced in 1970 when part of Johnson's rich and remarkable collection of art was showcased in an exhibition entitled, 'Flora and Fauna painted by Allied Prisoners in Siam 1942–1945' at the Sladmore Gallery in London. Regrettably, the whereabouts of the original watercolour portrait remains unknown. Organised by the gallery owner, 'Flora and Fauna' is the only known exhibition of Johnson's unique and vast collection. Johnson was 47 at

Figure 8. Anonymous butterfly study, Thailand
(© *courtesy the Johnson family*)

the time his portrait was painted, though perhaps unsurprisingly he looks older. Old signed it, noted it was painted at Chungkai and dated it. The date is difficult to decipher but it is most likely 1944.

Johnson's daughter, Wendy Bird, is now custodian of his impressive FEPOW art collection. This comprises dozens of small watercolour and pen and ink studies (up to A6 paper size) of the many different species of tropical butterflies. There are a few watercolour sketches of birds and several studies of orchids. Many of them are still in the mounts used for the 1970 exhibition.

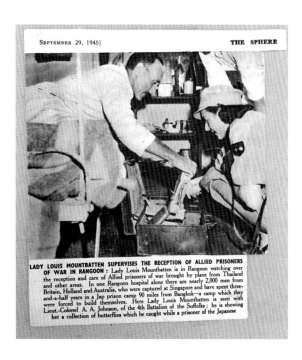

Figure 9. Press photograph (*Sphere* magazine), Johnson showing Lady Mountbatten his biscuit tin full of butterflies, Rangoon Sept 1945 (© *courtesy the Johnson family*)

Figure 10.   Portrait of Lt Col. A. A. Johnson
M.C. Thailand 1944, by Gnr G. Old
(© courtesy the Johnson Family)

In notes he made for a talk about
his wartime captivity in later life,
Johnson recalled a spectacular natural
phenomenon:

> *"During the spring of 1943, when*
> *in Siam as an unwilling guest of the*
> *Japanese Emperor, I witnessed a most*
> *remarkable sight, a migration of*
> *millions of butterflies. This migration*
> *continued in a northerly direction, for*
> *more than a fortnight, starting off each*
> *day at first light and continuing until darkness fell, with never a slightest*
> *pause. The line of flight coincided roughly with the route of the Burma Siam*
> *railway, which itself followed, for much of its path, that of the Meklong River,*
> *so we, so to speak, had a seat in the stalls for this extraordinary phenomenon.*
>
> *Sometimes they flew in dense clouds but more often, since the country*
> *generally was enclosed, they made their way slowly but with grim*
> *determination, follow-my-leader fashion, through all avenues in the jungle."*

Not only does Wendy have her father's collection of butterfly, bird and orchid
watercolours, but also his actual tropical butterfly collection! In this modern age
many may recoil at the notion of capturing, killing and displaying wildlife, but
this collection ought to be viewed in terms of its history. Johnson and many of
his fellow FEPOW belonged to a generation of collectors, of literally anything
and everything – stamps, rocks, shells, fossils, insects and yes, butterflies
and birds' eggs. Curiosity about the wider world, it's history, geography and
nature knew no bounds in the early twentieth century. And this collection
undoubtedly helped to keep men focused on something other than their
threadbare, meagre and risky daily existence.

Figure 11. Photograph of the specimen cabinets in Wendy's study (© *courtesy M. Parkes*)

These tropical butterflies were collected over 76 years ago, during a war that had seen thousands of men incarcerated in the Tropics, far from home. During captivity Johnson kept his precious collection in an old biscuit tin; post-war he had it professionally displayed in three wooden specimen cabinets (Figure 11), each delicate butterfly painstakingly pinned in place, in serried ranks – drawer after drawer of exquisite tropical butterflies.

Johnson cared for the collection and later this responsibility fell to Wendy. Some specimens are large, others very large (up to four inches between the wingtips); many are small, some are tiny (barely an inch wide at wingtips) – brown, green, white, black, red, ochre, yellow and blue. The colours of the small iridescent ones are still sharp, not dulled over the decades. They are simply incredible.

Robert Hardie: While some of the Johnson collection of watercolour studies of butterflies and orchids are unattributed, a number are signed by artists such as Captain Robert Hardie, a medical officer attached to the Federated Malay States Volunteer Force (see butterfly, Figure 12), Sergeant Jack Kemp and Lieutenant Robert Milner-Moore. Several were also done by the celebrated artist, Philip Meninsky. All spent some time at Johnson camp or nearby at Takanun Camp.

This study has some interesting notes by Hardie. As well as painting butterflies and orchids, he also created beautiful, serene watercolour landscapes in Thailand. These are now held at IWM, along with Hardie's detailed diaries. His memoir, *Burma Siam Railway,* was published posthumously by the Imperial

Captain Robert Stevenson Hardie

Medical Officer, FMSVF

Captured:	Singapore 15.2.42
Camps:	Changi; Thailand: Ban Pong, Kanburi, Wan Tow Kien, Takanun, Chungkai, Tamuang
From:	Edinburgh
DoB:	1904
Died:	1973

Figure 12.   Butterfly studies from Thailand,
(© courtesy the Johnson family)

War Museum in 1983 and contains black and white copies of his watercolour and pen and ink sketches. A tranquil view of the riverbank at Tarsao (Chapter 4, Figure 30), nestling in what appears to be an idyllic setting, belies the reality that he and the other doctors faced daily within the bamboo and attap hospital huts shown at the riverside.

Jack Kemp has already featured in Chapter 1, Figure 32. A clerk pre-war from Lowestoft in Suffolk, he painted several butterflies (Figure 13) and studies of orchids (Figure 14) for Colonel Johnson.

Tribute was paid to Kemp's artistic abilities by Ronald Hastain OBE. Both men had had experience working on newspapers pre-war though in Kemp's case he only rose to junior reporter on the Lowestoft Journal. On his return Hastain published one of the earliest FEPOW memoirs, *White Coolie*, in 1947. In it he acknowledges Kemp's contribution:

"... [thanks] to Jack Kemp for use of his neat, painstaking and minute maps

Figure 13.
Butterfly study,
by Sgt J. E. Kemp
(© courtesy the
Johnson family)

Figure 14.
Study of orchid,
by Sgt J. Kemp
(© courtesy the
Johnson family)

of the P.O.W. camps in Siam, which enabled me to reconstruct our progress through the jungle during the building of the Bangkok-Moulmein Railroad."

Kemp was also an illustrator of theatrical programmes. This one (Figure 15), signed by some of the cast, is from Somerset Maugham's comedy, *The Circle*, produced by Fizzer Pearson and performed on two nights at Chungkai on Friday and Saturday 31 March and 1 April, 1944.

Kemp had arrived back at Chungkai a month earlier from upcountry camps, escaping the cholera outbreaks there.

Robert Milner-Moore: Apart from the fact that Robert was an Intelligence Officer in the FMSVF, little else is known, barring what can be gleaned from his Liberation Questionnaire. This states that he was born in

Figure 15.
Programme for
production of *The
Circle*, by Sgt J. E.
Kemp (© courtesy the
Pearson family)

Lieutenant Aubrey Robert Milner-Moore

IFMSVF 11th Indian Division (Intelligence Corps)

Captured: Singapore 15.2.42

Camps: Singapore: Changi POW camp

Thailand: Nong Pladuk, Arrow Hill, Wang Yai, Kanburi and upcountry camps

From: Malaya

DoB: 4.7.05

Died: not known

Figures 16.
'White crested babbler' by
Lieutenant R. Milner-Moore
(© courtesy the Johnson family)

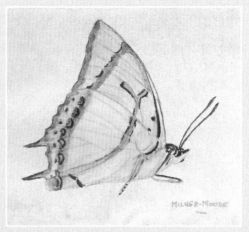

Figures 17 & 18.   Butterfly and orchids,
by Robert Milner-Moore
(© courtesy the Johnson family)

1905, had a postal address in Wheatley in Oxfordshire and that he went from Changi up to the railway. He was an amateur artist and had a particular interest in natural history, judging by his studies done for the Colonel. This is his lovely watercolour of a white created babbler (Figure 16) and he also did several studies of butterflies and orchids (Figures 17 & 18).

Johnson also had several watercolour studies of different species of orchid, some of which are quite a bit larger than the rest. This one (Figure 19) is signed by Mike Hardy, the artist featured in Chapter 2 for whom we have found several pieces of art. Sadly we have found no information about the man.

Colonel Johnson's daughter Wendy recalled:

> "Prisoners were encouraged to build my father an orchid house and then encouraged to collect orchids and to paint pictures of the orchids ..."

This extension, built on to the back of his bamboo and atap hut while Johnson was at Takanun North Camp, became known as 'The Colonel's Orchid House'. What a vibrant and scented oasis this must have created for all who visited the Colonel.

Robert 'Rob' Brazil: Another artist who was involved in theatricals, Rob Brazil like Kemp also did a poster for a play entitled, *The Circle* (Figure 20). He was in the same unit as Jack Chalker and during captivity when in the same camp they worked as a team painting stage sets and backdrops.[8]

Brazil also created this superbly-illustrated programme for the Christmas 1943 variety entertainment at Chungkai produced by FEPOW Wilf Pearson, known to all as 'Fizzer'

Figure 19.   Orchid, dated 26 February 1943, by M. Hardy (© courtesy the Johnson family)

Lance Bombardier Robert Guthrie Brazil

118th Field Regiment RA

Captured:	Singapore 15.2.42
Camps:	Changi
	Thailand: Tonchan, Chungkai, Tamuan, Nakom Paton
From:	London
DoB:	19.8.19
Died:	not known

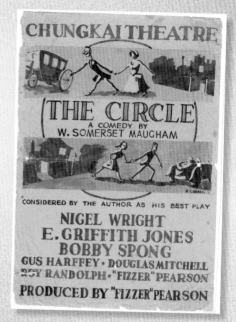

Figure 20. Poster for *The Circle*, by Gnr R. Brazil (© *courtesy the Pearson family*)

(Figures 21 & 22). The allusion to the railway, with an engine pulling huts made of bamboo and attap over a bridge, against a backdrop of mountains, is brilliant. Again, it's signed by members of the cast including, a young magician 'Wizardus' aka, Gunner Fergus Anckorn.[9]

Someone called 'Felicity' signed the programme with the message: 'To Fizzer, with happy memories of passionate nights, Felicity', and in brackets 'Bobby Spong'. Spong was one of the best-known female impersonators in captivity in Thailand and 'Felicity' is assumed to be one of the characters he played in a production.[10] Spong was one of over 1,500 FEPOW en route to Japan on 12 September 1944. He, like Kenneth Elwell, was on board the *Rakuyo Maru* which was torpedoed and sunk by the USS *Sealion*.

Brazil also made this wonderful birthday card (Figure 23) which was given to Fizzer on his birthday – 28 November – at Nakom Paton. In this one the dedication reads: from Felicity Trentan, Flick to you Fizzer, A. S. The initials A. S. were thought to stand for Angela Spong, another of Bobby's aliases. According to Sears Eldredge,

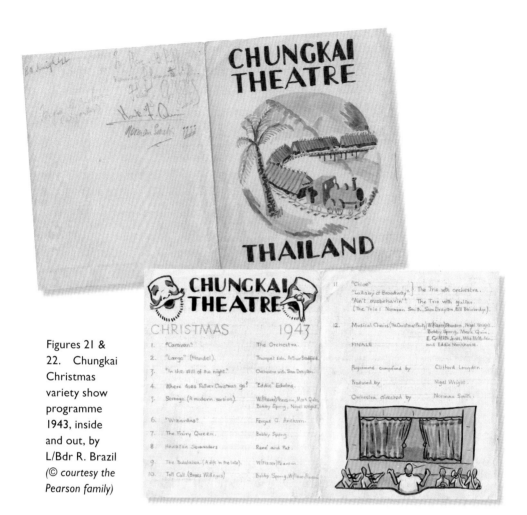

Figures 21 & 22. Chungkai Christmas variety show programme 1943, inside and out, by L/Bdr R. Brazil (© *courtesy the Pearson family*)

"[this card] *documents the journey Pearson as an entertainer took from performing in construction camps up the line, then down to Tamarkan (with a thumbnail sketch of the theatre)* [the lower of the two right of centre], *then across the river to Chungkai (again a good thumbnail sketch of theatre before it was rebuilt after monsoon rains of 1944)* [left of centre opposite Tamarkan], *and finally down to Nakom Paton* [bottom]."

However, the dedication 'Flick to you Fizzer' is a mystery. It is known that Pearson received this card in November 1944 on his 28th birthday. It could not have been from Bobby (A. S. or the Flick short for 'Felicity') as he was never at Nakon Pathom, having left the troupe in the July of that year for Singapore and later Japan. But we know he never reached there. In an email Sears Eldredge shed light on who 'Flick' may have been:

BIRTHDAY WISHES from "Felicity Trenton Flick to you Fizzer A·S. NAKOM PATON ₀ THAILAND

"There was a performer named Sam Flick at Chungkai. Don't know now if he was transferred to Nakhon Pathom [sic] or not ..."

This was Major Samuel Godfrey Flick 4th Suffolks. Was he the Flick who sent the card?

Basil Ferron: In Chapter 7 of Sears Eldredge's e-book on entertainments and entertainers, *Captive Audiences: Captive Performances*, he mentions a well-known female impersonator called Basil Ferron. An Anglo-Indian who was an RAMC medical orderly in the 11th Indian Division, Ferron's Liberation Questionnaire gives his address as Newmarket, Suffolk. He was first involved in entertainments while working at Robert's Hospital, Changi. Due to his short stature and slim physique, sleek, dark curly hair and his fine, almost feminine facial appearance, from the outset he took the leading lady roles. On 6 November 1942 he was drafted with L Party to Thailand. There he worked at Nong Pladuk for over two years before being moved to Ubon at the end of February 1945, from where he was liberated.

Ferron was also an artist. Despite few of the 37 works shown to the enquiry being signed or dated, making it uncertain when they were done, his composition and storytelling is informative and his illustrative style clear.

This sketch of the interior of a hut at Ubon (Figure 24) gives a sense of the width, height and sheer length of some of the huts built by the POW, each housing up to 300 men. Ferron peoples his sketches with activity – this looks like a mealtime with men returning to their bed space with mess tins and billy cans containing rations. The details of the construction are clearly visible: high roof trusses with the joints held by tight bindings, sloping bed platforms (or bali-bali), flattened earth floor and side entrances opposite each other, with the far end of the hut barely visible. Clothes slung over the lower roof supports, kit rolled up at the head end and shoes underneath the bali-bali, all create the impression of an orderly if spartan existence. There are more of Ferron's sketches in Chapter 4.

Malcolm Rivron: Here is another artist about whom very little is known. He and his brother, Peter, both served in the East Surreys and survived Far East captivity. Malcolm was only 18 when captured during the Battle of Malaya. Held in several gaols, he was sent to Singapore in November 1942. Both men went to Thailand, Peter in October 1942 and Malcolm in March 1943.

Pvt. Basil Elvin Ferron
RAMC, 11th Indian Division

Captured:	Singapore 15.2.42
Camps:	Singapore: Roberts Hospital Changi
	Thailand: Nong Pladuk, Ubon
From:	Newmarket
DoB:	15.9.20
Died:	not known

Figure 24. Inside a hut at Ubon Thailand, by Pvt. B. Ferron (© courtesy S. Smith)

Malcolm Boakes Rivron

Private, 2nd Btn East Surrey Regiment

Captured:	Singapore 15.2.42
Camps:	Malaya: H.M. State Gaol Alor Star
	Malaya; Taiping; Kuala Lumpur,
	Singapore
	Thailand: various, including Nakom
	Paton
From:	Grantham, Lincs
DoB:	22.4.24
Died:	not known

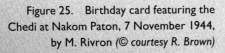

Figure 25. Birthday card featuring the Chedi at Nakom Paton, 7 November 1944, by M. Rivron (© *courtesy R. Brown*)

This birthday card (Figure 25), painted in camp and dated 7 November 1944, is clearly now very fragile. It depicts the large, golden-domed Buddhist temple, the Chedi, which dominated the camp at Nakom Paton and which also featured in AKKI's card (Chapter 1, Figure 26). This temple was an iconic symbol known to, and remembered by, many FEPOW.

Fred Ransome-Smith: Known to all as 'Smudger' Smith, Fred was a trained commercial artist who was involved with both theatricals and medical work (see Section II). He did this poster (Figure 26) for the last concert, held on 28 August at the Kanburi Theatre at Kanchanaburi was liberated. The poster is painted but appears to be unfinished. All the elements are there, outlined in pencil but only some of them have been finished. On the reverse he has listed the evening's entertainments and added a dedication to 'Fizzer' the producer, dated the following day.

The poster, which is painted, appears to be unfinished. It has his signature in the bottom right-hand corner and all the elements are there, outlined in pencil. But

Lieutenant Frederick William Henry 'Smudger' Ransome-Smith

5th Suffolk Regiment

Captured:	Singapore 15.2.42
Camps:	Singapore: Changi
	Thailand: various, including Nakom Paton Hospital camp
From:	London
DoB:	8.9.19
Died:	4.8.19

Figure 26. Poster for the Victory Concert at Kanburi camp, Thailand, August 1945, by Lt F. Ransome-Smith (© *courtesy the Pearson family*)

some of them have not been finished. On the reverse he has listed the evening's entertainments which appears to have been a multinational line-up, with the three main nationalities' anthems sung, one imagines with great gusto, at the end of the evening. In the bottom righthand corner he has added a personal dedication to 'Fizzer' the producer, dated the following day.[11]

Bill Norway's artwork was introduced in Chapter 2. He managed to continue sketching and designing ideas for business stationery after he was sent to Thailand. One striking piece to survive is this imaginary advertising poster featuring a motorbike (Figure 27).

A keen motorcyclist, Norways did this sketch entirely from memory and wrote this caption on the reverse:

> *"Wasn't feeling to* [sic] *good when I did this, so thought I would fill in time by seeing if I could remember what a motorbike looked like."*

Figure 27.   Poster of motorbike done in camp in Thailand, 1943, by Cpl W. Norways
(© courtesy the Norways family)

It is worth noting that the last time Norways had seen his motorbike would have been over four years earlier. His younger son Toby:

> *"I think the motorbike is remarkable – the detailed drawing is not a 'still life' reproduction of a motorbike in front of him in Singapore, but his memory of his bike back in England."*

Having been drafted back to Singapore, in early 1944 Norways was again immersed in theatricals, when he wasn't required to sketch in the medical huts. Here (Figure 28) is yet another striking example of the quality of Norway's skill as a graphic artist, two posters for the play, 'Journey's End'. The one of the

Figure 28. Left, original poster for 'Journey's End', Kranji, Singapore, 1944 and right copy done post-war, by Cpl W. Norways (*© courtesy the Norways family*)

left appears to be an original, given its tattered state, the one on the right a later copy, most likely done post-war. Toby Norways, Bill's son, sought advice from the expert on entertainments in Far East captivity, Professor Sears Eldredge, who commented:

> "Even in its tattered condition, the original is still a wonderful piece of graphic art … and is best 'explained' by, the later programme cover … [the play] seems to be about what when on in Kranji later in the war, but not about a production of 'Journey'.

> … [in] my file on the 18th Division's production of 'Journey's End' [there's] a very funny description of what happened during one of the performances. So, the script of that play was making the rounds of the POW camps in Changi (and up on the railway also). Extraordinary that they should do that play because it has distinct anti-war sentiments."

As a footnote to 'Journey's End', the play was first performed in Changi in February 1943 when, according to Toby's research, it was not universally appreciated:

> "'Journey's End' is a story from WW1. It was performed both in Kranji Theatre and The Palladium, Changi in Feb 1943. My Dad did the programme for the Kranji performance, Des Bettany did the programme for the Changi performance [which] the Changi performance wasn't well received. It was a thoughtful play with lots of dialogue, performed in torrential rain. The actors were heckled by the Aussie spectators and nearly didn't come out for the final act!"

Hong Kong

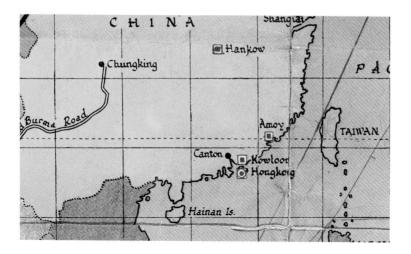

Most British FEPOW captured at the Fall of Hong Kong were held at some point in one of several large camps including, Stanley, North Point, Shamshuipo and Argyle Street (which became the officers' camp) as well as many smaller ones. From the autumn of 1942 several thousand men were shipped to Japan to run the industrial heartland of Japan's empire – the shipyards, steelworks, foundries and coalmines.

LSTM recorded four interviews with FEPOW veterans of Hong Kong captivity, one of whom was former Lt James T. 'Jim' Wakefield RE. Jim showed me a facsimile of an album of artwork that he had won in a raffle in 1944 (Figure 29). Number Four POW is a large format, homemade, hardback book with cloth binding, containing a large number and variety of artwork. Jim donated the original to the IWM in the late 1990s. This was the fourth such album to

Figure 29.   Frontispiece of Album 4, with signatures of featured artists
(© courtesy J. Wakefield)

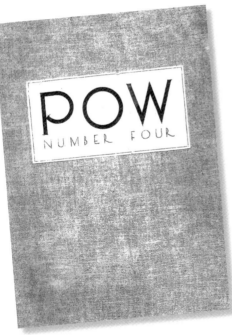

be compiled by artists, the money raised from the 1,100+ subscribers buying much-needed and illicit medical and cookhouse supplies.

Godfrey Bird: One of the contributing artists was Jim's friend, architect Godfrey Bird, who was one of the third generation of 'Bird' architects who helped create modern (early twentieth century) Hong Kong. The other British artists whose work featured in Album 4 were Hindmarsh, Tebbutt and Poltock. Hindmarsh and Tebbutt, like Bird, were architects and Poltock was a tea planter.[12]

Captain Godfrey Vernon Bird GM

RE, appointed GSO3 (Int)

Captured:	Hong Kong 25.12.41
Camps:	Queen Mary Hospital, Bowen Road Hospital, Argyle Street, Shamshuipo
From:	Hong Kong
DoB:	10.11.07
Died:	not known

Figure 31. A selection of art used for lecturing on architectural history, by Capt. G. Bird
(© courtesy the Bird family)

The album had been bound by British Royal Navy officer Mervyn Scott-Lindsley. He used a fundo-shi, or 'Jap Happy' (a POW loincloth) for the cover. The poor quality, loose woven, fabric is clearly visible (Figure 30). Jim was handed his prize on 20 May 1944, the day they left Argyle Street to return to Shamshuipo camp. In captivity Bird produced dozens of pieces of artwork (some of which are pictured in Figure 31) related to the classes and lectures he gave in camp on the history of architecture.

Another pencil and watercolour wash shows the new La Salle College building (Figure 32) as seen from Argyle Street POW camp. The fine modern building with a large square tower with its huge clock, is slightly obscured by trees and a rocky outcrop. Bird's firm designed and built the college. How strange must it have been for him to view it from the confines of captivity, knowing every nook and cranny of the building.

There are more sketches by Bird in Chapter 4.

John Harris: Yet another member of the Hong Kong architectural community, John Harris was a friend of Jim's and Godfrey's and he was also an accomplished artist. He too, did copious architectural drawings in captivity to keep his mind occupied but also scenes like this (Figures 33 and 34) remembering happier days past, and hopefully to come.

Figure 32. 'La Salle College', dated 22 August 1943, viewed from Argyle Street camp, by G. V. Bird (© courtesy D. Bird)

2nd Lieutenant John Harris

Royal Engineers

Captured:	Hong Kong 25.12.41
Camps:	Shamshuipo, Argyle Street, Shamshuipo?
From:	Surrey/Hong Kong
DoB:	5.6.19
Died:	15.3.08

Figure 34. Salisbury Cathedral, by John Harris (© courtesy John R. Harris/Mark Harris)

Figure 33. Copy of watercolour of Chinese junks, 1945, by 2/Lt J. Harris (© courtesy John R. Harris/ Mark Harris)

John's son, Mark, also an architect, said:

> *"My father used to say he was fortunate that the Japanese officer guard allowed him to keep his small water colour set. The one of Salisbury cathedral is remarkable in its accuracy given that it was done entirely from memory. He drew the junks at the end of the war."*

Mervyn Scott-Lindsley: As well as being a proficient book binder (reference POW Art Album 4 above, p. 156), Scott-Lindsley was also an accomplished artist. A sketchbook of his detailed sketches from captivity is held in the Royal Navy Museum archives in Portsmouth. Many of his drawings are of everyday life in camp, the ways in which the POW adapted and coped. Figure 35 clearly shows the sturdy wooden hut and homemade furniture that was home to many at North Point camp in Hong Kong while Figure 36 shows a more informal scene, gathered round a brick built boiler in what appears to be warmer weather, judging by the casual attire on display.

Lieutenant Mervyn Scott-Lindsley

RNVR

Captured:	Hong Kong 25.12.41
Camps:	North Point and Shamshuipo
From:	St Albans
DoB:	18.11.14
Died:	not known

Figure 35. North Point camp, naval officers in hut, March 1942, by Lt M. Scott-Lindsley (© Dr. B. Harris and courtesy the National Museum of the Royal Navy)

Figure 36. 'Hot water, toasting, or a light for your butt', North Point camp, by Lt M. Scott-Lindsley (© Dr. B. Harris and courtesy the National Museum of the Royal Navy)

His detailed pen and ink sketches of various everyday scenes at North Point camp present the viewer with a clear visual record of the kinds of makeshift solutions that the POW created.

Albert Joseph Poole was born Joseph Albert Poole in March 1918 in Walthamstow, London. He switched his Christian names and lied about his age to join Middlesex Regiment as a regular in 1935. Having served in China he was eventually posted to Hong Kong where he was captured. Known as 'Tookie', Poole was not an artist, but another collector of other people's art. Poole's small autograph book is a treasure trove of work by many different artists of different nationalities. One is known to be British and that is Ronald Barnes.

R. D. Barnes: A sketch, captioned 'Rations' and signed in a highly stylised way by R. D. Barnes, is believed to have been done by Able Seaman Ronald Barnes of HQ China Command in Hong Kong. He sketched in pencil a FEPOW (Figure 37), wearing a Jap Happy (loincloth) and carrying what looks like a sack of rice on his back adding definition by lightly colouring in crayon.

Comparatively little British artwork has emerged from Hong Kong captivity and, until Tookie Poole's book came to light, none so far has referenced the

Able Seaman Ronald David Barnes
HQ China Command

Captured:	Hong Kong 25.12.41
Camps:	Hong Kong: various, including Camp 'N'
	Japan: Osaka III
From:	Tilehurst, Berkshire
Date of birth:	11.1.18
Died:	Not known

Figure 37.   'Rations', Hong Kong, by A/ Seamn R. Barnes (© courtesy the Poole family)

Figure 38. 'Shamshuipo Memories' 1.11.44, signature of artist unclear (© courtesy the Poole family)

entertainments that are mentioned in the literature. One colourful sketch appears to be a montage of theatrical subjects from Shamshuipo POW camp under the title, 'Shamshuipo Memories' (Figure 38). This work comprises several female characters – are they caricatures? Dated 1 November 1944 it is signed 'Good Wishes Major [the artist's name is indecipherable] officer in charge entertainments'. Initial enquiries as to who the artist is have drawn a blank, but this work warrants further research.

Alfred Mitchell: Gunner Geoffrey Coxhead had been a teacher working in Hong Kong, who joined the HKVDC when war loomed. Early on in captivity, at Shamshuipo POW camp, he taught geography and also spent many hours teaching POW how to play chess, a game he both excelled in and was passionate about. In January 1943, Coxhead was drafted on a party leaving for Japan. One of the men who had learned to play chess, Alfred Cromar Mitchell of the RAOC, presented Coxhead with a home-made wooden chess set as a mark of gratitude (Figure 39). One set is coloured with black boot polish, the other left natural wood.

The chess set was kept in what appears to be a small Army issue canvas water bottle bag, bearing the following hand-written inscription:

> *Given to G. S. Coxhead HKVDC leaving H.K. in a draft to Japan January 1943 by A. C. Mitchell, RAOC*

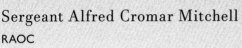

Sergeant Alfred Cromar Mitchell

RAOC

Captured:	Hong Kong 25.12.41
From:	Hong Kong: Shamshuipo
	Japan: Narumi, Toyama
From:	Stockport
DoB:	19.3.07
Died:	not known

Figure 39. Canvas bag and chess
pieces made by Sgt A. Mitchell
(© courtesy J. Coxhead)

Taiwan

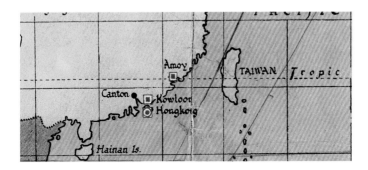

Gunner **John Clement's** Changi artwork was introduced in Chapter 2. Drafted,
along with Padre Stallard, from Singapore to Taiwan aboard the *England
Maru* in October 1942, Clement arrived at his first camp in Taiwan, Taihoku,
in November 1942. Within a week or two he had moved camps and was on a
working party. The work was hard, initially building a small rail track running
for nearly two miles from the camp to clay pits and then, working in pairs,
pushing trucks loaded with clay back and forth for months, depositing the load

across a small valley to form the base of a reservoir. Once done, they moved to another camp where the work was shifting stone in a similar manner, to change the course of a river.

Luckily for Clement, he was not on one of the parties sent to work in the notorious the copper mines at Kinkaseki (one of the worst work camps in the region).[13] But, at the end of his first year in Taiwan, he was down to under eight stone in weight (having lost three stone). He began to cough up blood and the POW doctor diagnosed TB (tuberculosis). Too sick to work, Clement was quarantined for much of the rest of his captivity. Recounting this in a recorded interview given to his grandson Paul in 1991, when Clement was 75, he said:

> "... No medication. Men were dying all around, three a day. Not old men. These were just young lads [with emphasis on the word 'young']."

It would be hard, if not impossible, to fully comprehend how sick, weak, hungry and bored he and other TB patients with him, must have been. The Japanese, being terrified of infectious disease, kept away from the TB huts, leaving care of patients to the Allied POW doctors and orderlies.

John's son Frank recalls being told that *"the notebooks were made in camp. He begged and bartered cigarettes for the paper and pencils."* Being quarantined gave his father time to keep his diary and make and illustrate the notebooks. Some,

Figure 40. An example of illustrated notebook depicting the different vegetables they ate, by Gnr F. Clement (© courtesy Glasgow Life: Glasgow City Archives and the Clement family)

like this example (Figure 40) were small and some even smaller (Figure 41); homemade booklets were carefully bound with decorated brown card covers.

By turning the homemade, landscape-oriented autograph book-sized notebooks through ninety degrees and ruling the long page into two columns of differing widths, he created a linear journal. The left side illustrated some of the noteworthy diary extracts on the right. His artwork while simple in style is graphic, clear and informative.

This entry (Figure 42) is worthy of mention (note, the horizontal line of the fold is visible near the top of the page). At Shirakawa camp, in February 1945 over half way down, he recorded an encounter with an officer. On the 27th, his brief diary entry notes that *"... Padre Stallard shows me his portfolio of portraits he has sketched."* To the left and above this entry, Clement drew a small square box around the head and shoulders to denote a picture.

Down the left side of the page the word 'WHEEE' is repeated. Clement explained in his diary that this was the sound of air raid sirens. He consistently utilised this comic-book style in his notebooks, visually documenting key moments each day. His artwork, neatly formatted into readable, absorbing even, miniature logs of each camp that he was held in for nearly three long years, is quite simply, extraordinary.

Figure 42.   Notebook entry 27 February 1945 re Padre Stallard, by Gnr J. Clement (© courtesy *Glasgow Life: Glasgow City Archives* and the Clement family)

His journey home was by hospital ships, trains and medical facilities, until he reached Bangour sanitorium south of Edinburgh where he spent the next year. When fully recovered he applied for and gained a place at the famous Glasgow School of Art where he studied for four years. The impact of his time as a POW affected his health, but it also changed his life in positive way as he spent the rest of his working life as a commercial artist.

Fred Stallard: His gloriously vibrant watercolour of his tent at Changi appeared in Chapter 2, along with his pencil sketch of below decks on the hellship, *England Maru*. While in Taiwan Stallard did some fine pencil portraits of fellow POW and some of the guards. This one of Colonel Meade (Figure 43), lying propped up and reading, his swollen ankles and lower legs clearly indicative of cardiac beriberi, a vitamin-deficiency disorder. He also made portraits, like the ones of David Piper (Figure 44) and one of the Japanese guards, Corporal Fuija (Figure 45).

Stallard also did at least one cartoon, this one (Figure 46) given to Captain Wyndham Forbes, 5th Field Regiment. The play on words hints at the approachability of the padre. Forbes also sketched and collected artwork while in Taiwan by other British artists, like Archie Bevan.

Figure 43.   Portrait of Colonel Meade suffering from beriberi, by Padre F. H. Stallard *(© courtesy the Stallard family)*

Colonel Meade with beri-beri

IV

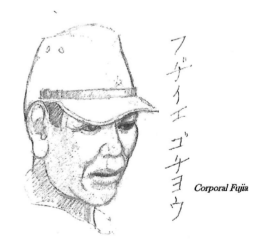

Figures 44 & 45.   Portrait of David Piper and Japanese guard, Corporal Fujia, by Padre F. H. Stallard *(© courtesy the Stallard family)*

Corporal Fujia

Figure 46. Cartoon, by Padre F. H. Stallard
(© courtesy D. Forbes)

But perhaps Stallard's most evocative work is this watercolour (Figure 47). It was hurriedly worked at dusk on his final evening in Taiwan, in September 1945.

Looking out across the cemetery at Shirakawa, the viewer sees what Stallard saw that evening: the earth mounds in neat rows, simple handmade wooden crosses, each marking the last resting place of so many young men. Under a lowering sky of mauve and grey, green fields melt away into valleys and woodland toward the distant hills. It is so powerful, so moving. It speaks of a padre wanting to ensure that all his flock returned home. None would be forgotten. Their friends, their padre, would make sure of that.

Figure 47. 'Shirakawa cemetery, dusk', by Padre F. H. Stallard (© courtesy the Stallard family)

Captain Gerald Archibald Johnstone Bevan

Welsh Guards, attd HQ 18th Division

Captured:	Singapore 15.2.42
Camps:	Singapore: Changi
	Taiwan: Heito, Shirakawa
	Japan: Miyata
	China: Mukden Manchuria
From:	London
DoB:	18.5.12
Died:	not known

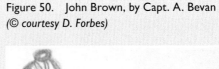

Figure 48. Maltby brothers reunited, by Capt. A. Bevan (© courtesy D. Forbes)

Figure 49. 'Forbes weighing sugar?' by Capt. A. Bevan (© courtesy D. Forbes)

Figure 50. John Brown, by Capt. A. Bevan (© courtesy D. Forbes)

Archie Bevan: One of several artists who gave artwork to Captain Forbes while in Shirakawa camp, was Captain Gerald Archibald Johnstone Bevan (known to all as Archie). His initials are his signature. His rather strange two-headed cartoon character (Figure 48) marks the reunion of the two high-ranking, be-spectacled and moustachioed, Maltby brothers. Paul, in his Air Vice Marshall's uniform faces left and Michael wearing the uniform of the General Officer Commanding British Forces in Hong Kong, faces right. Coloured with crayons the caricatures are convincing.

The reunion took place at Shirakawa camp in Taiwan when all the most senior Allied commanders had been gathered there from across the region, by the Japanese. Another cartoon (Figure 49) in Forbes' small autograph book appears to allude to him weighing something, possibly sugar (as this was in very short supply at Shirakawa). And yet another of Bevan's cartoons (Figure 50) features FEPOW John Brown.

Brown is sitting at a table on which is a stack of books, a pen and ink bottle. He strikes an elegant pose, cigarette holder in hand, giving a clue to his pre-war occupation in sales working for the Oxford University Press (OUP). Post-war he rose to become the publisher of OUP and was knighted in 1974.

Wyndham Forbes: The interior of the *England Maru*, (Figure 51), the hellship that transported members of the 5th Field Regiment including Padre Stallard, from Singapore to Taiwan, was one of the first sketches made by Captain Wyndham Forbes in his small pocket book.

The sketch shows that the men lay on platforms around the sides of an open hold where presumable bulk cargo was normally held, at the bottom of which there appears to be enough water to bathe in. A smaller sketch at the bottom of the page is entitled 'the "weekly" wash', and shows men stripped off and jumping into the water. This configuration below decks is interesting and has not been described before. Two more detailed pencil sketches in the same notebook, also coloured with crayon, and by Captain Forbes, provide views of the living quarters at Taihoku and Shirakawa camps.in Taiwan (Figures 52 & 53). It is interesting to note in the Taihoku sketch, that the huts are referred to as 'bungalows' and that church services were held outdoors between the buildings.

Captain Wyndham Kinloch Forbes

5th Field Regiment, 9th Indian Division

Captured:	Singapore
Camps:	Singapore: Changi Birdwood camp
	Taiwan: Taihoku, Shirakawa
From:	India
DoB:	26.6.09
Died:	not known

Figure 51. Sectional drawing of the *England Maru*, by Capt. W. Forbes *(© courtesy D. Forbes)*

For Shirakawa he provides a camp plan – at great risk. The detail is interesting, for example he refers to a moat at intervals around the camp. Was it a moat? Or perhaps, a deep trench, to be used if the camp, or Taiwan, was threatened by Allied invasion?

Figure 52. Views both inside and outside in Taihoku camp, by Capt. W. Forbes *(© courtesy D. Forbes)*

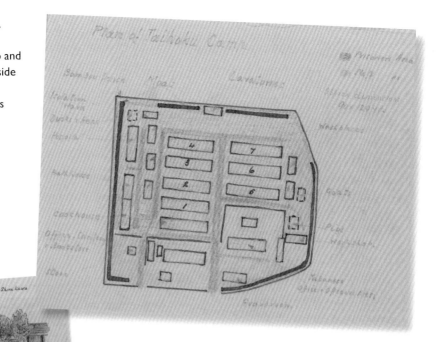

Figures 53 & 54. Right, plan of Shirakawa camp and below, views inside and outside, by Capt. W. Forbes (© courtesy D. Forbes)

The sketches of Shirakawa camp depict a clean and orderly, if spartan, scene, both inside and outside the low building. The presence of a row of trees close to the building softens the impression of what must have been a bleak captivity, providing a softer focus to life – attracting birds and insects, providing the sound of rustling leaves; nature's barometer for the changing seasons.

Captain Forbes' nickname was Windy. The following is the first entry in his notebook.

> *Who day by day grows thinner, frailer, and more flat*
> *In bamboozling, digging, but especially in that*
> *Never is this food real food, that satisfies –*
> *Despair not – for one day I'll meet yet recognise*
> *You not: so lewdly, lovely gross, so beastly fat.*

This acrostic verse (the first letter of each line spells the name WINDY) was composed by Forbes' friend, David Piper, whose portrait was done by Padre Stallard (see Figure 44). Post-war Piper was to have an illustrious career as an art historian becoming first, Director of the National Portrait Gallery, then Director of the Fitzwilliam Museum in Cambridge and finally Director of the Ashmolean Museum in Oxford. He was knighted in 1983.

George Harrison: Serving in the 5th Field Regiment, Lance Bombardier Harrison was held initially at Changi before being drafted to Taiwan, sailing on 20 October 1942. There he worked as a medical orderly at Taihoku, Kinkaseki and Kukutsu camps assisting the doctors. Harrison had qualified as a commercial artist pre-war and in captivity used his skill to secretly record many of the challenges of daily life in captivity. He was the only orderly working in Kinkaseki mine able to assist the injured.

Harrison worked closely with Canadian Major Ben Wheeler RAMC who was revered by the men under his care. Wheeler's daughter Anne, a Canadian film producer who made the film 'A War Story', based on her father's diaries (already referenced), said of Harrison's artwork:

Lance Bombardier George William Harrison

5th Field Regiment RA, 11th Indian Division

Captured:	Singapore
Camps:	Singapore: Changi
	Taiwan: Taihoku camp 6, Kinkaseki and Kukutsu
From:	Bromley, Kent
DoB:	5.5.20
Died:	December 2006

Figure 55. POW being beaten up by guards, by L/Bdr G. Harrison (© courtesy Taiwan POW Camps Memorial Society)

"… it was very detailed and lovingly executed … he was considered the camp artist."

Regrettably, despite searches, as yet none of Harrison's artwork has come to light in private collections. We are grateful that Michael Hurst, Director of the Taiwan-based 'Never Forgotten' organisation and website[14] who has shared a sketch by Harrison (Figure 55) which will be known to researchers of captivity in Taiwan. The pencil and charcoal sketch shows the daily ritual beatings of men who had not fulfilled their daily quota in the mines.

Regarding the rest of Harrison's sketches, Hurst said:

"… this is one which George is famous for and rather than just rough sketches like some artists did, George's were very detailed and accurate … It is certainly a shame that his drawings were all 'lost' after his death."

Japan

There is no precise figure for the numbers of British POW held in Japan. They were either sent there immediately after capture, for example senior naval personnel from HMS *Exeter*, who initially were sent to the Japanese Navy Interrogation camp at Ofuna, or were drafted in from camps in Hong Kong, the Dutch East Indies and Singapore. Allied POW were sent to Japan as early as autumn 1942 and were used to supplement Japan's industrial workforce in the shipyards, coalmines and smelting works across the country. Despite there being less artwork from Japan to have so far come to light, the quality and range is remarkable, given the risks men took to document what how they lived and what they saw.

Derek Clarke and Harry Berry: Derek Clarke was another man known as 'Nobby'. He served as a Sapper in the 5th Field Regiment. Derek and Harry Berry (known collectively as Harber and Nob!) first teamed up in Taiwan where they spent a year after being drafted from Changi. They then moved to Japan, to Omori camp, a much-feared labour camp.[15] There, the pair continued to entertain with Clarke's amusing cartoons, 19 in all (see example Figure 56), forming a collection entitled, *Ballads of the Barons*. Harber created the words and Nob the cartoons, the 'Barons' referring to the men who were adept at thieving. Harber also wrote songs for shows (both in Taiwan and Omori) and produced them.

These cartoons were created using flimsy brown paper, roughly postcard size, but as the paper was so thin the drawings done on the reverse of each sheet show through. The verses were typed and can be difficult to read in places. The verse shown reads:

> *Baron Fergy was an outlaw*
> *A reckless one was he*
> *Who's held up many A 'Kaisha'*
> *For the sake of having sweet tea*
> *And they say it's more than likely*
> *That – when he gets the knack*
> *He'll be walking down the Yama Sen*
> *With the engine in his sack!!*

Edward Burch: A Sapper in the Royal Engineers, Edward Burch left Changi with Z Party on board the *England Maru* bound for Taiwan. He spent time in both Taichu camp and the Kinkaseki copper mines, before being drafted in late February 1945 to Japan, on board the *Taiko Maru*. He arrived at Fukuoka camp 24B in early March. The POW there worked at the Sumitomo coal mining company. Only one watercolour painted by Burch has so far come to light, (Figure 57), a portrait of John and Maurice Green's mother Mary, done from a photograph that John had kept with him throughout captivity. (Maurice's artwork features in Chapter 2).

Sapper Derek Clarke

251st Field Park Company, 18th Division

Captured:	Singapore, 15.2.42
Camps:	Singapore: Changi
	Taiwan: Taichu
	Japan: Omori (from November 1943)
From:	Watford, Herts
DoB:	3.8.21
Died:	2000

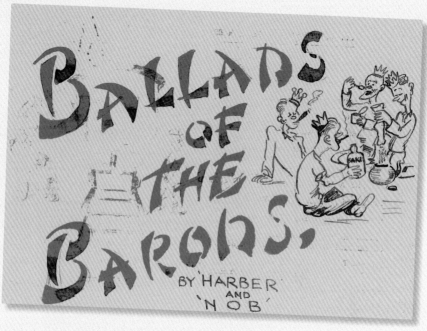

Figure 56.   Cover and one of the comic verses and cartoon, by
'Harber' & 'Nob'; sketches by Sapper D. Clarke, words by H. Berry (© *courtesy L. West*)

Gunner Henry William 'Harry' Berry

5th Field Regiment, RA

Captured:	Singapore: 15.2.42
Camps:	Singapore: Changi
	Taiwan: Taihoku
	Japan: Omori
From:	Islington, London
DoB:	1.12.16
Died:	19.1.04

Sapper Edward Burch

288 Field Company, RE

Captured:	Singapore 15.2.42
Camps:	Singapore: Changi
	Taiwan: Taichu, Kinkaseki
	Japan: Fukuoka camp 24B
From:	Norbury, London
DoB:	7.11.16
Died:	not known

Figure 57. Portrait of Mary Green, Japan 1945, by Sapper E. Burch (© *courtesy M. Green*)

Captain Atholl Duncan Argyll & Sutherland Highlanders, was captured in Java and later shipped to Japan. Duncan was not an artist but had been trained in technical drawing while studying engineering at university.

The first of his three detailed camp plans, of the large transit camp at Tandjong Priok in Java, is in Chapter 1 (Figure 35). At Zentsuji Officers' camp on the island of Shikoku in Japan, Duncan documented the buildings both inside and out. This was a former Japanese Army barracks occupied initially by American POW captured on Guam and Wake Island. A small British contingent of senior officers from HMS *Exeter*, sunk during the Battle of the Java Sea, joined the Americans in late spring 1942, followed in July 1943 by Duncan and a party of fellow officers from the Java party sent initially to the coalmines on the southern coast of Honshu.

His sketch of the POW barrack block (Figure 58) shows a substantial brick and timber construction with a pitched roof, whereas the benjo hut (latrines, Figure 59) is made of wooden partition walls, again with a pitched roof. This afforded little protection during the freezing winter months.

Figure 58. Barrack block at Zentsuji POW camp, Japan, by Capt. A. A. Duncan (© courtesy the Duncan family)

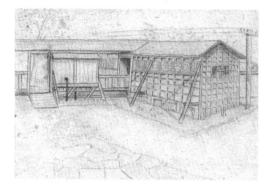

Figure 59. Benjo hut at Zentsuji POW camp, Japan, by Capt. A. A. Duncan (© courtesy the Duncan family)

He wrote in diary No.3 towards the end of 1943, that he had acquired drawing paper for these sketches:

"Last night, I managed to buy a drawing book from Freddie Murdock for five packets of Nip cigarettes so this afternoon, feeling very bored with life and having nothing better to do, settled down and managed to reproduce a fair likeness to the old 'benjo' using Studer's [American POW] *sketch as a guide, and intend to try and get a few more drawings of life in this camp in the future."*

Duncan's sketch of the inside of his barrack room features in Chapter 4 (Figure 15). He also did detailed plans of the layout and facilities at Motoyama coalmining camp (Figure 60) on Honshu Island and Zentsuji on Shikoku (Figure 61), both neatly drawn to scale, coloured in crayon and with compass bearings.

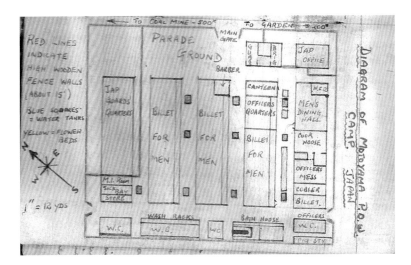

Figure 60. Capt. Duncan's scale plan of Motoyama coalmining camp, Honshu Japan, 1943 (© courtesy the Duncan family)

Figure 61. Capt. Duncan's scale plan of Zentsuji officers' camp, Shikoku, Japan, 1944 (© courtesy the Duncan family)

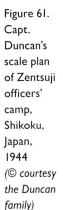

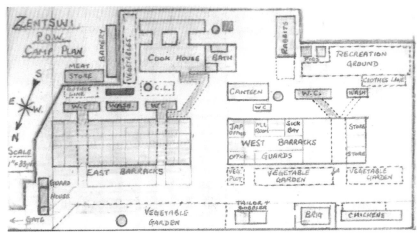

These were drawn in 1943 and 1944 respectively in his small brown leather-covered pocketbook. He knew the risks he was taking which is why even his closest friend at Zentsuji had no idea he kept a diary, it was never shared or discussed for fear of implicating others. He also did small sketches in his diary, like this one (Figure 62) done of the *Lisbon Maru* sinking (the first hellship to be sunk by Allied submarines, in September 1942 en route from Hong Kong to Japan). Again, it was drawn in diary No.3. This homemade notebook was made from small booklets cut down from a larger pad, bound together using mosquito netting and tapioca root glue. He was told about the sinking by a survivor in 1943, while at Motoyama camp.

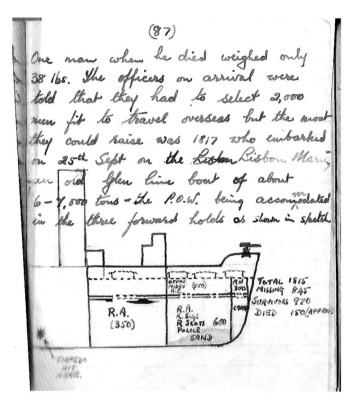

Figure 62.
Sketch of *Lisbon Maru* in Diary 3, showing numbers of POW on board, by Capt. A. A. Duncan (*© courtesy the Duncan family*)

POW Officers at Zentsuji were required to do agricultural work. They were on half-rations as the work was not heavy labour and these rations reduced over time as the net tightened around Japan's home islands. During the two years Duncan spent there his weight, energy levels and resistance to illness fell markedly, all charted in the diaries and notebooks that he secretly kept. However, it was too dangerous to record his fourth and final camp, the Miyata coalmine on the island of Kyushu.

Norman Power: A naval lieutenant on the ill-fated HMS *Exeter*, Norman Power was known as 'Freddie'. He was among the first British POW to be sent to Zentsuji in spring 1942 and was one of the leading lights in entertainments, performing in, and writing, plays and shows. He and Duncan got to know each other during late 1943. Freddie trained in law pre-war and was a gifted amateur artist. Amongst other things he did comic greetings cards, like this one (Figure 63) given to Duncan on 4 March 1944, signed by the men in his hut, on his 26th birthday.

Lieutenant Norman Hickey 'Freddie' Power RN

HMS *Exeter*

Captured:	Battle of Java Sea
Camps:	Japan: Ofuna interrogation camp, Zentsuji, Mitsushima
From:	Coventry
DoB:	18.5.17
Died:	14.2.92

Figure 63. Birthday card to Andy Duncan, by Lt Freddie Power (© *courtesy the Duncan family*)

It is a well-crafted graphic design in 1940s comic style, the image alluding to Duncan's all-consuming desire to be airborne (he had wanted to join the RAF and become a pilot but was not accepted in 1939). Freddie used watercolours and inks to great effect (they are still vivid 74 years on). The card has a piece of patterned cellophane-type paper taped to the back and folded over to cover the front, possibly added later. On 10 January 1944 in diary no.4 he wrote this about Freddie's artistry:

> "... *Freddie Power is engaged on making a series of cartoons depicting our life here in Zentsuji for the souvenir book which Strang is hoping to produce – these drawings of his never fail to amuse me.*"

Geoffrey Coxhead: Having trained as a teacher pre-war, Geoffrey Coxhead was working in a school in Hong Kong as war loomed. He joined the Hong Kong Volunteer Defence Corps and went into captivity at Shamshuipo camp following Hong Kong's capitulation on Christmas Day 1941. Coxhead was the recipient of a hand carved chess set, given to him by Sergeant Mitchell when he left Hong Kong for Japan (Figure 39).

Gunner Geoffrey Shervill Coxhead

HKVDC

Captured:	Hong Kong 25.12.41
Camps:	Hong Kong: Shamshuipo
	Japan: Hiroshima 5
From:	Gerrard's Cross, Bucks
DoB:	10.5.11
Died:	August 2000

Figures 64 & 65.   Above, notebook with two coastal views: top, 'Innoshima 3.7.43' and above, 'May 1945', by Gnr G. Coxhead (© *courtesy the Coxhead family*)

Coxhead filled his small pocket book with pencil sketches, coloured with crayon, of camp scenes and the local scenery (Figures 64 & 65) like these below. There are more of his sketches in Chapter 4, Figures 16 & 17).

Korea

The Lancashire Infantry Museum at Fulwood Barracks in Preston holds the largest collection of British art work from POW camps in Korea. The officers and men of the 2nd Btn The Loyal Regiment left Changi on 12 August 1942 and among them were a few talented artists.

Harold Kingsley: A Private in the 2nd Btn The Loyal Regiment Harry enlisted in 1933 aged 19. From his Army pay book we know he had been a window cleaner. He was a prolific artist in captivity producing caricatures and portraits in pencil on cheap local paper. Some are now in Preston's Harris Museum collection, but over 200 are held by the Lancashire Infantry Museum. The curator, Jane Davies, says of Kingsley's work:

> "The paintings and drawings produced by PoWs like Kingsley, undoubtedly remain of the greatest historical significance to us today ... often these pictures represent the only extant, or most authentic, visual depiction we have of camp life ... Consciously or not, PoW artists thus captured their experiences for posterity, leaving an enduring record of the realities of everyday existence in the camps ... composed under grim circumstances, with inadequate materials, [it] stands as testament to the resilience and resourcefulness of the human spirit in adversity."

Kingsley did many caricatures in his own distinctive style, like this one (Figure 66) depicting a visit to the camp dentist.

Private Harold 'Harry' Kingsley

2nd Btn The Loyal Regiment

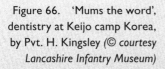

Captured:	Singapore 15.2.42
Camps:	Singapore: Changi
	Korea: Keijo
From:	Manchester
DoB:	6.9.14
Died:	not known

Figure 66. 'Mums the word', dentistry at Keijo camp Korea, by Pvt. H. Kingsley (© courtesy Lancashire Infantry Museum)

Kingsley's captions are clever. In Figure 66 'Mum' refers to Captain C. F. Mummery the dentist,[16] who is poised with carpenter's pliers in hand, ready to extract!

The caricature is of two officers, Lieutenants David and Jakeman, playing a rubber of bridge (Figure 67). Both were in the FMSVF having lived in worked in Malaya for many years[17] and Malaya was synonymous

Figure 67. 'Rubber', by Pvt. H. Kingsley (© courtesy Lancashire Infantry Museum)

Figure 68. 'Weighing in'. Capt. Paque at the left-hand end of the queue, by Pvt. H. Kingsley (© *courtesy Lancashire Infantry Museum*)

with rubber production. This next one (Figure 68), captioned 'Weighing In', is a line-up of emaciated officers at Keijo camp, probably sometime in 1944. From left, Major Lawrence (Gordons), Major Lydden (122nd Field), Major Beaumont (RASC), Lt Bell (2nd Loyals) and the diminutive Captain Paque (2nd Loyals). Paque also features in one of Lieutenant Wade's caricatures that appeared in the camp magazines, *NIB* (Chapter 6, Figure 7 & 8).

On 13 November 1942 Kingsley suffered an injury to his leg while tunnelling at Kia Kosha and was in hospital for several weeks. This left him with a noticeable limp and thereafter he referenced himself in sketches as a small monkey with caricature face wearing a peaked cap, and with a bandaged leg, as in this sketch (Figure 69) on the left. Kingsley appears to be sketching medical officer Major

Figure 69. Self-portraits, Kinglsey depicted as a monkey conversing with Major O'Donnell, medical officer, Keijo camp, by Pvt. H. Kingsley (© *courtesy Lancashire Infantry Museum*)

O'Donnell of the Indian Medical Service. Perhaps he was the doctor who had looked after him? In his sketch on the right, he is again with O'Donnell, this time his bandaged leg is not obvious, and he seems to be showing the doctor one of his sketches.

From 1947 to 1951 Kingsley studied art at the Manchester School of Art and made a career in teaching. He was a member of the Salford Art Club. Little else is known of this gifted, private man. However, his work came to public attention in 2005, when he was one of the Lancashire FEPOW artists whose work formed part of the 'Nor Iron Bars' exhibition at the Museum of Lancashire in Preston, to mark the 60th anniversary of VJ Day. The exhibition title is taken from a collection of satirical magazines of the same name, secretly written by a handful of 2nd Loyals' officers during captivity. The line comes originally from a poem, *To Althea, from Prison*, by Richard Lovelace, the fourth stanza of which starts with:

> *Stone walls do not a Prison make,*
> *Nor Iron bars a Cage;*

The first editions of *Nor Iron Bars* (quickly shortened to *NIB*) were written in Changi. Later editions were created in Keijo camp in Korea. There was only one copy of each edition made and it was published intermittently, due to lack of materials. Each copy was eagerly-anticipated, being circulated discretely among the officers' mess. The editorial team relied on contributions from the 30 to 40 officers in the mess and there were twelve editions in all, each richly illustrated. These two caricatures (Figures 70) by Harry Kingsley show two of the editorial team, Lieutenants Turner and Given-Wilson, studying recent editions.

Figure 70. 'Their Nibs', Keijo Korea, by Pvt. H. Kingsley (© *courtesy Lancashire Infantry Museum*)

Tom Henling Wade: The artist credited for illustrating the first few editions of *NIB* was Lieutenant Tom Henling Wade. He was missing from Kingsley's caricature above, presumably because it was drawn after Wade had left for Japan. Here (Figure 71) is Wade's own caricature of the editorial team entitled 'ED.', which appeared in an early edition of *NIB*, and includes himself.

This sketch (Figure 72) featured in an early edition of *NIB*, and depicts conditions below decks on board the 3,800-ton cargo steamer, *Fukkai Maru*, used to carry 1,000 POW, including members of the 2nd Btn The Loyal Regiment, from Singapore to Korea.

In Section III (Chapter 6) Jenny explores Wade's contribution to the production of *NIB*.

Donald Teale: Another member of *NIB*'s editorial team was Captain Donald Teale. A pencil and charcoal portrait signed by Teale of a woman (Figure 73), which is in the Lancashire Infantry Museum's archives, was thought to have been the wife of one of the older officers.

Lieutenant Tom Henling Wade

Intelligence Officer, 2nd Btn The Loyal Regiment

Captured:	Singapore 15.2.42
Camps:	Singapore: Changi
	Korea: Keijo
	Japan: Omori
From:	London
DoB:	6.6.20
Died:	2016

Figure 72. 'Fukkai Maru', by Lt T. H. Wade *(© courtesy Lancashire Infantry Museum)*

Captain Donald Eric Teale

2nd Btn The Loyal Regiment

Captured:	Singapore
Camps:	Singapore: Changi
	Korea: Keijo
From:	St Annes on Sea
DoB:	14.11.15
Died:	not known

Figure 73. Gloria d'Earie, July 1944, sketch by D. E. Teale *(© courtesy Lancashire Infantry Museum)*

However, the portrait was not drawn from a photograph but from life, the sitter being Gloria d'Earie, aka Lance Bombardier Arthur Butler. Butler was one of the Singapore garrison's best-known female impersonators (see Introduction) and had been a member of the 'Stand Easy' Concert Party on the island, pre-war. Emeritus Professor Sears Eldredge, who has made a detailed study of entertainments in Far East POW captivity, wrote of Butler:

> "With his 'delightful tenor voice,' he sang on Singapore Radio every Sunday and at society birthday parties, and he even gave a command performance for the sultan of Johor. 'Butler was slim and gracious, with small features and ardent brown eyes,' wrote Tom Wade. 'He was always known as Gloria and the jokes about him were almost as numerous as they once use[d] to be about Mae West. It was said that when he gave an order to the gunmen in his artillery battery, they would always reply, 'Yes, darling.'"[18]

Donald Teale was also immortalised by Kingsley, in this caricature (Figure 74) entitled, somewhat hopefully, 'If I could only stay the course'.

Alan Toze: Working closely with fellow artist Sgt Stanley Strange, Lance Bombardier Alan Toze created detailed, informative pen and ink sketches (see example Figure 75). The two men adopted a similar style, presenting their drawings individually, in a montage format using a comic-book style. This one, by Toze recalls scenes around Changi and was done in March 1943 when he was in Korea.

Figure 74. 'If I could only stay the course' portrait of Capt. Teale, by Pvt. H. Kingsley
(© courtesy Lancashire Infantry Museum)

Lance Bombardier Alan Vernon Toze

122nd Field Regiment RA

Captured:	Singapore 15.2.42
Camps:	Singapore: Changi, Caldecott, Roberts Hospital
	Korea: Pusan, Keijo, Jinsen; plus 17 days' work in Takao Taiwan, en route to Japan
	Japan: Omine, Kyushu
From:	Virginia Water, Surrey
DoB:	4.5.15
Died:	not known

1. TYPICAL "CHANGI BUGGY" LEAVING ARTILLERY SQUARE WITH RICE RATIONS.
2. WATER FATIGUE ENTERING SOUTHERN AREA. (NOTE INTER-AREA "CONVOY" & SIKH SENTRY)
3. R.C. CHURCH IN COURSE OF CONSTRUCTION.
4. RUINS OF BOMBED R.C. GARRISON CHURCH, CHANGI.

DRAWN BY L/BDR. A.V.TOZE. 122. R.A. MAR. 1943

Figure 75.   Scenes around Changi, March 1943, by L/Bdr A. Toze
(© courtesy Lancashire Infantry Museum)

Sergeant Stanley Strange

2nd Btn The Loyal Regiment

Captured:	Singapore 15.2.42
Camps:	Changi
	Korea: Keijo
	Japan: Kobe, Fukuoka 26 and 27 camps
From:	Chorley, Lancashire
DoB:	19.2.14
Died:	not known

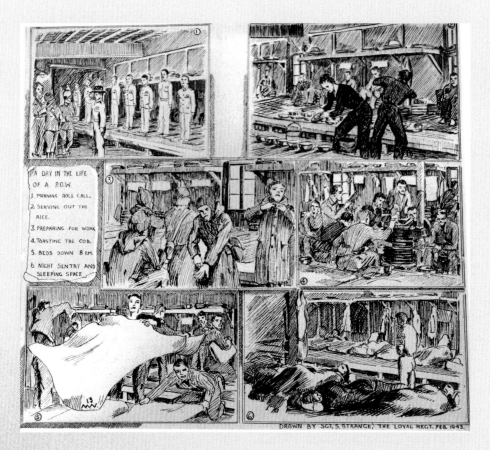

Figure 76. 'A Day in the life of a POW' Keijo camp, Korea, Feb 1943, by Sgt S. Strange
(© courtesy Lancashire Infantry Museum)

Toze did several more of these montages.

Stanley Strange: A career soldier, Stanley Strange, like his artist friend Alan Toze, did similar style montages of events and scenes during captivity (Figure 76). This example dated February 1943, according to the caption depicts 'A Day in the life of a POW'. This was drawn at Keijo camp in Korea. His pen and ink drawings are full of action, giving a real sense of the overcrowding and general conditions in camp.

Conclusions

The first three chapters of this book have introduced the work of 69 'unrecognised' British FEPOW artists. This wealth of new visual material adds greatly to our collective knowledge of the history of Far East captivity during the Second World War. There is undoubtedly more to discover and certainly more to be learned. Hopefully, by shining a light on this topic it will encourage more work to come to the surface and further study.

In Tom Wade's 1994 memoir, *Prisoner of the Japanese, From Changi to Tokyo*, his dedication reads:

> *"To my family above all, four generations of them; to those prisoners of war who did not return from the Far East and to those survivors, scarred but sturdy, who returned to an uncomprehending country."*

Thanks to the courage and determination of the 'scarred but sturdy' men like Wade, who documented what they saw but were largely unable to share it during their lifetime, we are now able to comprehend better what they endured and survived. In the next two sections Geoff Gill and Jenny Wood will explore this artwork further, under the themes of camp life, environment, medicine, survival and finally, the changing post-war attitudes to war art.

SECTION II

Geoff Gill

CHAPTER 4

Camp Life – A Pictorial View

This chapter will take an overall view of Far East camps, based around depictions by POWs. It will include the geography and structure of such camps, as well as living amenities and accommodation, working patterns, survival strategies and movement between camps. As previously stated, approximately 140,000 Allied troops were captured by the Japanese in late 1941 and the first part of 1942. This occurred throughout Southeast Asia, but major concentrations of prisoners were at Singapore, Hong Kong, Java and Sumatra. Later movements brought many POWs to Thailand, Burma, Borneo, Taiwan, Korea and Japan.

An important point is that there was no one inclusive POW camp experience. There were similarities, but also marked differences. Some began as tented encampments, bamboo and thatch huts were constructed elsewhere, and in some areas accommodation was in more substantial buildings. The latter included pre-existing jails, administrative buildings, workers' dormitories or barracks. The next section will examine these camp structures in different areas – the locations are not inclusive but are selected to demonstrate the geographical differences which occurred. The descriptions will be complemented by contemporary artwork by prisoners at these camps.

Camp structure

Singapore

The largest garrison captured by the Imperial Japanese Army (IJA) was at Singapore, which capitulated on 15 February 1942. Several camps developed on Singapore Island, but by far the biggest was at Changi, on the east of the island. In its early days this was overcrowded with very basic cooking and sanitation facilities, and not surprisingly diarrhoeal diseases such as dysentery soon broke out (see Chapter 5). Figure 1 shows an example of early accommodation at Changi. This drawing by Driver Don Clarke was produced in April 1942, not long after captivity. It shows his unit's camp, with the tents erected in line under a degree of shade.

Figure 1. 'Part of E Troop Lines, Changi Camp, April 1942', by Dvr D. Clarke
(© courtesy C. Tuffrey)

In time, Changi POW camp became a more permanent, mostly hutted structure, and later accommodation moved to the adjacent Changi Gaol. As we have already seen, several artists sketched the huts and tented encampments at Changi POW camp during the early years. Figure 2 is a pen and ink sketch done in 1944 of the interior of a new hut in Changi Gaol POW camp, drawn by medical officer Capt. Toss Wilson. This shows the more substantial (but still very overcrowded) living quarters which were constructed. Poignantly, Toss has entitled his drawing 'Home. 28.7.44–?'. Figure 4 is a view from his laboratory, looking out towards Changi Goal, the large white building with the tower. By that time it housed POWs.

Figure 2. 'Home. 28.7.44 – ?', by Capt. T. Wilson (© *courtesy the Wilson family*)

Figure 3. 'View of Changi Goal building from the Laboratory', with a vegetable garden in the foreground, by Capt. T. Wilson (© *courtesy the Wilson family*)

In the foreground are the POW vegetable gardens. These evolved widely at Changi to supplement the rice-based diet which was dangerously low in B vitamins.

Thailand and Burma

The construction of the railway between Thailand and Burma was a major project involving about 60,000 POWs and many more local labourers. The railroad was 415 Km long when completed and traversed difficult jungle terrain. Not surprisingly, camp conditions were often primitive. Colonel Cary

Owtram, on arriving at Ban Pong camp in Thailand (near the start of railway construction), described it as a 'poor exchange' from Changi camp which he had earlier left by train. The accommodation was in overcrowded bamboo thatched huts, with no water supply, and *"the stench was indescribable".*[1]

The huts Owtram described were the common accommodation currency on the Thai–Burma railway. They were known as 'atap' (sometimes spelled 'attap') huts and were described by POW John Coast as *"an inverted V-shaped roof, thatched with atap and supported on a crude bamboo framework"*. Atap was a thatch made from palm leaves, which when packed tightly provided reasonable rain protection. Coast continued,

> *"down the middle of each hut was a central gangway, flanked on both sides by a split bamboo shelf … raised a couple of feet above the ground."*[2]

Sleeping space was very tight and bed bug infestation was common. Figure 4 is by **Gunner Will Wilder** and shows some of the atap huts at Nong Pladuk camp in Thailand. Note also the primitive washing facilities in the right foreground.

An interesting representation of atap hut construction is shown in Figure 6. This is a cartoon by Bombardier Basil Akhurst (known as 'AKKI') and gives a comic representation of POWs building an atap hut at Nong Pladuk camp in Thailand. An accompanying caption, probably written by Akhurst's friend Jack Sutter, comments that,

Figure 4. Nong Pladuk Camp, Thailand, showing atap hut accommodation, Gnr W. C. Wilder (© courtesy Anthony Wilder [not to be reproduced without permission])

Figure 5. 'Jerry Builders?' by Bdr 'AKKI' Akhurst (© courtesy IWM. IWM ART.LD 7342 1–22)

"part of our job was to build huts ... we used bamboo and atap – palm leaves dried and placed over a piece of bamboo. They were tied on with 'rattan' – bamboo stripped down to the thickness of tape. The tools were the world's worst".[3]

The AKKI cartoon shows atap hut construction at Nong Pladuk camp in Thailand. Note the POW on the top right about to get his fingers hammered, and at the top left a prisoner sitting on the wrong side of the bamboo spar he is sawing through!

Figure 6. 'Bath Time at No.1 POW camp Nong Pladuk', Thailand, by Pvt. B. Ferron (© courtesy S. Smith)

Further depictions of camps on the Thai–Burma railway are shown in Figure 7, bath time at Nong Pladuk and in Figure 8, a view of Chaungayya Camp, Burma. The latter is interesting as little in the way of POW art work has been found from the Burma side of the railway. This camp had several alternative names and was close to Three Pagodas Pass on the Thai–Burma border.

Sumatra

A lesser known railway project of Japanese imprisonment was the Sumatra Railway, designed to connect Pekanbaru to Maaro. This was about 200km long and involved a predominantly Dutch workforce together with British POWs, as well as many more local labourers. The line was forced east to west across the island as a supply line, through dense jungle terrain.[4] Conditions were, if anything, worse than on the Thai–Burma railway, and mortality was very high. Camps on the Sumatra Railway were similar to those in Thailand and Burma, and similarly, the POWs themselves generally built their own atap huts. There were relatively few British POWs present, but one, Aircraftsman Derek Fogarty, commented as follows about camp building:[5]

Figure 7. 'No.5 Camp, Chaungayya, Burma July 1943', by Lt J. White (© *courtesy J. Aldridge*)

Figure 8. 'Bridge over the Kanpari Kiri, Sumatra', 1944 by Lance Bombardier W. Cullen (© *courtesy the Cullen family*)

200

"We got into camp and – you had to build it! …. somebody dug the holes … somebody got the bamboo … and you split that and you made the pieces across to hold the atap."

Because of the conditions, and the smaller numbers of POWs involved, artwork from the Sumatra Railway project was limited. However, Lance Bombardier Wally Cullen recorded scenes from this desperate POW scenario. For example, his sketch of railway bridge construction (Figure 8) demonstrates the very difficult terrain and rudimentary engineering methods.

Hong Kong

The city of Hong Kong fell to the IJA on Christmas Day 1941, with some 8,000 Allied troops taken. They were held in a variety of buildings including former British and Canadian Army barracks and schools. The POWs were overcrowded, underfed and forced to work. Many Hong Kong POWs were later moved elsewhere in the Far East, but British POW, Captain Godfrey Bird (Royal Engineers), made artistic records whilst in Hong Kong, including one of the hospital at Shamshuipo camp (Figure 9), and the interior of a hut at Shamshuipo at night (Figure 10). The two rows of beds are shrouded in draped mosquito nets tucked neatly into the bed foot boards.

Figure 9. 'Hospital – Shamshuipo POW camp' – Hong Kong, by Capt. G. V. Bird (© courtesy D. Bird)

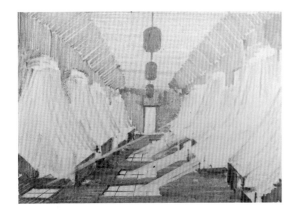

Figure 10. 'Night 17/12/43', Hong Kong, by Capt. G. V. Bird *(© courtesy D. Bird)*

Figure 11. 'My bed space', Hut 10, Argyle Street camp Hong Kong, by Capt. G. V. Bird *(© courtesy J. Warrack)*

Of particular interest is a personal painting entitled 'My Bed Space' done in Argyle Street camp (Figure 11). The bed space referred to was not Bird's but that of his good friend, RAMC officer Alexander ('Sandy') Warrack. It was given to Warrack by Bird as a birthday present in December 1943. The structure of the hut is more substantial than those made of atap and bamboo, and there are camp beds to sleep on. Nevertheless, there is still great overcrowding and the atmosphere is somewhat oppressive.

Java and Borneo

This area of captivity also includes the Molucca Islands (north east of Java), including the Spice Islands of Ambon and Haroekoe. Conditions in this area for POWs were difficult in different ways from those in the railway camps of Thailand, Burma and Sumatra. As an example, RAF medical assistant Arthur Turbutt described his arrival at Haroekoe[6] –

> *"It was monsoon season, torrential rain came down in sheets, and we were taken off the boat … to a cleared area … it was about three inches deep in mud … and we were told to lie down and go to sleep."*

Figure 13.   Interior of the officers' hut at Jaarmarkt
camp in Java, by Fl/Lt L. J. Audus *(© courtesy H. Audus)*

Things did not improve greatly, as subsequently the POWs were set to work reducing two nearby hills to a flat area for construction of an airstrip – using primitive tools including hammers, trowels and spoons.[7]

HAROEKOE

RICHARD PHILPS

Figure 14. 'Doctors' Hut' on Haroekoe, by Fl/Lt F. R. Philps *(© courtesy the Philps family)*

Depictions of these areas of imprisonment include work by Flight Lieutenant Leslie Audus – Figures 12 and 13 are watercolours of Jaarmarkt camp in Java, an exterior view of the camp area and an interior of the officers' mess. This was a hutted camp and Audus depicts how the officers lived in very cramped quarters.

Flight Lieutenant Richard Philps (a medical officer) painted the 'Doctors' Hut' on Haroekoe (Figure 14) which was an atap and bamboo construction. This was the hut he shared with fellow medical and dental officers. At the top of his bed space can be seen the small carved kingfisher that is referred to in Chapter 2 (Figure 29).

Japan

Large numbers of prisoners were transported to Japan during captivity. Taiwan, Korea and Manchuria were other destinations. The POWs were largely moved as a workforce replacement for the growing numbers of Japanese needed to serve the war effort overseas. POWs were often housed in poor quality wooden huts (workers' dormitories) in industrial work camps. As well as continuing food shortages (which worsened as time passed), the cold winters were a major problem.

Figure 15 shows the inside of a barrack room in the Officer's camp at Zentsuji, on the island of Shikoku in southern Japan, drawn by Captain Atholl Duncan. It is a pencil sketch showing a typical wooden hut interior, drawn as seen from

Figure 15. 'View from my bedspace', Zentsuji 1944, by Capt. A. A. Duncan (© courtesy the Duncan family)

Duncan's bed space. It shows the spartan living quarters, as well as remarkable detail, for example, in the wood grain. What the picture cannot show, however, is the infestation with bed bugs and fleas which *"made life a misery for us"* (recorded in Duncan's diary).[8]

There were a great many camps throughout Japan. One was at Innoshima, a port on the Inland Sea in central Japan (about 100 Km from Hiroshima). One of the prisoners there, Gunner Geoffrey Coxhead, was a talented artist and Figure 16 shows his interesting drawing of the pier at Innoshima. Figure 17 was drawn in his small pocket book and is of particular interest, given the date; POWs were at last free to swim in the waters of the Inland Sea.

Figure 16. 'P.O.W. camp on the Island of Innoshima, Inland Sea of Japan', by Gnr G. S. Coxhead (© *courtesy J. Coxhead*)

Figure 17. 'Innoshima. August 17th 1945', by Gnr G. S. Coxhead (© *courtesy J. Coxhead*)

Camp organisation

The IJA generally left internal organisation of camps to POWs themselves, and Allied camp commanders did their best to maintain discipline and infrastructure. Personal hygiene was difficult, but earlier in this chapter was an image of 'bath time' at Nong Pladuk camp in Thailand (Figure 6) demonstrating an attempt to maintain cleanliness under difficult circumstances. In Japan, Geoffrey Coxhead drew a view of the spartan benjo hut (latrines) at Innoshima (Figure 18). Some camps even had 'barber shops' and an example is shown in Figure 19, a pencil sketch by Captain Godfrey Bird in Hong Kong.

Food was of course a major preoccupation in prison camps, and cookhouses were very important. Cooks did their best to vary the dreary rice-based diet, and as time went on learnt to grind rice and produce cakes, doughnuts, and sweet rice flour tarts widely known as 'doovers'. In his lovely pencil sketch

Figure 18.   The benjo hut at Innoshima, Japan, by Gnr G. S. Coxhead
(© courtesy J. Coxhead)

Figure 19.   'Barber's shop' at a camp in Hong Kong, by Captain G. V. Bird
(© courtesy D. Bird)

Figure 20. 'Doovering' by Lt J. W. B. White *(© courtesy J. Aldridge)*

Figure 21. 'P.O.W. Canteen, Ubon 1945', by Dvr Don Clarke *(© courtesy the Clarke family)*

Lieutenant Stanley E. Bagnall, RA

Captured	Java 9.3.1942
Held:	Batavia: Boie Glodok, Tandjong Priok
	Singapore: Changi
	Borneo: Jesselton and Kuching
From:	not known
DoB:	not known
Died:	not known

(Figure 20), Lt Jack White drew two POWs, seated either side of a small stove, one of them holding a frying pan. In faint handwriting, written diagonally across the bottom left-hand corner, is the word 'Doovering'. It is undated, but from the scenery it is likely this was drawn in Changi Gaol POW camp sometime after May 1944.

Figure 21 is a drawing by the talented artist Driver Don Clarke, and depicts the canteen at Ubon camp in Thailand. This was not a railway camp but was in the north of the country and mostly populated by POWs after completion of the Thai–Burma railway.

Lieutenant Stanley Bagnall RE: Interestingly, the officers' cookhouse at a POW camp in Kuching in Borneo (Figure 22) by Bagnall reflects the standard military practice of separating officers and men, maintained in many POW camps. The depiction is in pencil and crayon and is the scene inside of the officers' cookhouse at Batu Lintang POW camp in Kuching. The roofing above the ovens is probably of corrugated iron, to prevent the atap thatch igniting.

An interesting painting of Changi concerning food supply is shown in Figure 23. The artist was Lt Eric Stacy and it shows the movement of a large ration wagon across the camp in 1943. The picture is entitled, 'The ration wagon passes Java Lines, Changi 1943' – presumably referring to an encampment of POWs

Figure 22. 'Officers' cookhouse, Kuching P.O.W. camp '45', by Lt S. E. Bagnall (© courtesy IWM.IWM DOC.398)

moved in from Java. As well as the ration wagon itself, Stacy's picture gives beautiful detail of the accommodation amongst the palm trees.

Some form of medical and hospital facilities were present in most camps, and these will be discussed and illustrated in Chapter 5 which deals specifically with camp medicine. Associated with disease and medicine, there was sadly the need for camp cemeteries. These were situated near to, or on the outskirts of camps, and were usually a series of simple burial mounds marked with a cross. The cemetery at Kanburi camp in Thailand exemplifies this in Figure 24 which is a pencil sketch by POW Robert Gamble, probably drawn sometime between August 1943 and April 1944. One of the camp padres described the cemetery as *"a plot of rough ground ... given by the Thais ... one regrets the fact that cattle trample the area"*.

Figure 23. 'The ration wagon passes Java Lines. Changi. 1943' by Lt E. F. Stacy (© courtesy IWM. IWM DOC.18648)

Leading Aircraftman Robert James Gamble

RAF 153rd MU (Maintenance Unit)

Captured:	Java 9.3.42
Camps:	Java; Singapore; Thailand: Hintok, Kanburi; Singapore (other camps unknown)
From:	Sheffield
DoB:	27.2.18
Died:	not known

Figure 24. 'Kanburi Cemetery' in Thailand, by LAC R. Gamble (© *courtesy the Cordingly family*)

Where there were padres they led simple burial services, and many kept secret burial registers. Jewish services were held at some camps on the Thai–Burma railway, sometimes led by the dental officer Captain David Arkush, who acted as an unofficial rabbi at Chungkai Hospital camp.[9]

Some camps also had chapels, and even theatres in the larger ones – notably at Changi in Singapore, and Chungkai in Thailand. These and other aspects of pastoral care and recreation will be discussed in detail in Chapter 6.

A major POW activity was of course labour for the Japanese, who constantly demanded work parties. Sickness was not normally accepted as an excuse, and medical officers had regular arguments with the IJA guards over who could or could not work. The type of work varied with camp and location. In Thailand, Burma, and Sumatra railway construction was of course a major activity. Earlier in this chapter, Figure 8, showed a railway bridge being built by POWs in Sumatra. Figure 25 shows a work party in Thailand – the men are carrying railway building materials, and interestingly their standard loincloth dress can be seen (these were

widely known as 'Jap Happies'!). The artist is Don Clarke, who was later sent to
Ubon camp in northern Thailand. Note the elephant, bottom right.

A scene at Ubon camp (Figure 26) by artist Basil Ferron shows vegetables being
prepared near the cookhouse. In the foreground a work party is mustering – in
this location probably for airstrip construction. Ferron has actually described
these details in a handwritten annotation on the back of the picture:

> "The men at the tables are preparing vegetables for the meals – 'veg-bashing'.
> Men in the foreground are a small working party about to go out to work".

Work in other areas of captivity varied greatly and included, for example, loading and unloading ships (particularly in Singapore, Java and Japan), factory work (in Japan), and mining (usually for coal or copper).

Transport between camps

If conditions in the prison camps were difficult and challenging, transport between camps often brought new levels of misery and privation. Overland, POWs were usually force-marched from camp to camp. One of the most notorious of these movements was that of F Force on the Thailand side of the railway. In May 1943 they were moved from the base camp at Kanburi to the remote up-country Sonkrai Camp, in 13 night marches – a total of 193 miles.[10] Food was short, the monsoon season had started, and daytime rest was often in jungle clearings. Major Cyril Wild (a member of F Force) recorded that the march would have been *"arduous for fit troops in normal times,"* but with the difficult terrain, lack of adequate food, and large number of sick *"it proved a trial of unparalleled severity".*[11]

Lance Bombardier John Mennie: Not surprisingly, few visual records exist of such marches, but John Mennie did paint a scene that he had witnessed of a detachment of Gordons and Argylls marching towards the Three Pagodas Pass and on to the Burma side of the railway in May 1943 (Figure 27). Interestingly in a post-war interview, Hugh de Wardener, an RAMC doctor on the Thai–Burma railway, recalled witnessing this march and said how remarkable and uplifting it was to hear the sound of bagpipes in the jungle, and to see the men marching past in step – proud and disciplined. *"It was a brave sight"* he recalled, becoming quite emotional at this point of the interview. In Section III Jenny Wood explains more about Mennie's work.[12]

Movement of POWs from Changi in Singapore to the base of the planned railway in Thailand was by train. Large numbers of prisoners were involved and the journey was to say the least unpleasant. The men were crammed into steel railway wagons with sliding doors – about 30 men per wagon. The journey was approximately 1,000 miles and took four to five days and nights. POW Geoffrey Adams recalled that *"there was not room in them (the trucks) for thirty people to lie or even sit down, so we took it in turns to rest."*[13] Many men had dysentery, including Len Toseland who described the predicament:

Lance Bombardier John 'Jack' Mennie

2nd HKSRA

Captured:	Singapore 15.2.42
Camps:	Singapore: Changi Sothern Area
	Thailand: Kanu, Chungkai, Nakom Paton, Tamuan, Pratchi
From:	Aberdeen
DoB:	26.11.11
Died:	24.8.82

Figure 27. 'Detachments of POW Gordons and Argylls, going towards Burma, Thai–Burma Railway May 1943', by L/Bdr J. Mennie (© courtesy IWM.IWM ART.LD 7297)

"I, being a dysentery sufferer, was not in control of my bowel movement and needed to be near the door, as did many others. We had a little trick … the man in need would move backwards to the edge of the doorway, then he would drop his trousers and stoop, at the same time clasping the hands of a friend who would face him. It was far from funny at the time, but I am left wondering what the local Malay and Thai people thought as they watched a row of bums going by!"[14]

The POW artist Jack Chalker also travelled by train from Singapore to Thailand in October 1942. Figure 28 shows his depiction of the rail trucks at one of the relatively infrequent stops on the journey. POWs are climbing out of the steel trucks and a sick prisoner is collapsed in the foreground.

The final form of transport to discuss was arguably the worst – by sea. Large numbers of prisoners were moved between countries in ships. Conditions were similar to those of the eighteenth- and nineteenth-century slave trade – the men were battened down below decks, terribly overcrowded and with minimal or no sanitary facilities. The Japanese ships also carried no markings to show they were transporting prisoners of war and so were fair game for Allied air

Figure 28.
'The train
journey from
Singapore
to Thailand'
by Gnr J. B.
Chalker
*(© courtesy
Jack Chalker)*

and torpedo attack. The first tragedy was the sinking of the *Lisbon Maru* on 2 October 1942, as it sailed between Hong Kong and Japan. The ship was torpedoed with the loss of 843 POW lives. Not surprisingly, these boats became known as 'hellships'. In a post-war interview, Denis Morley (a survivor of the sinking of the *Lisbon Maru*) said,

> *"All I can remember is the blackness of the hold and the stink and the stench ... we were battened down, hence the darkness and the stench."[15]*

Similarly, John Tidey, who was shipped to Japan after working in Thailand, recalled being in

> *"the bowels of the boat ... we were crammed in, man for man and we weren't allowed to go up on deck until things got worse when they had to allow people to go to the latrines."[16]*

Padre Fred Stallard drew a scene in the hold of the *England Maru* travelling from Singapore to Taiwan, showing the dark and overcrowded conditions (Figure 29). He simply entitled it 'Inside the Coaler'.

With the dark, overcrowding, sweat, rats, dysentery outbreaks and associated stench, conditions on board the hellships were probably the worst and most fearful of all Far East POW experiences.

Figure 29. 'Inside the Coaler', by Padre F. H. Stallard (© courtesy the Stallard family)

Beauty amongst misery

The final section of this chapter will end on a more positive note. Despite the dreadful conditions of living, working and transport; a number of POW writers and artists appreciated that often the countryside, flora and fauna around them were outstandingly beautiful. Thus, on the rail journey from Singapore to Thailand, Jack Chalker recalled a

> *"stop at Kendong, a pretty little station full of exquisite flowers. It was brilliantly sunny and we could see Malay families in the padi fields ploughing with water buffalo … a great vista of blue hills rising from the mist beyond".*[17]

The Thai–Burma railway went through some outstanding country, as shown by Captain Robert Hardie's watercolour landscape of the view from Tarsao camp (see Figure 30).

Captain Lyons, who like Hardie was a medical officer, related an event during a march up the railway line on the Thailand side, where he and his party came across a

Figure 30. 'View downstream from Tarsao, 1943', by Captain R. S. Hardie (© *courtesy IWM.IWM DOC.18746*)

"cloud of the most beautiful butterflies … some were very, very large, the size of big birds … there was every conceivable colour one could think of … you literally walked through them … I've never seen anything so beautiful in my life".[18]

Butterflies were the subject of a number of POW artists' work and Figure 31 shows a study by Jack Kemp.

On the Sumatra Railway, Aircraftsman Derek Fogarty, in a post-war interview recalled travelling with wagon supplies, and after crossing some hills, he and his party

"came out the other side and there was just a panoramic view of hundreds of miles … of Sumatran jungle … it was wonderful … you could not but admire the beauty of Sumatra."[19]

Figure 31. 'Birdwing' butterfly study, Thailand, a birdwing, by J. E. Kemp (© *courtesy the Johnson family*)

In Java Fl/Lt Leslie Audus was also artistically aware of his surroundings. Figure 32 shows the Gunong Lawu volcano in the east of Java, drawn at dusk with fading light and rising mist (for two other studies done on the same day see also Chapter 2, Figure 5). He also painted several botanical studies on both Java and Haroekoe – see Figure 33 for examples. Also, on Haroekoe Fl/Lt Richard Philps produced a number of remarkable scenic watercolours, one of which is shown in Figure 34.

Figure 32.   Volcano on Java at dusk, by Fl/Lt L. J. Audus (© *courtesy H. Audus*)

Figure 33.   Botanical study, Haroekoe, by Fl/Lt L. J. Audus (© *courtesy H. Audus*)

Figure 34.   Landscape on Haroekoe, by Fl/Lt F. R. Philps (© *courtesy Philps family*)

Conclusions

This chapter has explored camp life in Far East imprisonment, particularly from the view of the brave and talented POW artists who recorded their experiences for future generations. Their work has shown us how the POW camps were constructed, and the everyday activities of camp life – including cookhouses, work parties, cemeteries and even hairdressing! They also documented the appalling systems of transport between POW camps – by foot, rail and sea. Finally, their records have shown us the beauty of the surrounding countryside, flora and fauna. For providing these records we owe these men an enormous debt of gratitude.

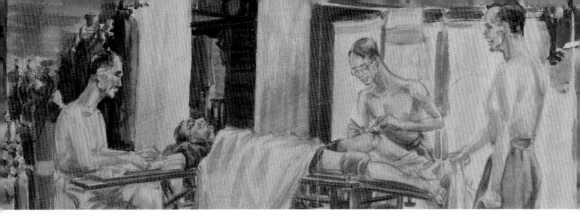

CHAPTER 5

Medicine and Art
in Captivity

Disease was a major cause of debility and death in Far East imprisonment.
Throughout Southeast Asia and the Far East, there were large numbers of
war prisoners (POWs) held by the Japanese. The diet was universally poor in
both quantity and quality, resulting in frequent syndromes of malnutrition.
Lack of adequate sanitation and clean water supply predisposed to a variety of
diarrhoeal diseases. Many tropical diseases, notably malaria, were indigenous to
locations of imprisonment. Drugs and medical equipment were in short supply
and some important therapeutic tools were yet to be discovered or introduced –
for example penicillin and effective anti-tuberculosis treatments.

Medical issues were common subject matter for prisoner-of-war (POW) artists
– including both depictions of disease and methods of treatment. This may
partly be because this was an ever-present subject matter, but also some medical
officers (MOs) did request POW artists known to them to record medical
scenes to provide a post-imprisonment record.

Major tropical diseases

In terms of frequency and mortality risk, there were five major diseases affecting Far East POWs, as outlined below.[1]

Malaria

Many (but not all) of the locations in which POWs were interned were malarial. High risk areas were particularly the jungle regions of the Thai–Burma and Sumatra railway camps, and across the Dutch East Indies. Changi camp in Singapore was low risk, and the Japanese camps were not affected, though POWs there did suffer relapses from malaria caught elsewhere. There are several strains of malarial parasite – all transmitted by mosquitoes. The commonest type in Southeast Asia was *Plasmodium vivax*, causing what was known as 'benign tertian malaria'. As the name suggests, this was rarely fatal, but caused a very unpleasant and debilitating feverish illness. Quinine was effective but was frequently not available in sufficient amounts. On the Thai–Burma railway, POWs all had several attacks of malaria – often 30 or more during their captivity. The more severe malarial strain – *Plasmodium falciparum* – was present, particularly in the remote jungle camps where it constituted about 20% of cases.[2] This caused 'malignant tertian malaria', including the frequently fatal syndromes of cerebral malaria and blackwater fever.

Dysentery

An affliction of POWs regardless of location was dysentery – often with similar frequencies of attack as malaria. The commonest type was bacillary dysentery – a severe diarrhoeal disease due to bacteria of the *Shigella* species. Symptoms were usually severe with frequent diarrhoea, passage of blood and mucus, abdominal cramps, and a particularly distressing symptom called tenesmus – which was described by one POW as *"like having a pineapple stuck up your*

Figure 1. 'Dysentery Hut' Kranji Hospital Camp, Singapore, by Cpl W. Norways
(© courtesy the Norways family)

bottom"![3] Not surprisingly, attacks of dysentery were extremely debilitating, and were also a major cause of mortality. Bacillary dysentery could be treated with the drug sulphapyridine ('M&B') but this was mostly unavailable, and the disease had to run its course. The number of dysentery patients was so high that many camps had dedicated dysentery wards or huts (see Figure 1).

A less common form of the disease was amoebic dysentery, caused by the protozoan organism *Entamoeba histolytica*. This tended to occur in jungle camps and was especially common in Thailand and Burma. It ran a very chronic and particularly debilitating course and was sometimes fatal. It could be treated at least partially by the drug emetine, but again, supplies were short. More inventive ways of treating amoebic dysentery will be discussed later in this chapter.

Beriberi

There are several types of vitamin B deficiency, but perhaps the most important is a shortage of thiamine (vitamin B_1) which causes beriberi – a very common problem of Far East captivity. The condition was related to the POW diet mainly consisting of poor quality rice, with very little vitamin content. Beriberi exists in two forms – 'wet' and 'dry'. The dry form causes damage to peripheral nerves, particularly in the legs, leading to tingling, numbness and sometimes weakness. In wet beriberi the body swells with fluid – especially in the legs and abdomen. This is due to weakness of the heart muscle leading to congestion of blood, with fluid leaking through capillary blood vessels into the tissues. The condition could be fatal, and death sometimes occurred suddenly – presumably due to cardiac rhythm disturbances. Figure 2 shows a POW with severe wet beriberi. Note the emaciation of the upper body, and gross swelling of the abdomen with fluid (ascites) as well as swollen legs. A tube can be seen in the abdomen which is to drain fluid.

Beriberi could also affect the brain, usually in the form of a condition called 'Wernicke's encephalopathy', characterized by confusion and double vision. On the Thai–Burma railway, the POW doctor Captain Hugh de Wardener made close records of several cases, which he termed 'cerebral beriberi'. Details were published in the medical literature post-war.[4] As well as beriberi, a variety of

Bombardier Philip Meninsky

B Company, 5th Btn Bedfordshire & Hertfordshire Regiment

Captured:	Singapore 15.2.42
Camps:	Singapore: Changi
	Thailand: Tarsao, Chungkai, Tamuan, Nakom Paton
From:	London
DoB:	1.11.19
Died:	5.8.07

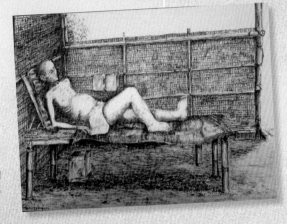

Figure 2. 'Beriberi case being drained', by Bdr P. Meninsky (© courtesy IWM.IWM ART.LD 6523)

other syndromes of malnutrition occurred due to lack of other vitamin B sub-types which included skin inflammation, in particular affecting the mouth, tongue and even the scrotum.

Other neurological syndromes also occurred, for example 'camp eyes' where vision was reduced due to optic nerve damage, and 'burning feet' – a distressing and painful lower-leg neuritis. It should be emphasised that considerable generalised weight loss occurred in all Far East POWs as the diet was deficient in calories as well as vitamins. An extreme example is shown in Figure 3 – an emaciated prisoner, Mr Stanley, painted in September 1945 on release from Changi Gaol in Singapore. Having been flown to Rangoon this man had to be hospitalised as he was too weak to continue his journey home.

This remarkable illustration of the effects of chronic malnutrition, is by Gunner George Old and the level of anatomical detail is fascinating. Old was not medically trained, though he had done an anatomical art course at Art College. A copy of the watercolour was subsequently annotated by Philip Wilson, a member of the Medical Artists Association of Great Britain (interestingly

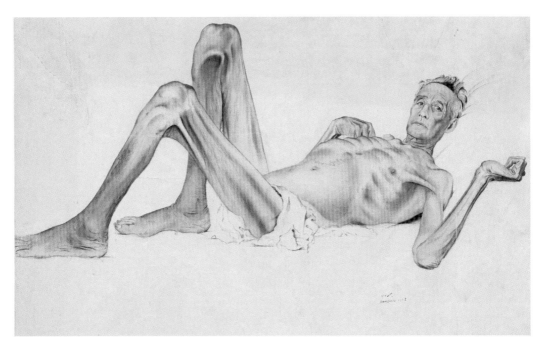

Figure 3. 'Mr Stanley' Rangoon September 1945, by Gnr A. G. Old, Below: annotated sketch by Philip Wilson (© *Bartholomew family, courtesy of the Council of the National Army Museum NAM. 1989-04-116-677*)

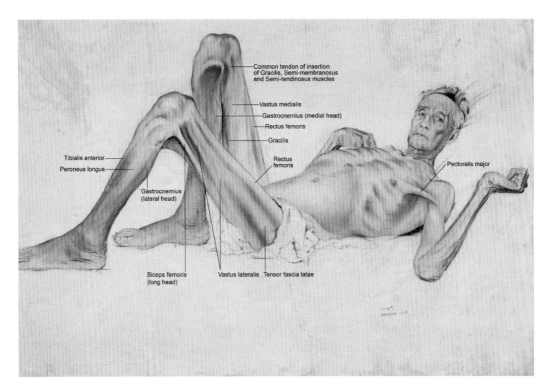

FEPOW artist Jack Chalker was an Honorary Fellow of the MAA), after the painting was discovered, unattributed in the archives of the National Army Museum (NAM) in London in 2013. The medical artist gives names to the muscles and tendons shown by the severe loss of subcutaneous fat.

Cholera

This severe diarrhoeal disease is caused by the bacteria *Vibrio cholera*. It is water-borne and characterised by profuse watery diarrhoea sufficient to cause death from dehydration within 24 to 48 hours of onset. Cholera mainly affected the remote jungle camps and it tended to occur in epidemics. It was a much-feared disease, both by POWs and their Japanese and Korean guards. When outbreaks occurred, patients were usually quarantined in a separate area outside the main camp. The best attempts at rehydration were made – oral or intravenous – but the mortality was high. The bodies of those who died were either buried in mass pits or cremated on horrific 'cholera pyres' to try to prevent spread of infection. The associated horror of this disease cannot be understated – Private F. Whalley in his diary recorded his experiences on arriving at Konyu camp in Thailand:[5]

"There were only a few skeleton-like travesties of humanity left and the signs of a big fire where they burnt their dead. These fires flared at every camp where cholera struck."

Figure 4. Cholera prevention poster, by Spr G. B. Gee (© courtesy IWM.IWM DOC.19778)

When cholera occurred, it was a major therapeutic challenge to POW doctors. By its very nature it tended to occur in remote and ill-equipped camps. Rehydration was given but was often difficult. Preventive measures were applied as vigorously as possible and Figure 4 shows a poster drawn by Sapper Geoffrey Gee in Thailand, giving messages such as sterilising mess tins and avoiding fly contact with food. Cleverly, the picture uses cartoon images to attract attention, to spread very serious preventive messages.

Tropical ulcer

This distressing and debilitating condition occurred mostly in jungle POW camps, particularly on the Thai–Burma railway. The condition often started with relatively minor trauma to the foot or lower leg, which then became infected and spread to the deep tissues, sometimes as far as bone. Poor nutrition, with associated lowered immunity, was likely to be a risk factor. Tropical ulcers were intensely painful and the deep infection often serious. Local measures included crushed M & B tablets (if available) and scraping the slough from the ulcers with an instrument such as a sharpened and sterilised spoon. However, amputation was not infrequently needed. An example of a tropical ulcer painted by George Old, is shown in Figure 5. It is sub-titled 'tropical ulcer with sinuses and bone involvement'; perhaps not surprisingly the leg was subsequently amputated.

The number of patients in the railway camps with tropical ulcers was such that dedicated 'ulcer wards' were needed. A drawing of one of these at Chungkai by Gunner Will Wilder, is shown in Figure 6. The depiction is interesting as it shows 'spoon scraping' in progress in the centre (an intensely painful procedure

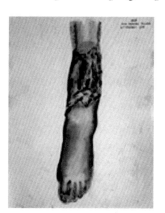

to remove dead tissue and slough, as previously mentioned). To the left is a patient with a recent amputation at thigh level.

Figure 5. 'Tropical ulcer of the lower leg in POW at Chungkai, 21 February 1944', by Gnr A. G. Old
(© courtesy State Library of Victoria, Australia)

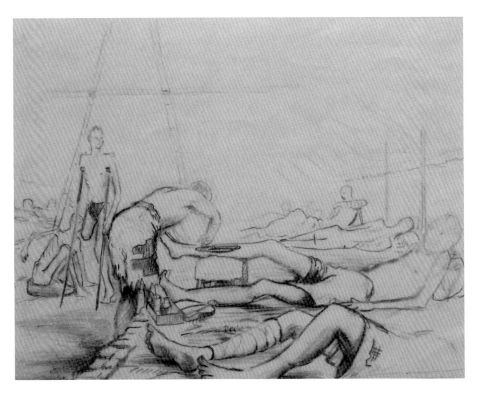

Figure 6. 'Ulcer ward at Chungkai camp, Thailand', by Dvr W. C. Wilder (© *courtesy Anthony Wilder [not to be reproduced without permission]*)

Amputation was usually done as a life-saving procedure because of overwhelming infection. One doctor – Captain Jacob Markowitz RAMC – said simply *"in brief the indication was to save life"*. Markowitz had enormous experience in amputations for tropical ulcer and in 1946 wrote a medical paper with details of over 100 such operations.[6] A consequence of the operation was that it relieved the often agonising pain. In Captain Harry Silman's diary, he recorded visiting one of his men on an ulcer ward in Thailand and recorded, *"he pleaded with me with tears in his eyes for his leg to be taken off"*. Silman finished his entry with the words, *"what a terrible thing a tropical ulcer is"*.[7]

Other medical and surgical challenges

Other tropically-based diseases included dengue, typhoid and diphtheria. In addition, there was plenty of more routine illness including bronchitis, pneumonia, appendicitis, fractures and sprains. Dyspepsia, constipation and haemorrhoids were quite common, possibly related to the low-residue rice-based diet. Perhaps surprisingly, at least in the early months of imprisonment in Singapore, a 'Venereal Disease and Scabies Department' existed at Roberts Hospital in Changi POW camp, treating 18 in-patients and 151 out-patients between 20 February 1942 and 15 February 1943.[8]

Infections (mostly syphilis and gonorrhoea) were presumably acquired prior to capitulation! The clinic was run by Captain C. D. Chilton RAMC and it is most likely he who is shown as the doctor in Figure 8 – a cartoon depiction of the VD clinic in progress, by FEPOW Basil Akhurst (known as 'AKKI'). After release during the early post-war years, Akhurst became a regular cartoonist for the West Lancashire Evening Gazette, his local newspaper in Blackpool.

Surgery and anaesthesia presented problems, given the general lack of drugs and equipment. Anaesthetics used were usually simple inhaled agents such as chloroform or ether; or spinal anaesthesia was used with dental local anaesthetic agents. Occasionally surgery was done without any anaesthesia. Surgical instruments and antiseptic agents were often home-made and will be discussed later in this chapter. Successful surgery was carried out in most sizeable camps, including in the jungles of Thailand and Burma.

Flight/Sergeant Fred Margarson
232 Squadron RAF

Captured:	Singapore 15.2.42
Camps:	Singapore: Changi POW camp
	Thailand: Chungkai, Kanchanaburi, Tarsao, Tamarkan
From:	Grimsby
DoB:	20.4.18
Died:	8.12.00

Figure 7. 'Op Theatre Chungkai', 26 December 1943, Thailand, by Fl/Sgt Fred Margarson (© courtesy the Margarson family)

Fl/Lt Fred Margarson: This lovely pencil sketch (Figure 7) of the exterior of the operating theatre at Chungkai was done by Fred Margarson on Boxing Day 1943. The operating theatre was situated at one end of a long bamboo hut

Figure 8 shows an operation taking place at Kranji Hospital camp in the north of Singapore island in 1944, where reasonably sophisticated equipment was available, for example the overhead theatre lamp. The surgeon facing is Lieutenant Colonel Julian Taylor RAMC, who post-war returned to University College Hospital, London. In 1946 he was made Commander of the Most Excellent Order of the British Empire (CBE), and later became professor of surgery.

As well as there being doctors amongst the POWs, there were also dentists. In the British Army they were part of the Royal Army Dental Corps (RADC). Dental services were clearly necessary for the many thousands of young men

Figure 8. The venereal disease clinic at Roberts Hospital, Changi POW camp Singapore, in the early months of captivity 1942, by Bdr 'AKKI' Akhurst (© courtesy J. Sutherland)

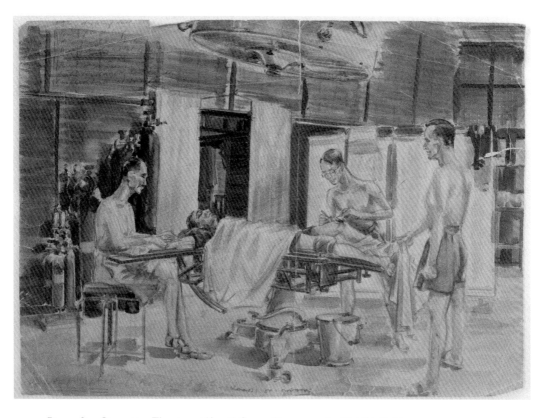

Figure 9. Operating Theatre at Kranji Camp, Singapore, by Cpl W. G. Norways
(© courtesy the Norways family)

imprisoned for over three years (particularly with a lack of toothbrushes and toothpaste). Many large camps had makeshift dental departments with home-made dental chairs and sometimes even pedal drills. One such clinic is shown in Figure 10 – at Chungkai camp in Thailand, drawn by Driver Kenneth Elwell. Captain David Arkush, RADC worked in this clinic and reported excellent results with temporary filling materials, though he had to restrict local anaesthetic doses because of shortages of Novocaine.[9]

The large and more sophisticated camps sometimes had medical laboratories to support the work of the doctors and medical orderlies. Smaller camps may have had a microscope to detect malaria parasites in the blood, or the eggs or larvae of worms in stool samples. Larger camps (such as the Thailand base hospital camps, or Changi POW camp in Singapore) could measure haemoglobin levels

Figure 10. View of the Dental Surgery at Chungkai camp in Thailand by Dvr F. K. Elwell (© courtesy Museum of Military Medicine)

or simple biochemical tests. These laboratories were usually staffed by medical scientists of the RAMC, supported by trained volunteers. The laboratory at Changi Gaol POW camp is depicted in drawings by Captain Thomas ('Toss') Wilson RAMC (see Figure 11). Wilson was medically trained, but also an expert malarial parasitologist. With his colleague Major John Reid (an entomologist Wilson knew from the Malayan Medical Service) he carried out remarkable malarial research in the up-country camps in Thailand.[10] Interestingly, Toss

Figure 11. 'Laboratory, Changi Gaol Hospital, April 1945' exterior, by Capt. T. Wilson (© courtesy the Wilson family)

Laboratory, Changi Gaol Hospital. April 1945.

Figure 12. 'Our laboratory, Changi Gaol Hospital, March 1945' interior, by Capt. T. Wilson (© *courtesy the Wilson family*)

Wilson was later to become a professor at the Liverpool School of Tropical Medicine. The remarkable illustrations (Figures 11 & 12) show the exterior and interior of the laboratory hut at Changi Gaol POW camp, in the latter part of captivity.

Meeting the challenge – 'making do'

The Citizen's Army

From the previous sections of this chapter, it can be seen that imprisonment under the Japanese brought about a major medical crisis. Large numbers of patients were presenting with complex tropical illnesses and serious syndromes of under-nutrition. However, the necessary drugs and medical equipment were in very short supply, and insufficient to meet the massive therapeutic challenges. The Imperial Japanese Army (IJA) provided only very small amounts of drugs, and many camps had to resort to smuggling and buying supplements from outside the prison camps.

An extreme example of the inadequacy of IJA supplies was recorded by Major T. M. Pemberton RAMC, who reported that in one large camp only a single bedpan had been given by the IJA and *"all other equipment was improvised"*.[11] By 'improvised' this meant constructed from basic materials in the prison camp, and this brought into play a major survival factor in Far East imprisonment, the so-called 'Citizen's Army'. This term reflects the fact that in the Second World War, Allied armies were largely volunteers and conscripts, as compared to modern mainly professional armies. Therefore, in all Far East POW camps there were men from a variety of professions and trades – scientists, mechanics, plumbers, metal workers, glaziers, carpenters etc. As ex-POW Steve Cairns remarked,

> *"there was everyone from earl's sons to doctors not finished their university courses, solicitors, bricklayers – you name it, they were all together".*[12]

Jack Chalker even recalled a POW at Changi who in civilian life was a part-time cat-burglar and who used his skills to steal drugs and equipment from the Japanese (at great risk to himself)![13]

POW doctors and camp commanders rapidly realised that the resources of skill and expertise in their camps could be used to counteract the medical shortages they were faced with. Camp workshops rapidly arose, and the rest of this chapter will demonstrate the diversity of invention and innovation which undoubtedly saved a great many lives.

Medical equipment

A great deal of medical equipment was produced in the camp workshops. These included scalpels (adapted from kitchen knives), retractors (from metal strips), and a variety of orthopaedic equipment. Figure 13 shows a raised bed (made from bamboo, padded with sacking), and remarkably complex pulleys and traction gear, used for the treatment of fractured femurs. This was depicted by the gifted POW artist George Old, who also created the illustration in Figure 14 of a post-operative patient receiving fluid therapy by both the intravenous and rectal route. The saline for intravenous delivery is in the sterilised bottle, and for rectal delivery in the unsterilised can. The tubing may well have come from stethoscopes, and the intravenous needle could have been a thin, engineered piece of sterilised bamboo shoot.

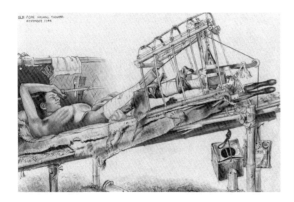

Figure 13. 'Extension for fractured femur', Tamuang camp November 1944; by Gnr A. G. Old (© courtesy State Library of Victoria, Australia)

Figure 14. 'Post-operative nursing – intravenous and rectal saline', 15 August 1944, Tamuang camp, by Gnr A. G. Old (© courtesy State Library of Victoria, Australia)

Larger equipment (e.g. operating tables etc) utilised bamboo, of which there was usually a plentiful supply. Bamboo was straight, sturdy, but relatively light. A bamboo dental chair, drawn by POW Fred Ransome-Smith, (known as 'Smudger') is shown in Figure 15. This was made at Chungkai camp in Thailand and used by Captain David Arkush RDC, mentioned earlier. The chair had an adjustable back-rest, head support, spittoon and instrument tray. Arkush said that the number of POWs who he treated in the chair *"must have run into thousands"*.[14]

Figure 15. Improvised bamboo dental chair at Chungkai camp, Thailand, by Lt F. W. H. Ransome-Smith (© courtesy the artist)

233

Yeast and distillation

There was a desperate need for vitamin B preparations to treat beriberi and other vitamin deficiency syndromes. The use of naturally occurring yeasts became widespread. These were cultivated and concentrated in various ways to produce what was often known as 'Camp Marmite'. One of the most sophisticated production systems was created by POW Leslie Audus (who prior to the war as an academic botanist) in Java and later on the island of Haroekoe.

The project started secretly at Jaarmarkt Camp, Soerabaya in Java, when the medical staff asked Audus if he could produce yeast extract to treat patients with visual loss due to B vitamin deficiency. He himself was similarly affected which gave added impetus to his endeavours. Using his botanical knowledge, he helped set up a yeast manufacturing laboratory at the back of the camp hospital. It was soon producing high quality yeast extracts which were greatly beneficial to the patients with visual disturbance and other syndromes of B vitamin deficiency.[15]

Audus was also an amateur artist and Figure 16 is one of his cartoon-type drawings showing an assistant at work in the laboratory. Audus' colleague in this yeast project – Bill Altson – should also be mentioned; he had been a

Figure 16. 'Yeast production at Jaarmarkt camp, Java, 1942–43', by Fl/Lt L. J. Audus (© *courtesy H. Audus*)

mycologist (expert in fungi and yeasts) at the Rubber Research Institute in Kuala Lumpur and worked closely with Leslie. He was largely responsible for the isolation and maintenance in culture of suitable yeast strains.

Natural yeasts could also be used for the production of alcohol, essential for effective surgical antisepsis. Rice or various fruits were generally used as the source of yeast, and relatively sophisticated distillation equipment was constructed in many camp workshops. One system used at Tamarkan in Thailand is shown in Figure 17 – the main containers being discarded kerosene or guala malacca (molasses) tins, and the tubing at least in part from doctors' stethoscopes. As well as producing surgical alcohol, these systems were used to make distilled water. With the correct amount of added salt, this made an excellent saline solution for intravenous infusion (see also Figure 14).

Lieutenant Gordon Smith: Artist with no formal training, Smith not only sketched but also made this still (Figure 17) at Tamarkan Hospital camp in Thailand. Another artist, **Lt Stanley Gimson**, produced many sketches, including the distillery at Chungkai which he described as *"a contraption which saved many lives".* Gimson regarded his own work as simplistic and 'too clean'.

Lieutenant Gordon Smith
2nd Btn Argyll & Sutherland Highlanders

Captured:	Malaya, January 1942
Camps:	Malaya: Pudu Gaol
	Thailand: Tamarkan, Nong Pladuk, Nakom Paton, Kanburi
From:	Edinburgh
DoB:	23.10.20
Died:	22.4.14

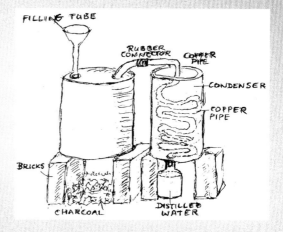

Figure 17.   The still made at Tamarkan camp in Thailand by Lt Gordon Smith
(© courtesy J. G. Smith)

Limb prostheses

In those areas of imprisonment particularly affected by tropical ulcers, many patients had leg amputations, leading to a need for lower limb prostheses. These amputations were frequently at thigh level – creating a particular challenge to the camp workshops. Nevertheless, remarkably successful artificial limbs were produced. In the jungle camps materials such as wood, bamboo, leather and canvas (from kit bags and rucksacks) were used, and various examples from Thailand are shown in Figure 18, painted by Jack Chalker.

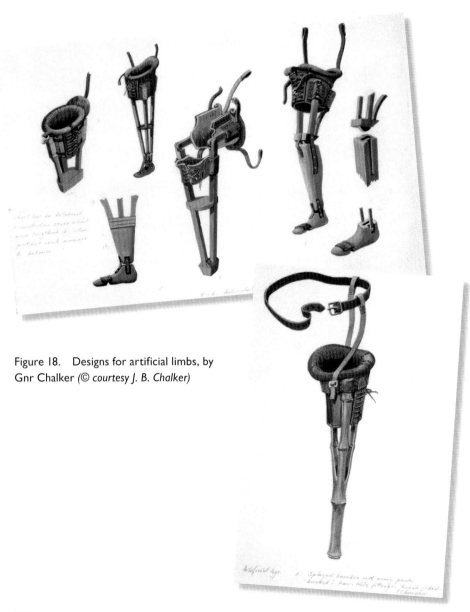

Figure 18. Designs for artificial limbs, by Gnr Chalker *(© courtesy J. B. Chalker)*

As time went on, even more sophisticated designs emerged (Figure 18). At Nakom Paton Jack Chalker recorded a 'Thigh Amputation Model 7' which included articulations at the knee, ankle and toes. In Changi POW Camp, Singapore, a 'Prosthetic Limb Factory' existed, recorded in the illustration (Figure 19) by Desmond Bettany. Note the workshop engineer who also has an artificial leg. Here the available materials even included sheets of aeroplane fuselage metal.

Blood transfusion

Donation and transfusion of blood presented special difficulties, but these were overcome, enabling transfusion to be widely practiced, particularly in the railway camps of Thailand. The equipment for collecting and giving the blood was similar to that for intravenous infusion. 'Needles' were often thin, hollowed-out bamboo shoot skilfully engineered or adapted from small, glass droppers. The receptacle for the donated blood was frequently a discarded bottle with the tubing from stethoscopes attached (as mentioned earlier in this chapter). Equipment was sterilised by boiling, or by immersion in alcohol.

The specific problems were, however, anticoagulation and cross-matching. Anticoagulant solutions (such as sodium citrate) were rarely available, so an old system of defibrination was more usual. This was often done with bamboo, split and shredded and made into a 'whisk'. After sterilisation of equipment, the donated blood was stirred with the whisk for several minutes, and the fibrin clot deposited onto the bamboo fibres. Cross-matching was usually done crudely by examining mixed droplets of donor and recipient blood under the microscope, looking for 'clumping' of the red blood cells.

Figure 20 is a remarkable representation of the blood transfusion hut at Chungkai camp in Thailand done in 1944, by the POW medical artist George Old. Donation is in progress on the right, and a transfusion is on the left. The donors of blood were men regarded as 'healthy' (a relative term during POW life!) but there was no shortage of volunteers. This is demonstrated in another drawing by Old, showing a line of POWs waiting to have their blood 'typed' (Figure 21) after returning from a day's work on the railway. The level of detail in both of these drawings is quite remarkable. Old also noted that at the time of his illustrations, about six transfusions each day were being carried out at Chungkai, by trained lay staff under medical supervision.

Interestingly, at Chungkai camp a written note of appreciation was given to the donor, signed by the Camp Commandant. One of these was later donated to the

Figure 20.   'The blood transfusion hut at Chungkai camp Thailand 1944', by Gnr A. G. Old (© *courtesy State Library of Victoria, Australia*)

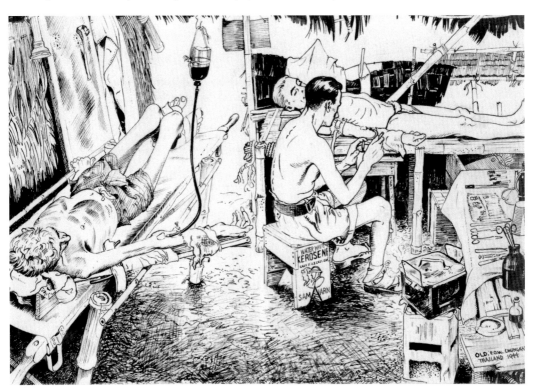

Figure 21. 'Routine blood typing at Chungkai', by Gnr A. G. Old
(© courtesy State Library of Victoria, Australia)

Liverpool School of Tropical Medicine by Private Grassick, dated 17 October
1943, and read,

> "*I note that you have given your blood for your comrades, an act which under
> the present circumstances as a prisoner of war is highly commendable.*"[16]

Large numbers of transfusions were carried out at the Thai–Burma railway
base hospital camps. Captain Markowitz kept records of 250 procedures
done at Chungkai and published the results after release.[17] The indications for
transfusion were tropical ulcer (44%), amoebic dysentery (31%), malnutrition
(13%), malaria (7%) and miscellaneous (5%). In terms of beneficial affect, 60%
of patients were 'much improved' or 'improved' by the transfusions.

Self-retaining ileostomy tube

Amoebic dysentery was a major problem from a therapeutic viewpoint – it often ran a chronic indolent course, was difficult to treat, and patients became debilitated and malnourished, with a fatal outcome not uncommon.

The disease affects primarily the large bowel. Treatment with the surgical procedure of ileostomy was introduced initially on the Burma side of the Thai–Burma railway. The rationale was to rest the large bowel to allow it to heal. This was often highly effective. However, dealing with the ileostomy drainage fluid was difficult. Private Gordon Vaughan, a former Post Office engineer, was a medical orderly who worked closely with Captain Markowitz at Chungkai.

Figure 22.   A self-retaining ileostomy tube, artist uncertain (© *courtesy LSTM*)

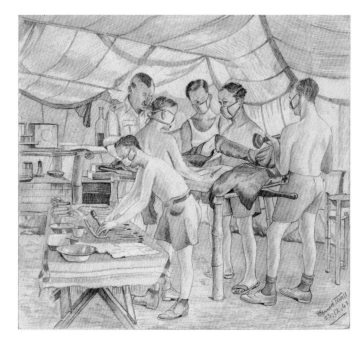

Figure 23.   A scene from the operating theatre at Chungkai, December 1943, by Dvr F. K. Ellwell (© *courtesy IWM.IWM ART. LD 7189*)

Vaughan used his engineering skills working alongside Fl/Sgt Fred Margarson, a plumber from Grimsby, to make and repair all manner of medical and surgical equipment. Between them they turned their talents to the ileostomy problem. A simple rubber drainage tube would not stay in place, so Vaughan attached a piece of rubber condom, or the finger of a surgical glove, over the end of the tube and tied it firmly in place to form a 'balloon'. Once inserted into the stoma, a needle and syringe was used to inflate the balloon and hold it in place.[18]

The device is shown in a pencil sketch (Figure 22), though regrettably the name of the artist is uncertain. It is thought it may have been drawn by Driver Kenneth Elwell who had done several other medical sketches at this time (late 1943), like Figure 23 which shows Captain Markowitz (2nd from right) about to carry out an above-knee amputation. Opposite him assisting (in mask) is medical orderly Private Gordon Vaughan (RAMC).

As well as his remarkable work as an instrument designer and producer, Gordon Vaughan frequently assisted Markowitz at surgical operations and even carried out minor procedures himself.

During captivity Markowitz gave Vaughan a highly complementary written testimonial to help him undertake formal medical studies after the war. Unfortunately, a bursary for a place at the Liverpool School of Medicine could not be obtained, but Gordon Vaughan did eventually qualify as a dental surgeon and had a successful career in Merseyside and Cheshire. He was a patient at LSTM in later life.

The Nakom Paton Camp Scientist Report

A final and remarkable example of the Citizen's Army in operation is a report on the 'Work of the Nakom Paton Camp Scientist, April 1944 to August 1945'. This document is held at the National Archives in Kew (London) and makes fascinating reading. Nakom Paton was one of the biggest of the Thai–Burma railway base hospital camps.[19] The report was written by the Camp Scientist, Private G. W. Chapman, and is signed by him as 'G. W. Chapman MA, PhD (Pte)'. He was a Cambridge graduate, and highly-respected for the scientific support he provided to medical staff. Despite being only a private, he was in charge of a staff of 10 POWs of varying ranks and skills.

The report details extensive activities, including distillation – in December 1944, 12 gallons of 95% pure alcohol was produced (from 'waste and condemned rice') for surgical antisepsis, with a further 90 gallons produced during 1945. Chapman records the fermentation process in detail, and also pays particular tribute to one of his staff – a tinsmith who was responsible for constructing the distillation apparatus. Distilled water was also produced for saline infusions, and interestingly catgut sutures from the peritoneal membranes of cows or yaks.

From this report, it is clear how important camp workshops were, and that they were staffed according to skill rather than rank. The coming together of such varied expertise produced remarkable results – Chapman commented that they were able to *"make something from nothing without the aid of magicians"*.

Conclusions

The final words of this chapter will be those of Jack Chalker who perceptively remarked,

> *"you put a geneticist and a pharmacist and a tinsmith – all these people together – and you've begun to move a bit of a mountain."*[20]

He went on to add that this was

> *"a kind of corporate effort of survival simply because of all the different skills that we all had … if you had enough energy and enough guts and enough of a willingness to do it, then it worked, and I think that was pretty magical."*

SECTION III

Jenny Wood

"ELY CATHEDRAL"

Maintaining Morale

Camp morale

During the 1990s the Print Room at the IWM was home to a knowledgeable and varied crew of researchers. They came to look at war artists' drawings and paintings and the associated archive of documentary material. In the quiet, well-lit space we could spread out drawings from different boxes and folders, learning always from our visitors – publishers, historians and artists' families.

One day we played host to an American academic, a quietly authoritative man with a vast experience and knowledge of theatre and a specific interest in FEPOW theatricals – Professor Sears Eldredge. I learned that he had been researching this topic for several years and intended to publish his research on the internet, making it freely available through his college in the USA. *Captive Audiences/Captive Performers: Music and Theatre as Strategies for Survival on the Thailand–Burma Railway 1942–1945* appeared in 2013 and is the most wide-ranging and deeply researched oeuvre, including images and sound-clips which immerse the audience in the musical and theatrical creativity of the camps. The introductory flyer states:

Figure 1. 'Chungkai Entertainments. New camp Theatre 1944', by Lt G. S. Gimson
(© courtesy IWM.IWM ART.16854)

"It is about the value of the performing arts to prevent minds and emotions
from atrophying; to foster a collective identity in the midst of a world where
solitary withdrawal leading to despair was a death sentence. It is about the
necessity of the performing arts for survival."

Lieutenant George Stanley Gimson

1st Indian Regiment HAA

Captured:	Singapore
Camps:	Singapore: Changi
	Thailand: Kanu, Chungkai, Tamuang,
	Nakom Paton Hospital, Kanburi,
	Nakon Nyok
From:	Glasgow
Dob:	6.9.15
Died:	30.8.03

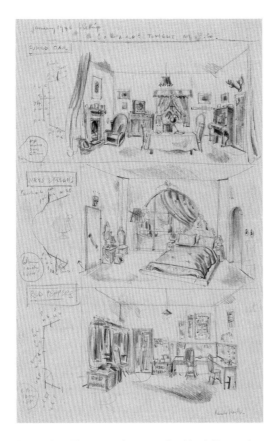

Figure 2. Three set drawings for Noel Coward themed evening, Jan 1945, by Spr R. W. F. Searle (© the artist, permission The Sayle Literary Agency. IWM. IWM ART.15747 199, image 28 of 58)

Figure 3. 'The Star', costume design, Jan 1945, by Spr R. W. F. Searle (© the artist, permission The Sayle Literary Agency. IWM.IWM ART.15747 200 a-m, image 11 of 29)

Professor Eldredge was particularly interested in the final box of Ronald Searle drawings – a hotch-potch of odd costume and set designs and illustrated notebooks covering the period when Searle returned to Singapore from his experiences working on the railway. These had been set aside during the preparations for the big exhibition and book which marked Searle's generous gift of his drawings in the mid-1980s. At that time the emphasis was on his experiences prior to captivity and then in the railway camps.

I remember Sears' mounting excitement as he reviewed the drawings and notebooks. He already had a good idea of the other artists involved in producing playbills, designs, programmes and posters for concerts and theatrical productions in up-country camps. He was in a good position to identify not only the Changi theatre locations but also the individual plays. It was the first time I had looked at these drawings with a knowledgeable researcher. I could see the style and expertise of these drawings but now I became aware of the wider background – how Searle was burying himself in staging theatre as a way of imposing order on desperate circumstances and using his art, as he himself said, as an anchor. Searle contributed constantly to plans and designs for productions (Figures 2 & 3), but he was part of a creative team realising these works. John Beckerley, mentioned in Chapter 2, worked closely with him on set-construction and notes the professional quality achieved.

Theatre presentations and concerts were a lifeblood in the FEPOW camps and the different activities associated with them appear throughout this book. Stories of the performers themselves come from John Clement, from Basil Ferron and Donald Teale. Bill Norways was active in producing and acting in theatre performances and Robert Brazil and Fred Ransome-Smith ('Smudger') produced posters. Programmes, such as those made by Jack Kemp, were almost always hand-made, sometimes hand-coloured single productions, scrupulous in listing participants and their roles. The plays of Norman Power in Zentsuji show how widespread the theatrical impetus was throughout the FEPOW camps and the songs composed to celebrate the camp entrepreneurs by 'Harber and Nob' (Derek Clarke and Harry Berry) in Omori (Taiwan) illustrate the work of comic songs in fostering a shared view of camp life.

Figure 4. 'Three interpretive dance costumes for Henri Encoma', by Spr R. W. F. Searle. (© the artist, permission The Sayle Literary Agency. IWM.IWM ART.15747 199 a-u. Image 16 of 58)

In a captivity devoid of women, these theatricals offered a much-needed comic relief and such female impersonators as Gloria D'Earie (Lance Bombardier Arthur Butler), Bobby Spong and Basil Ferron were valued actors. In Changi, Henri Encoma worked with Ronald Searle (Figure 4) in realising ever-more sophisticated dance and drama roles.

Norman Pritchard: Originally taken prisoner at the fall of Singapore Pritchard had worked as stage manager for performances by the 'Optimists' troupe in Changi. Transferred to Thailand in 1942 he was assigned to the railway supply depot camp at Nong Pladuk. He had trained as an architectural draftsman and the numerous programmes he produced for the 'Harboured Lights' shows in Nong Pladuk and later Ubon indicate a love of experiment in print and art techniques, working with stencils and toothbrush-spatter. His programme for the July 1944 show *Any more for sailing?* (Figure 4a) is unusually colourful as he had just acquired 8 watercolours from a Dutch POW. Sears Eldredge commented:

Figure 5.   Programme cover, July 1944 Nong Pladuk camp, Thailand
(© courtesy Sears Eldredge)

Lance Bombardier
Norman Pritchard

118th Field Regiment, Royal Artillery

Captured:	Singapore 15.2.42
Camps:	Singapore: Changi
	Thailand: Nong Pladuk, Kanburi, Ubon
From:	London
Dob:	not known
Died:	not known

Figure 6. 'Our publicity office',
1945 Ubon camp, Thailand
(© courtesy Sears Eldredge)

"his programmes represent an extraordinary artistic output produced, as they were, under increasingly extreme conditions with few resources."

Music and concerts were also part of the impetus to find a shared perspective on camp life. From comic songs to classical music, camp musicians worked hard to create and promote ideas of a shared norm. Hard to transport and to maintain, there were few regular musical instruments in the camps and musicians worked with engineers to fashion working instruments from the materials to hand. Camp concerts, both impromptu (Figure 5) and highly-organised, became a staple of entertainments offered in the camps. The illustration by John Mennie is captioned in pencil:

"these were the early efforts organised by Fizzer Pearson and Norman Smith which developed into the larger shows at Tasso [sic], Chungkai etc."

Another staple of life in the camps were talks given by FEPOWs with a huge variety of expertise. Men who knew about subjects as diverse as botany or

Figure 7. 'Marks and Waller. POW camp fire concert', Kanu river camp, early 1943. Thai–Burma railway, by L/Bdr J. G. Mennie *(© artist's estate, courtesy IWM, IWM Art 17877 39)*

architecture were encouraged to teach classes for those who wished to learn. Listening and learning offered a way to focus on something outside daily concerns and reassured captives that a civilised world of knowledge still existed

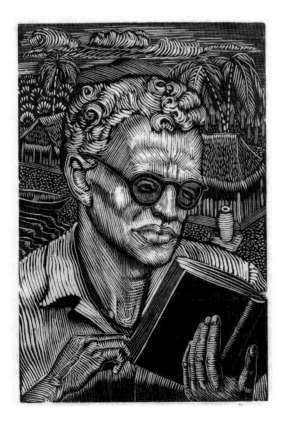

Figure 8. Lance Bombardier Alexander Oppenheim, Professor of Mathematics at Raffles College, Singapore, by L/Bdr J. Mennie *(© artist's estate, courtesy IWM.IWM ART.LD 7308)*

beyond camp confines. Papers now kept in family collections and public archives contain study lists and notes on languages, on literature and on the sciences. Eric Lomax refers to this as 'a therapy of lists'.

FEPOW artists were also involved, teaching portraiture and passing on drawing skills. Philip Meninsky and John Beckerley are amongst those who acknowledged how much they learned from fellow artists. The story is told in Chapter 3 of Lt Col. A. A. Johnson MC who, whilst in the hardest of conditions in remote railway camps, built a natural history collection, asking his men to collect butterflies and persuading FEPOW artists to illustrate his fascinating discoveries.

In Changi Divisional Headquarters established a 'camp university', making use of the teaching skills of lecturers, now FEPOWs, from Raffles College in Singapore (Figure 8). The church leaders in the camp staffed a 'Free Church Faculty' and lectured on aspects of Theology. Bill Norways lectured on Advertising and Art, calling on his pre-war commercial art training. This teaching initiative was replicated by the civilian internees at Changi Gaol. A 'university' is also recorded by Stanley Bagnall at Kuching in Borneo.

Camp journals

Camp journals bridged the gap between the larger shared experiences reflected in theatre, music and teaching and the more localised shared perception of life in the individual camps.

They were made in many FEPOW camps and IWM has examples from Hong Kong, Java, Japan, Shanghai, Singapore and Thailand. They fed an overwhelming need for shared information and often followed the format of popular newspapers or magazines, including sections on camp 'sport reports' and regular caricatures of individuals. This lampooning of camp figures, making fun of eccentricities familiar to fellow prisoners, was a valuable expression of popular affection and support for camp 'authorities'. Information on camp groups and events, times of church services and accounts of life in peace-time could be included but the editors were careful to omit or hide anything the Japanese guards might consider evidence of underground news.

The format may have followed popular papers but the materials available dictated a very small circulation. Paper and the means of reproduction were hard to obtain, and these journals might exist only as single copies, written or typed and hand-illustrated. For example, the *Jungle Journal* produced in Tandjong Priok camp in Java ran for eight issues from March to December 1942. In Issue 6 the editors noted *"we remain dangerously short of paper. If you*

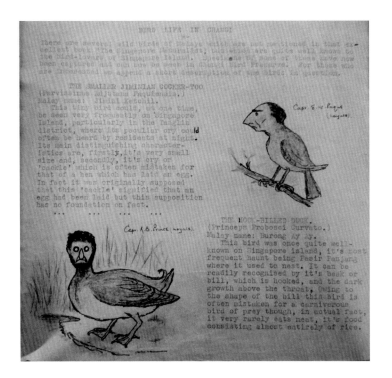

Figure 9.   Changi edition of *NIB* ornithological studies, by Lt T. H. Wade *(© courtesy Lancashire Infantry Museum)*

Figure 10.   Enlarged copy of Paque caricature, believed to be by Lt T. H. Wade *(© courtesy Lancashire Infantry Museum)*

value JJ remember us on your next work party – there may need to be some begging."
These journals were passed from hand to hand around the camp and so suffered
from over-handling so that copies are now very rare.

At the other end of the spectrum were productions such as *POW*, made
in Argyle Street camp, Hong Kong. These were lavishly illustrated issues
containing artists' original competition designs for inn-signs and wine labels.
POW issues no 2 and no 4 were raffled off within the camp.

A selection of titles gives an idea of the wry intentions of these journals. *Prisoners'*
Pie (Hong Kong), *Pow Wow* (Thailand, also Japan), *Mark Time* (Bandoeng, Java),
Wireville Gazette (Tandjong Priok, Java), *Exile* and *Clink Chronicle* (Changi camp,
Singapore). *Nor Iron Bars* (*NIB*) is of particular interest (Figure 7). The artist
Tom Henling Wade, mentioned in Chapter 3, is credited with much of the early
illustration of this journal which ran for 12 issues.

This page from the Changi edition of *NIB* (Figure 9) and the close-up, illustrate
the wit and skilful caricature work exemplified throughout each magazine. This
series of animal caricatures, featuring what is believed to be Wade's handiwork,
ran in early editions. It took notable characters in the Mess, attributed
lengthy scientific Latin names and imbued them with precise ornithological
characteristics (in similar style to *The Times* cartoonist Peter Brookes'
contemporary 'Nature Notes' series). For example, below, this one parodying
Captain Ernest William Paque, the Adjutant, who was noted for his lack of
height and busy nature.

The ornithological description reads:

> *THE SMALLER JIMINIAN COCKER-TOO*
> *(Parvissimus Adjutans Paquiensis)*
> *Malay name: Jiminie Ketchil*

> *This tiny bird could, at one time, be seen very frequently on Singapore Island,*
> *particularly in the Tanglin district, where its peculiar cry could often be*
> *heard by residents at night. Its main distinguishing characteristics are, firstly,*

it's very small size and, secondly, it's cry or 'cackle' which is often mistaken for that of a hen which has laid an egg. In fact it was originally supposed that this 'cackle' signified that an egg had been laid but this supposition has no foundation in fact.

On a serious note, Paque was also well-known for his detailed mapwork.

In December 1943 Wade and McNaughton were two of the officers drafted to Japan. Lieutenant McNaughton had been one of the most prolific contributors to *NIB* and they were both keenly missed. Their departure was recorded by Harry Kingsley in this sketch (Figure 9) with the two Tokyo postmarked stamps bearing portraits of each man.

Wade was moved around several camps in Japan. Eventually, at Omori camp, he came under the reign of terror meted out by the infamous Japanese guard, Corporal Watanabe (who featured in the 2013 feature film, 'Unbroken'). In a newspaper interview at the time of the film's release, Wade aged 94, said:

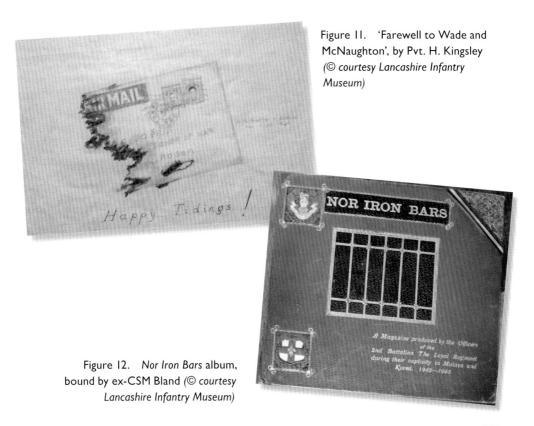

Figure 11. 'Farewell to Wade and McNaughton', by Pvt. H. Kingsley (© *courtesy Lancashire Infantry Museum*)

Figure 12. *Nor Iron Bars* album, bound by ex-CSM Bland (© *courtesy Lancashire Infantry Museum*)

"Watanabe treated us with terrible brutality and most of the time with no respect at all. He was a psychopath. Practically nothing the prisoners said coming out of that camp was a fabrication."

Of one incident in which he was attacked with a 4ft kendo sword, made of tightly bound bamboo, Wade said:

"He whirled it above his head with both arms outstretched and cracked it down on the top of my head. Then he swung it like a baseball bat against the left side of my head and then the right. He just went on and on – the Japanese never know when to stop."[1]

In 1946 the complete set of 12 *NIB* magazines was presented to the Regimental Headquarters at Fulwood Barracks, to ensure their safe-keeping. In 1947, a Mr Bland, ex-Company Sergeant Major, 4th Btn The Loyal Regiment, undertook the task of binding the magazines in one large leather-bound album.

Opening the beautifully crafted, leather-bound and richly-tooled album reveals an extraordinarily vivid collection of writing and artwork from captivity. It is a lasting memorial to those who endured captivity at Keijo camp in Korea.

Personal morale

The camp initiatives described so far were aimed at an audience keen to share their collective derision of their captors and hungry for a 'normal' time. Individual FEPOWs also had very personal ties to home and family and had to find ways to cope with the protracted absence of news. Artists were in demand as prisoners asked for portraits of themselves and images of their loved ones, taken from treasured photographs (Figure 11), like these from the private papers of Wally Davis done by artist Geoffrey Gee (see also Chapter 1 Figure 34). These talisman images spoke of a hope for release. Leslie Audus, Will Wilder and George Old all drew many portraits which on a fundamental level reinforced a man's identity and sense of self-worth.

Figure 13.   Paired portrait, from the papers of Pvt., by Dvr G. Gee *(© courtesy IWM – 66/308/Box 6)*

Figure 14.   Portrait of Padre Cordingly signed H. C. Gordon, Changi, Singapore Oct 1942 *(© courtesy the Cordingly family)*

A FEPOW artist who signed himself 'H. C. Gordon' when he had completed this accomplished pencil portrait of Padre Eric Cordingly (Figure 14) in October 1942, is another man who, for now, remains a mystery.

Was the artist British? All that is known for certain is that the portrait was kept by the Padre for the rest of his life and is now treasured by his family.

Caricature images of both individuals and daily situations were an essential tool in the kit of survival and the insightful drawings of Leslie Audus in Java and Haroekoe, Richard Philps in Java, the Moluccas and Singapore, Rex Spencer in Sumatra and Archie Bevan in Taiwan, Japan and China all feature earlier in this book. Special mention must be made of Desmond Bettany whose sharp and irrepressible cartoons appeared regularly on theatre programmes and lampooned daily indignities.

Greetings cards were constantly required from the artists – birthdays, Christmas and leaving cards as FEPOWs were shipped to different camps. These personal cards in particular have survived in the papers and archives of FEPOWs (Figure 15). They are kept for their message and often the artist is unrecorded or unknown.

Figure 15. Hand-made Christmas card, Changi Gaol 1944 by R. W. F. Searle (© the artist, permission The Sayle Literary Agency. IWM.IWM ART.15334)

Figure 16. Anniversary card, by CQMS M. Green (© courtesy the Green family)

One particularly moving greetings card was made by Liverpudlian Maurice Green (Figure 16). He had married Doris Irene Rose in July 1940 and he did this drawing for her – a small bunch of roses was for Doris, his 'rose'. As each year of his captivity passed, in Changi and in Thailand, he added another year to the list of dates arching over the flowers, no doubt recalling their special day. It is such a sweet, simple, yet poignant symbol of hope for the future.

Jack Chalker interrupted his art training when he was called up. At Goldsmiths College before the war he had studied graphics and responded strongly to the design and colour he saw in a chance find in his early days in Singapore.

Figure 17.   Embroidery, Chungkai Hospital camp 1943, by Gnr J. Chalker
(© Jack Chalker)

In November 2018 when visiting Guy Chalker-Howells (Jack's older son) at his home, Meg was shown this piece of embroidery (Figure 17), newly-framed and hanging in pride of place. She asked what it was and was amazed to learn that it had been made by Jack during captivity. Guy recalled what his father told him about the embroidery: while helping his father sort out his art studio a year or so before he died, Guy picked up a rolled-up piece of cloth from a box full of items. It measured roughly 13.5 by 9.5 inches. As he unrolled the cloth and saw the bright colours, he asked his father what it was.

"Dad said he was in a Chinese house in Singapore torn apart by the bombing and some silk thread had spilled out of a chest … [later in captivity] in a big sick camp near the end of the war, an Australian POW had shown him how to do some embroidery."

On further investigation, on page 19 of Jack's first book, *Burma Railway Artist, The War drawings of Jack Chalker,* [2] he writes:

"… I was on my way to an observation post on the outskirts of Singapore Town and had to make my way through a bombed house that was on fire. In a corridor I saw through the smoke and dust some brilliant colours on the floor. A small chest of drawers had been blown apart, spilling small skeins of brightly coloured Chinese embroidery silks and pieces of canvas. I stopped for a moment, caught by the beauty of the colours, and wrapped a handful of silks in a small piece of canvas and stuffed them into my pocket. They were to bring pleasure later on."

Then again, on page 88, when describing being ill in one of the fever huts at Chungkai Hospital camp in Thailand, sometime towards the end of 1943, he says:

"I rediscovered the small skeins of Chinese silk that I had picked up in the burning house in Singapore. Surprisingly, my sick neighbour, an Australian farmer, said he had some experience of embroidery learnt from an aunt when a small boy in the outback. I had two small needles, and with his massive hands he showed me how to do some exquisite stitching. Neither of us was mobile, and this helped to pass the time. I spent some days producing a passable piece under his guidance and I still have it."

And Jack kept it for a lifetime, until that day when Guy rescued it from obscurity by asking his father if he could keep it. This mesmerizingly vibrant piece of creative art represents the artist in Jack who was captivated by the tropics and would not be cowed. When writing his memoir so many years after those events, perhaps the fantastical tropical bird surrounded by a riot of colourful flora, was just one more element in the light and shade of his captivity. It acted as a personal talisman, the colour, proportion and fine skills of embroidery providing a counterpoint to the chaotic drudgery of daily camp life.

The majority of surviving FEPOW drawings are about life in captivity but a small number envision a future and are specific about the home and ideals involved. Mentioned earlier in this book are the drawings of Reginald Newman detailing the plans for the caravan he aimed to build after the war and the wonderful recreation made in 2016. The story of Bill Norways drawing a motorbike he had last seen four years earlier is remarkable and Geoffrey Munton's drawing of a remembered Ely Cathedral (Figure 18) shows how profound and detailed were FEPOW memories of home.

Figure 18. 'A Far East POW's Dream', Ely Cathedral from memory, 29 October 1943, by Spr G. Munton (© courtesy the Munton family)

While most of Munton's drawings are in the IWM collection, this drawing was retained by the family and is one of the most meaningful. It was used in 1988 to publicise Ely Cathedral's 900th anniversary at which time Munton wrote the following caption:

A Far East POW's Dream
Sketched in November 1943 on the island of Blackang Mati, south of

Singapore under the very harrowing conditions of our Japanese captors.
Against strict rules we should not have pen or paper, however much did
survive and we buried it during routine searches by our Japanese guards and
moved it from camp to camp.
It gave us a bond between the hell in which we were living and the thoughts
of our homeland. It gave us the will to survive, alas so many of my friends did
not. It is they we should not forget – we were so young …
G C Munton, 560 Field Coy. Regt., 18th Division.

Maps and plans

The urge to make maps, to locate yourself in the universe, is a strong
compulsion for many artists. Giving a figure drawing background and context
allows, literally, the establishment of perspective. In addition to the FEPOW
artists there were many engineers in captivity, accustomed to drawing scale
plans so mapping was a strong element of FEPOW drawing despite the threat
of reprisals if the charts and plans were found. The plans drawn by Captain
Atholl Duncan, shown in Chapters 1 and 3, are good illustrations of this
impulse.

There are stories of maps ranging from the ridiculous – when military charts of
Singapore turned out to be of the Isle of Wight and Philip Meninsky drew swift
sketch maps using a map taken from a school wall – to the horrific, when railway
enthusiast Eric Lomax's chart of the course of the Thai–Burma railway was
discovered and led to torture and incarceration. He recorded

> *"I decided to carry it with me, wherever we were going. It was my talisman*
> *of certainty; it gave a sense of direction to the blind steps we were now*
> *taking."*

Stephen Alexander's very detailed map of a section of the Thai–Burma railway
and the river and camp locations at Tamarkan (Figure 19) was made in a style
known to British readers but unfamiliar to his Japanese guards. The drawing
mimics the unmistakable work of E. H. Shepard, evoking A. A. Milne's map
of the Hundred Acre Wood inhabited by Pooh Bear and his companions. To
a British POW familiar with the whimsicality of this style, the drawing would

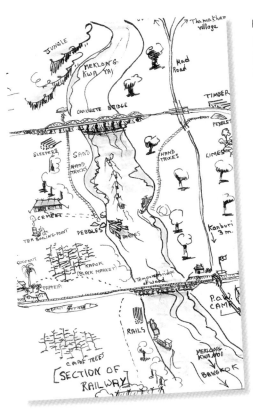

raise a smile. As a gentle mocking of Japanese railway ambitions, it is exceptional.

Spiritual morale

In published records and in archived papers there are moving accounts of the part played by chaplains and padres in trying to bring spiritual consolation to those in need. Distinctions of creed became less important in captivity as these men began to realise that their 'flock' encompassed many thousands of POWs. Of importance were regular services offering comforting memories of home, pastoral visits to the hospital lines and training men to conduct services in camps where there was no padre.

263

Chapels were established in the camps as numbers grew (see example Figure 18). The remarkable story of St George's chapel at Tandjong Priok in Java is told in Chapter 2 and chapels in Changi were drawn by Eric Stacy and by Toss Wilson. Where buildings remained long enough they became a focus for the creative efforts of the FEPOWs, for example Stanley Warren's fine murals for St Luke's chapel at Robert's Barracks Hospital in Changi.

The carved and painted chapel plaque shown below is by an anonymous artist. It was presented to Padre Cordingly for the first St George's chapel at Changi. The beautifully crafted hexagonal plaque, painted using oil paint, depicts St George slaying the dragon. It is a masterpiece of craftsmanship, as the fine detailing of the dragon reveals in Figure 21.

Measuring 45.5 x 45.5 cm. (depth 3.5 cm.) and now over 77 years old, the brightly coloured paintwork is still clear though the wood is cracked in places. The composition is based on the badge of the Royal Northumberland Fusiliers and it seems likely that the artist (unknown) was a member of the regiment. According to Cordingly's diary,

> "... the wooden plaque is carved in bas relief and depicts St George slaying the dragon ... it took the craftsman over a month to carve. He is by profession a sculptor, and this is his first venture in wood. It has been painted in oils and is probably one of the most lovely things yet made in the camp."

Figure 21.   Left: wooden plaque made for the first St George's chapel, Changi, centre and right detail, artist unknown (© *courtesy the Cordingly family*)

This tangible relic, much treasured by the Cordingly family, is a lasting reminder of both the skill of the artist and their father's work in captivity. Cordingly also made this interesting observation:

"We are perhaps a unique colony, having amongst us men who are skilled in all the arts, and here it is not commercialised and turned into work…"

The plaque was featured in *Down to Bedrock*, Cordingly's diaries and notes published by his daughter Louise Reynolds.[3] The plaque had accompanied Cordingly when he was drafted to Thailand but was mislaid, causing much distress. However, it reappeared in January 1944 when Cordingly was at Kanburi Hospital camp. He wrote,

"My church kit had been brought from store at Bampong [sic], the Communion Set and St. George's plaque which it had been necessary to abandon in the jungle-staging camp, turned up a little the worse for rain and sun."[4]

The plaque had also been used by the guards as a dart board.

Funerals and remembrance

The Allied military organisation in the FEPOW camps was accustomed to dealing with death and ensured that funerals and burials were carried out with dignity (Figure 22). Where possible the names of the dead were scrupulously recorded in lists and on grave markers. At times this system faltered, for example during the 1943 'speedo' period when the bodies of cholera victims in up-country camps were burned to minimise contagion. However, POWs were used to the formality of the funeral cortege and honoured their dead as circumstances allowed.

Artists honoured the dead in their own way by recording funeral processions and the extensive graveyards which were soon necessary (Figure 23). The neat formality of grave plots is a strange contrast to the riotous and luxuriant jungle but, like the landscape ever-visible beyond the camps, graveyards offered a place of quiet reflection.

Figure 22. 'Carrying the dead', Thailand 1943, by Spr R. W. F. Searle *(© the artist, permission The Sayle Literary Agency. IWM.IWM ART.17092)*

Figure 23. 'POW cemetery', Kanu camp, Thailand, January 1943, by L/Bdr J. G. Mennie *(© the artist, courtesy IWM. IWM ART.LD 7293)*

For artists, landscape drawing holds a particular place in art practice (for example Figure 24). British artists would know the lyrical pastoral watercolours of John Sell Cotman, John Constable and JMW Turner. They would be familiar with the prints of Samuel Palmer and their presentation of rural surroundings as a transcendent world of safety. The spirit of place is very strong in this tradition and FEPOW artists used this approach not only to document their locale but also to evoke a world beyond the camps.

266

Figure 24.   Haroekoe, view across water with barbed wire fence in the foreground, by Fl/Lt F. R. Philps *(© courtesy the Philps family)*

In this case the artists were not responding to demands from their fellow captives but, rather, spending time alone with nature and with their art materials, part of an abiding art tradition.

CHAPTER 7

Finding a Voice: Changing Post-war Attitudes

I still remember the shock of seeing Philip Meninsky's drawing of a shinbone eaten away by a tropical ulcer. (Figure 1). As a young art technician tasked with locating artworks for a planned exhibition of Far East POW (FEPOW) drawings, I had no idea what I would find. Previously, in the calm surroundings of the newly-furbished IWM Print Room, I had opened smart red boxes of mounted artworks, laying out lively watercolours of France and North Africa by officially commissioned Second World War artists or wonderful examples of poster design by First World War German and Russian artists. Meninsky's depiction of bodily suffering confronted me with a profound sadness about the significance of war art which has never left me.

When I joined the IWM Art Department a young team of curators were beginning to explore the huge art and poster collections which the Museum had been able to amass but not assimilate. In the 1950s and early 1960s the Keeper of Art, Philip Mayes, had achieved the monumental task of listing and publishing a basic catalogue of commissioned artworks from the two world wars. Now it was time to mine those riches and in the late 1970s a series of small

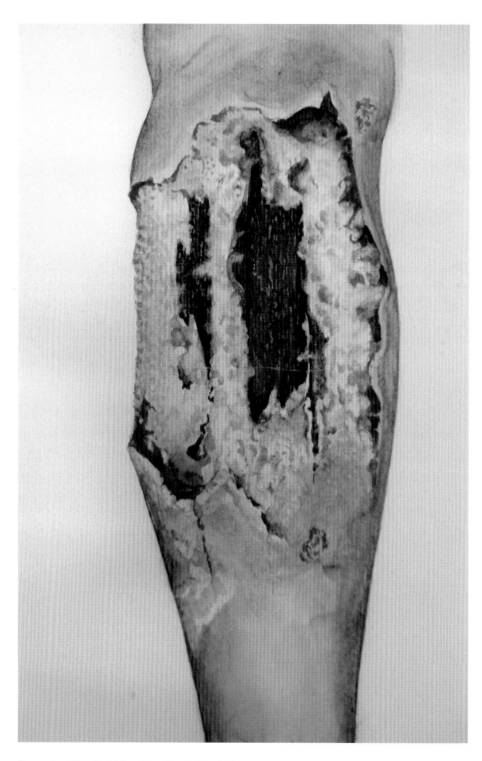

Figure 1. 'Tropical Ulcer', by Gnr P. Meninsky
(© courtesy Imperial War Museums, IWM.IWM ART.LD 6523)

but significant exhibitions began to illustrate the quality and diversity of the visual collections.

One of these exhibitions, entitled 'Captive' (1978), organised by Vivienne Crawford, showed an unusual aspect of the art collection – drawings made in captivity by 'unofficial' artists, particularly Far East prisoners of war. During the 1960s and 1970s drawings by these artists began to trickle in to the art collection. They were difficult to evaluate as they were outside the canon of trained British artists which formed the bulk of IWM's collection. The two criteria for assessing works for inclusion in the art collection were that they should show some artistic merit and that they should be authentic records, made at the time. The FEPOW drawings were of wildly differing artistic merit and expertise but were demonstrably done at the time and were valuable witness to the wartime experience of thousands of men.

Philip Meninsky was one of the artists who bridged this gap. Son of the First World War artist Bernard Meninsky he had grown up with a knowledge of artwork and techniques and in later life he built his reputation as an artist and teacher. After imprisonment in Singapore, Meninsky was sent north to work on the feeder road for the Thai–Burma railway. Various illnesses, including his own tropical ulcer (from which he never wholly recovered) necessitated his removal from Tarsao camp to the hospital camp at Chungkai hospital camp, then to

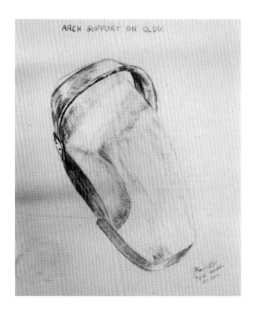

Tamuan camp for the disabled POWs and finally to Nakom Paton hospital camp. At Chungkai he encountered the Australian surgeon Major Moon who asked him to make drawings of the extraordinary medical challenges and improvised equipment in use. Moon ensured that Meninsky became a 'medical

Figure 2. 'Arch support on clog', by Gnr P. Meninsky
(© courtesy IWM.IWM ART.LD 6634)

orderly' so that he could continue to make drawings. Many of his sketches were made at the behest of medical men in the camps including Major Moon and, at the war's end, Colonel Ransom RAMC. In common with a number of FEPOW artists he kept the remainder of his wartime drawings aside, both physically and mentally, for 30 years before giving them to the Imperial War Museum.

Meninsky's drawings are compassionate but uncompromising. His works at the IWM include physical conditions – beriberi and tropical ulcers – and the improvised medical instruments in use – a rib shear, a nasal polyp snare, a mastoid clamp, a wooden arch support (Figure 2). Amputations became common due to tropical ulcers and Meninsky drew various types of artificial limbs developed in the camps.

In 1991 Meninsky was interviewed for the IWM's oral history programme and talked about a fellow artist Ashley George Old who was with him throughout captivity, nursed him though illness and was, in Meninsky's estimation, *"the best artist of us all"*. He remembered him with great fondness, saying *"he taught me a great deal about drawing – a natural teacher"*. In 1995 an exhibition was held at the State Library of Victoria in Australia showing the wartime drawings collected by Major Moon. These included work by Philip Meninsky and also drawings by George Old. The Moon collection had been *"painted in secrecy on Japanese toilet paper, buried with rat poison under the camp and* [later] *exhumed."*

Meninsky believed that Old had died after the war but was to learn otherwise. During the Australian exhibition's search for copyright holders it was

established that George Old was alive, cared for by the Royal British Legion in Canvey Island. A meeting at the IWM Print Room

Figure 3.   Meeting of Gnr P. Meninsky and George Old *(© courtesy IWM Print Room 1995. IWM95/40/6)*

was arranged (Figure 3) and in April 1995 Philip Meninsky was able to greet his fellow FEPOW artist whom he had thought dead for 40 years.

Ashley George Old's career is an example of much that is discussed in this book. The dislocation resulting from his wartime experience meant that a number of people had a piece of the jigsaw without anyone having a complete idea of his art. His pre-war training at Northamptonshire College of Art was followed by work as a commercial artist in the men's fashion industry. There is also an intriguing reference to him working on murals in the Japanese Embassy in London.

Joining the war as a gunner in the 5th Sherwood Foresters he was taken prisoner at the fall of Singapore and found himself part of a creative circle with other POW artists such as Ronald Searle, Jack Chalker, Philip Meninsky and Robert Brazil. All these artists early-on decided to draw openly so that their Japanese guards would get used to them drawing innocuous subjects while anything sensitive was hidden away. The artists drew greetings cards, cartoons and portraits, exchanging them often for tobacco, rations or art materials. This explains why, although some of Old's drawings from the camps were discovered and confiscated by the Japanese, there exist cards and individual portraits kept by prisoners in their personal collections. Indeed, now is the time to check again to see if any further works by this gifted artist may come to light.

A fellow FEPOW artist, Stanley Gimson, recorded in his diary in January 1944:

> *"had my portrait painted again – this time by a Northampton man named Old. He is a great hulking, fair-haired yokel with a face like a harvest moon – faintly reminiscent of Holbein's Henry VIII."*

Figure 4.   'G. S. Gimson' portrait, Thailand, by Gnr. A. G. Old *(© courtesy IWM.IWM ART.16923)*

This portrait (Figure 4) forms part of Gimson's papers in the IWM but many, like the compelling portrait of Charlie Proctor, 1st/5th Sherwood Foresters, or the distressing portrait of fellow artist Jack Chalker after a beating, are in private collections. Old, like Meninsky, made many drawings in the camps for Major Moon and later, in Rangoon, for Colonel Ransom, but these were retained for illustration of wartime medical practice or evidence in war crimes trials.

A rare exception in a public collection is the moving drawing 'Mr Stanley' 1945, in the National Army Museum and featured in Chapter 5 (Figure 3). Meninsky recalled that in 1945 he and George Old travelled from Nakom Paton via Bangkok to Rangoon where they spent two months working for Colonel Ransom as part of 136 Force (the War Graves Force). They drew skin conditions, medical equipment and emaciated men. Old's arresting watercolour of a reclining figure in an extremely emaciated state gives a nod to the reclining figures beloved of life drawing classes but accords the subject dignity by portraying, unembellished, his distressed body.

It appears that on Old's return to London he struggled to re-integrate, writing in 1952:

> *"like many of the FEPoWs I came home in a noticeable state of nervous tension and then was one of the few who are refused a chance of rehabilitation."*

And, in 1953, *"the after-effects of war completely changed me."* Conscious of his need for therapy he tried to focus on his art, having been awarded a grant to study at Camberwell School of Art in 1951. He clearly needed time alone and enjoyed an extensive trek along the South Coast to Cornwall but after the death of his parents he lost focus and a catastrophic Essex repository fire in the late '60s destroyed his studio works.

His lifeline during all of this time was a friendship he maintained with Ruth Bartholomew. He wrote regular letters detailing the hopes and reversals of his post-war life, his art insights and physical frailties including a fungal toenail infection dating from his FEPOW experiences when *"my toes were badly cut by falling rocks and were open wounds for at least ten months."* Plans to develop a pen-lettering business, and to teach in South Africa came to nothing and following the loss of his paintings in the fire he settled in Canvey Island and turned to factory work. Ruth's two sons remember him as a benevolent presence who visited regularly during their childhood, as David recalled in an email to Meg in 2013:

> "Ashley was a man with simple tastes and an extraordinary talent. He was modest in all things, except in respect of his art, where he believed himself to have true insight. Few who have seen his work would argue with that. Before the war, when Ashley was young, and he was painting my mother Ruth, she asked him 'What sort of artist do you want to be?'. 'Brilliant,' was his reply, and this exchange is echoed, at my mother's insistence, on his gravestone [Figure 5].
>
> My father described Ashley as 'one of nature's true gentlemen'... [he] was a great storyteller and could transfix a multigenerational audience. When my brother and I were teenagers (and he was in his sixties) he would come with us to the pub and our friends would hang on to his every word."

Figure 5. Ashley George Old's gravestone (© courtesy the Bartholomew family)

Corporal Charles Thrale

1st Btn Cambridgeshire Regiment attached to Intelligence

Captured:	Singapore
Camps:	Singapore: Changi POW camp; returned 1944
	Thailand: Kanburi, Sonkurai
From:	London
DoB:	7.3.18
Died:	1981

Figure 6. 'Self-portrait, Changi camp
Singapore 1944' by Cpl C. Thrale
(© courtesy IWM.IWM ART.15417 14)

Other FEPOW artists circulated their drawings to raise public awareness. One of my early jobs was to visit the executor of the artist **Charles Thrale** to assess the extent of the drawings and documents remaining from his travelling exhibition. The exhibition 'The Valleys of the Shadow of Death' opened in London in 1946 and circulated the UK until 1964. This exhibition of Thrale's FEPOW drawings was pasted onto a series of hardboard folding display panels with added typed paper captions. More than a hundred drawings were included, documenting Thrale's experiences in Singapore and working on the Thai–Burma railway. A small printed catalogue showed some significant images telling Thrale's story.

Originally made on paper of varying quality, in pencil, watercolours and other media, the drawings had suffered from exposure to light and the effects of the glue. In the exhibition catalogue Thrale documented some of his improvised materials, such as brass polish, crushed leaves, blood, boiled rags, medicine sediment, clay, shoe polish and mashed petals. It would be an expensive job to mitigate these conservation problems and to make them safe to archive and access. Happily, the IWM decided that those costs were bearable given the significance of the works.

Accompanying the panels of drawings were a series of 'visitors' books' which had grown as the exhibition circulated over the eighteen years. These were initially accepted as an adjunct to the drawings but were found to afford a fascinating portrait of British attitudes to the FEPOW experience. In particular, the early antagonism expressed towards the Japanese had evolved by 1964 as the awful effects of the bombings of Hiroshima and Nagasaki became more widely known, to a more nuanced, anti-nuclear viewpoint. One of the other FEPOW artists, John Mennie, went to view the show, commenting in the visitors' book that Thrale was not the only artist to have experienced these things.

Thrale was a professional portrait painter and commercial artist before the war. He joined up in 1940, serving with the 1st Btn the Cambridgeshire Regiment, attached to Intelligence. He sailed in October 1941 aboard the USS *Westpoint*, travelling to Singapore via South Africa, and with other artists who were part of the 18th Division, was soon to be imprisoned in Singapore, later being sent to work camps on the Thai–Burma railway.

In Scotland the artist **Stanley Gimson** personally circulated a display of more than sixty drawings he had made during captivity in Singapore and then Thailand. The exhibition notes reveal that in 1944, when it became more difficult and dangerous to keep the drawings from the Japanese guards, they were sealed in a bottle together with his diary and buried in the cemetery at Chungkai camp. Following the Japanese surrender eighteen months later, they were dug up, unharmed.

Gimson organised his exhibition chronologically, each group of drawings shown with an explanatory caption. The grouped drawings were first mounted and then fixed to small boards which were easily transported whenever Gimson arranged a temporary exhibition. He was an able speaker, his post-war career in Scottish law included responsibilities at War Pensions tribunals and he advised the Royal British Legion in Scotland on FEPOW matters. He was an active supporter of the Scottish FEPOW groups which hosted the exhibition (and later became chairman of the Scottish Association of FEPOW Clubs). It was important to keep the drawings together as a full record and they were promised to the IWM in 1985, finally accepted on his death when his wartime diary was bequeathed to the IWM Documents archive. Gimson was interviewed by the IWM Sound Archive in 1981.

Figure 7. 'Selarang Square Squeeze, Singapore, September 1942' by Gnr. J. Mennie
(© courtesy IWM.IWM ART.17877)

Gimson had no prior art training and the exhibition notes point to the
'increasing fluency which comes with practice'. His materials were a constant
problem. Early paper was taken from books and jotters, later works were on
flimsy paper 'acquired' from the Japanese office. Pencils were hard to find but
Gimson records an 'astonishing' occasion in 1944 when he bartered for a 3-inch
Venus 3B pencil. This accounted for the deeper shading to be seen towards the
end of his series of drawings.

He was one of several artists, in the early days of captivity in Singapore, to witness
the Selarang Incident which he describes in his IWM sound recording (Figure
7). From 2 to 5 September 1942 approximately 17,000 POWs were crowded into
the area of Selarang Barracks where they camped out in the square while refusing
to sign a 'parole' agreeing that they would not attempt escape. The overcrowding
led to swiftly deteriorating conditions and when the medical staff advised that
infectious illness was a high risk, the POW officers negotiated with the Japanese
that their 'request' to sign the parole should become an order. With this change it
was agreed that the men should sign this parole 'under duress'.

Figure 8.   'Kanyu riverside camp, 14 March 1943',
by Lt S. Gimson (© courtesy IWM.IWM ART.16892)

Gimson's drawings give an account of daily life in Kanu river camp and later
at Chungkai camp, illustrating the bedspaces, cookhouses, operating spaces,
church and camp theatre and particular medical and hygiene arrangements
from sterilisation to dentistry. After the Japanese surrender he passed through
Nakon Nayok camp and included in his panorama drawing the allied flags
flying. During the IWM art and documents review in 2011–12 Gimson's rare
panorama of Kanu ('Kanyu') camp, March 1943 (Figure 8) was compared with
a hand-drawn map in the papers of Lt D. A. Johnston to identify the different
functions of the array of huts shown. Gimson's exhibition caption notes 'the
whole site has now reverted to thick jungle'.

IWM's growing awareness of the range of FEPOW records did not always
lead to acquisitions as several artists preferred to retain their drawings and
documents. However, they were willing to let them be copied and in the case of
two artists – **Leo Rawlings** and William Wilder – a complete black and white
photographic record of their drawings was made by IWM's Photo Archive.
(Wilder's experiences are shown in Chapter 2).

Leo Rawlings had been working as a sign writer before the war, building on art
school training. He joined the Territorial Army in 1938 and drew throughout
his military career, documenting the Malaya retreat, the Fall of Singapore and
captivity in Changi. In 1943 he was sent north to work on the Thai–Burma

railway, travelling, as thousands of other POWs did, first to Ban Pong in overcrowded railway trucks (Figure 9).

In common with other recognised artists he was asked to document and record the deprivations and health problems of camp life, in his case being commissioned by Lt General Sir Louis Heath. Many of his drawings use black ink to record stark images of POWs suffering from cholera, tropical ulcers and paraplegia. He also recalled using clay, root juices and brushes made from his own hair. Some of his paper materials re-used the backs of Changi Prison sheets and were concealed from the Japanese guards in an old stove-pipe container buried beneath his bed space.

On his return to Lancashire, Rawlings' works were shown in 1946 at the Grundy Art Gallery in Blackpool which later acquired some of his drawings. He continued to show his drawings, first approaching IWM as early as 1952. In 1965 some drawings were auctioned and acquired by the Wellcome Foundation and IWM, when a b/w photographic record was made of the whole collection. IWM recognised the value of a complete record of his drawings but his work is patchy in quality and only thirteen drawings were acquired. Rawlings made his way as a professional artist in the post-war years, specialising in portraits

Gunner Leo Oscar Rawlings

137th Field Regiment (Blackpool)

Captured:	Singapore 15.2.42
Camps:	Singapore: Changi
	Thailand: Ban Pong, Khan Buri, Tonchan South, Tamarkan Bridge and back to Singapore
From:	Blackpool
DoB:	16.5.18
Died:	1990

Figure 9. 'Appalling conditions of ammunition trucks in which British and Allied POWs had to travel', by Gnr L. O. Rawlings (© courtesy IWM.IWM ART.LD 6032)

and paintings of racehorses. However, communicating his wartime captivity experiences remained a priority. He finally stopped the exhibitions in the early 1960s on doctor's advice and later published an illustrated memoir *And the Dawn came up like Thunder* (1972).

The teachers

Where artists such as Thrale and Rawlings continued in private practice or, like Old, struggled to make a living from their art, there were FEPOW artists who joined the post-war British art establishment as teachers, particularly John Mennie and Jack Chalker. They were confident in their abilities and were able to see their wartime work as a unique part of broader art careers.

John George Mennie, known to his family as Jack, was an established commercial artist in London in the 1930s after completing art training in his native Aberdeen and then London. He joined the Royal Artillery in 1940 and his experiences, after capture at the fall of Singapore, mirrored many other captives, with work at Kanu camp on the Thai–Burma railway followed by months at Chungkai hospital camp and Nakom Paton. He was in Pratchi camp when the war ended.

Figure 10. 'Dysentery ward, Kanu No. 1 P.O.W. camp Thailand June 1943 – Thai Burma Railway' by L/Bdr J. G. Mennie *(© courtesy IWM.IWM ART.LD 7292)*

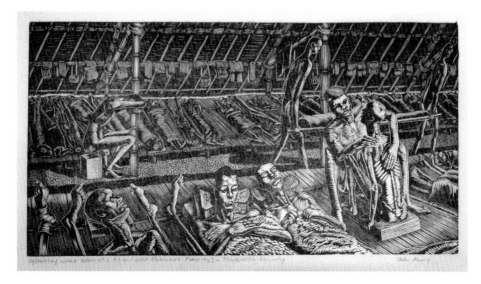

Throughout his captivity he kept drawings – a 'hidden' set showing the realities of incarceration and a more obvious collection of portrait drawings. The 'hidden' drawings were kept concealed in his bamboo walking stick. The portrait drawings were confiscated by his Japanese guards but not destroyed. They were found at the end of the war and, amazingly, were returned to him by post when he returned to Aberdeen.

In London he found an art teaching post with the Inner London Education Authority where he worked for most of his career. Using the original drawings from his captivity he made a distinguished series of linocuts and woodcuts printed onto Japanese paper. In a letter to IWM he wrote:

> "The prints were made from drawings of the same size on odd bits of paper, mainly taken from the blank fly-leaves you find in books. These I acquired (in exchange for cigarettes) together with a box of 12 tubes of Chinese watercolours from other prisoners."

His gift of prints and original drawings to IWM raised questions as the prints themselves were undoubtedly post-war productions. Post-war 'reconstructions' were not generally reliable, but these had been made from his own original drawings so could be admitted. The skilful mix of uncompromising imagery and seductively beautiful colour on fragile Japanese paper make these prints a thought-provoking meditation on his experiences.

Jack Bridger Chalker occupies a particular place in this field – he was one of the FEPOW artists who was not only known to the art world but also to the Liverpool School of Tropical Medicine. His wartime legacy of ill-health led him eventually to contact LSTM where he was seen for Tropical Disease Investigations in the 1980s.

During captivity he not only drew medical conditions and procedures, but as seen in Chapter 6 (Figure 17, in Chapter 6) he was also adept at the creative arts as well, as the hitherto unseen and glorious embroidery testifies. The artist in Jack was intoxicated by the beauty all around him in the tropics.

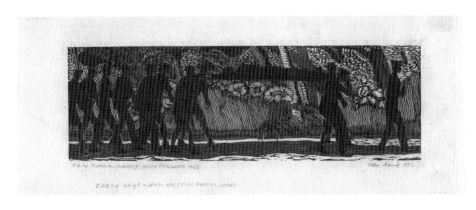

Figure 11. 'A POW funeral cortege, Kanu Thailand 1943' print by L/Bdr J. G. Mennie made in 1951 *(© courtesy IWM.IWM ART.LD 7305)*

Brought up in South London he always had an interest in medicine but was encouraged in art by his sister and her artist husband. After studying art at Goldsmiths College, Chalker was awarded a scholarship at the Royal College of Art (RCA). This was deferred as he was called up, and joined a Field Artillery Unit, training as an artillery surveyor and gunner.

Taken captive at the fall of Singapore he went from Changi to Kanu camp on the Thai–Burma railway and later to Chungkai hospital camp, then to Tamuan

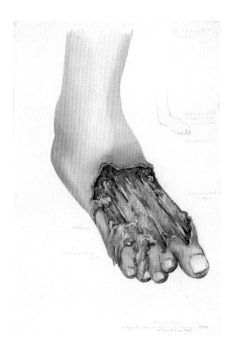

and ended the war in Nakom Paton. He made many drawings of medical instruments, procedures and disease (see Figure 12), working particularly for the noted Australian surgeon Edward 'Weary' Dunlop and the Canadian, Captain Jacob Markowitz RAMC. In 1945–6 he was attached to the Australian Army in Bangkok and some of his drawings were later used as evidence in war crimes trials. The Australian War Memorial retain a number of his works.

Figure 12. 'Tropical ulcer of the foot', by Gnr J. B. Chalker *(© courtesy Jack Chalker).*

He kept his drawings hidden in bamboo tubes which he buried (sadly losing early ones to termites) and once in the artificial leg of an amputee. However, some drawings were discovered at Konyu camp and led to a severe beating. The most powerful of his drawings are black ink and wash images of POWs suffering from dysentery and enduring reprisals and punishments in the jungle camps.

After the war he graduated from the RCA and taught at Cheltenham Ladies' College before becoming Principal at Falmouth School of Art in Cornwall and then later at the West of England College of Art in Bristol. For many years he could not look at his wartime drawings but in 1994 he published his memoir *Burma Railway Artist* and in 2007 *Burma Railway: Images of War*. He was interviewed by the IWM Sound Archive and the National Army Museum has an extensive collection of his work.

To the Kwai and back: Ronald Searle

The IWM's collection of FEPOW drawings came to prominence in 1986 with the exhibition 'To the Kwai and Back'. This exhibition and the publication of the associated book celebrated the remarkable gift by the artist Ronald Searle of over 400 of his drawings dating from his deployment with the 18th Division and subsequent experiences in captivity in Singapore and on the Thai–Burma railway.

IWM had long known of this important collection of drawings and had approached Searle with a view to acquiring them. Searle wanted to keep them with him and it was only in 1984 that he consented to pass them into IWM's care with provisos that they should be conserved, exhibited and available for future researchers. Once he had released the drawings he confessed that he felt a great weight had lifted from his shoulders.

It was a mammoth task to photograph, conserve, mount and document these works, and it was not until two years later that a selection were framed up to form the exhibition. Searle's drawings are a complete account, showing the outward voyage on the troopship to Singapore via South Africa, early encounters with Japanese troops during deployment, scenes of capture, daily FEPOW life in Singapore, in work camps on the Thai–Burma railway, later back in Singapore and early scenes of liberation.

Sapper Ronald William Fordham Searle

287th Field Company, RE

Captured:	Singapore
Camps:	Singapore: Changi; from Dec 1943: Sime Road and Changi Gaol
	Thailand: various including Ban Pong, Konyu 2, Wampo, Hintok, Kanburi
From:	Cambridge
DoB:	3.3.20
Died:	30.12.11

Figure 13. 'Self-portrait, Konyu camp, Thailand, July 1943' by Spr R. W. F. Searle (© *the artist, permission The Sayle Literary Agency. IWM.IWM ART.15747 76*)

Searle had been a student at Cambridge School of Art (CSA) before the war and when he returned from captivity over 300 of his drawings were immediately exhibited in December 1945 at the CSA gallery. A selection was then published in 'Forty Drawings' which appeared in 1946. The introduction to this book, by Frank Kendon, points out Searle's combination of terse directness with human sympathy, commenting that even in his portraits of Japanese guards they are 'understood'. Fellow artist Philip Meninsky emphasised in his IWM interview that although he decided himself never to draw the Japanese guards, Searle did.

In the book Searle wrote to accompany the 1986 show at IWM he is keen to explain the experiences he underwent and to communicate the scope of the years in captivity.[1] By this stage it had long been accepted that the war in the Far East was the 'forgotten war'. For understandable reasons FEPOWs were reluctant to talk of their captivity and the subject continued to be overshadowed by the better-known and understood war in Europe. The subject also lagged behind in the plethora of films about the Second World War which appeared in the 1950s and 1960s, with the exception of David Lean's 1957 film, 'The Bridge on the River Kwai'. In 1983 the film 'Merry Christmas Mr Lawrence' brought the subject to a new audience and so by the time of Searle's exhibition there was a growing appreciation and understanding of FEPOW captivity.

Searle wanted the public to see beyond the tales of camp atrocities and the 'notorious' railway to the daily lives and hardships of the prisoners suffering years of captivity in an unfamiliar landscape, malnourished and subject to disease. He drew compulsively and, when the threat of discovery by the Japanese guards was great he hid his drawings in the bedding of cholera sufferers, confident that none of the guards would risk going near.

The exhibition offered the public a new dimension to the creativity of an artist and cartoonist who was internationally known and loved for creations such as his 'St Trinians' images of an anarchic girls' boarding school. Works from the IWM's collection were requested for exhibitions at the Cartoon Gallery in London and a large Searle retrospective at Haus Ludwig in Hamburg. The timely gift of his drawings to the IWM did much to raise the status of FEPOW art in public awareness, making the point that 'unofficial' art was as important as the government-commissioned images in showing a unique perspective.

Public collections and perspectives

Other public collections in the UK have also collected drawings by UK artists. The National Army Museum holds around 70 works collected since 1989 including the artists Jack Chalker, John Mennie, George Old, Leo Rawlings and Ronald Searle. The Wellcome Collection focuses on medical and health subjects and includes work by Leo Rawlings.

Artworks and diaries have also found their way into regimental museums and archives, reinforcing the importance of regimental ties both during captivity and in post-war life.

The IWM collection of FEPOW drawings is seen to be unique when set in the context of the 'official' Second World War artists. These artists were sent by the British government into theatres of war to record conflict and latterly half a dozen artists worked in the Far East. Their work reflected the ending of hostilities and the state of released POWs and ranged from Burma to Singapore,

Figure 14. 'Orderly on his rounds, X-ward, Changi Gaol, Singapore, with Prisoners of War suffering from Starvation and Beriberi, 1945' by Leslie Cole (© courtesy IWM.IWM ART.LD 5618)

Borneo and Japan. One of these artists, Leslie Cole, painted sick and limbless FEPOWs at Changi Gaol (Figure 14) in the early days after release.

Cole's shocking images of skeletal figures and amputees should have reached a large UK audience built by regular exhibitions of War Artists Advisory Committee commissioned artists' work. However, his paintings reached the UK at the time when the WAAC was being wound up and artworks dispersed. This early opportunity to give FEPOWs the consideration they deserved was missed.

A re-assessment

I have outlined the sporadic growth of IWM's collection of Far East POW artworks and how public knowledge of the Far East captivity experience has changed in the past decades. In 2011–12 I undertook a ground-breaking and much overdue review of IWM FEPOW art in the different collections of art and documents. I worked in collaboration with Rod Suddaby, a much-valued colleague, previously Keeper of Documents and the curator responsible for an unparalleled collection of Far East POW documents, diaries and archive material. He knew the subject profoundly and could instantly identify the significance of various camps and rarity of drawings.

Figure 15. 'In the truck', Gnr P. Meninsky's drawing showing the rail journey to Ban Pong (© courtesy IWM. IWM ART.LD 6543)

We found, as suspected, that much of the collection of the FEPOW documents contained drawings or maps or greetings cards. The collections were listed by the individual donor's name but might contain a Christmas card designed by Ronald Searle, a portrait of the donor made by George Old or a theatre poster by 'AKKI' – Basil Parry Akhurst. Much like Meg Parkes' visits to Far East veterans' families, where cards, sculptures and drawings were produced along with papers and diaries, the review revealed the quality and unexpected quantity of FEPOW drawings in the archives.

We began by looking through the boxes of FEPOW drawings in the art collection and immediately made a discovery – a sketchbook by Philip Meninsky, previously listed just as 'sketchbook' proved to be a record of his journey from Singapore to Ban Pong (Figure 15), the base railway camp in Thailand. Rod knew that the pictures of men crowded into railway trucks, 30 to a truck, were unmistakable and confidently identified the drawings and the date.

Later we worked on Gimson's panorama of Kanu camp, identifying, with the help of camp maps in the papers of Lt D A Johnson, the function and probable date of the huts shown in the drawing. We found that at every stage the drawings and diaries reinforced each other, all parts of a jigsaw of witness where the truth showed through by constant correspondence of unconnected accounts.

The review showed the geographical spread of this material. Although there are a preponderance of reports from Singapore and Thailand, material was also collected from FEPOWs in Sumatra, Java, Formosa (Taiwan), Hong Kong and Japan. The review also separated out the material from civilian internee camps in Singapore and China and was able to identify the sitters in Changi Gaol drawings by referencing contemporary listings.

We looked at the drawings which showed the staples of artists' work – portraits, landscapes, humour, everyday life, travel, journals, entertainments and, unusually, medical care. However, these works had an additional dimension – the portraits might be done to barter for tobacco or rations; the landscapes might show an impossible notion of freedom from restraint; the cartoons lampooning figures of authority or the absurdities of daily life defused growing camp tensions; travel and transport were subject to ridiculously overcrowded conditions; camp journals, on restricted materials, were made as one-offs which were passed from hand to hand; the theatrical programme might be a rare hand-drawn listing of musical numbers and participants. The unusual aspect was the recording of medical conditions and procedures, largely prompted by the medical personnel themselves who needed to know that a record of such medical need and ingenuity in countering it would survive.

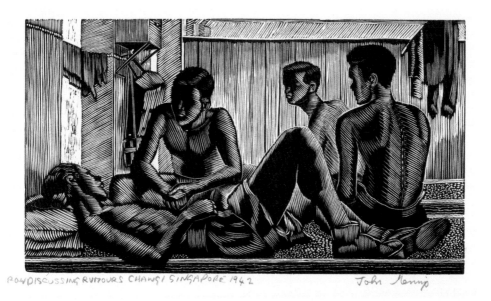

POW DISCUSSING RUMOURS CHANGI SINGAPORE 1942   John Mennip

Figure 16.   Gunner Graham Goulder-Hough discussing rumours, Changi 1942 by Gnr J. Mennie (© courtesy IWM.IWM ART.LD 7318)

The need to witness and record was clearly a primary motivation of the papers we examined in the Documents archive. Tiny diaries, their pages sometimes stitched together by hand and covered with minute pencil and ink descriptions of daily camp life show the determination to maintain order amid chaos and speak to us directly. It is hard to imagine, in our current 'connected' world, such a long period of disconnection where rumour and lack of reliable news could result in profound psychological distress (Figure 16).

Some of these collections have typescript versions made later by the FEPOWs themselves or their families. While these versions are easier to read, the presence of the original diary papers have a compelling immediacy and a meaning beyond the information they contain.

Why draw?

This is a fundamental question. In an uncertain time of captivity when there were risks of reprisals from the guards if people were caught recording sensitive subjects, why would anyone risk it?

With many thousands of troops taken prisoner, it was a given that some trained artists would be amongst those captives. Men such as Ronald Searle, Philip Meninsky and Jack Chalker turned naturally to drawing as their first, familiar point of refuge. Searle referred to daily drawing as his anchor. Medical personnel such as Major Moon took advantage of the ready pool of artistic talent to document the new and unusual challenges of the FEPOW camps.

There were many other talented amateur draughtsmen including those with map-making skills, men skilled in engineering, able to design and build anything from yeast-making apparatus to bridges, from musical instruments to theatre sets. There were also men with no arts training but a wish to learn. Initially there were opportunities to steal pencils and paper and a quantity of free time which needed to be filled. Philip Meninsky characterised his estimation of the FEPOW community as

"20% creatives including artists, designers, lecturers and makers and the entrepreneurs who obtained materials and medicines; 70% formed a willing audience and the remaining 10% would not engage, closing in on themselves."

He said that those were the ones who died, that some form of optimism was fostered by the creatives and those who joined in and was essential for survival.

Feeling a compulsion to draw in threatening circumstances speaks to the fundamental nature of creativity and underpins the challenge faced by all war artists. In addition, due to the particular lack of materials in the camps, and the attitude of the Japanese authorities in allowing very little photography and filming (for propaganda purposes only), the FEPOW drawings have earned an extra significance as being the primary record and witness of conditions suffered by many thousands in captivity. This function as documentary evidence has masked the underlying therapeutic use of drawing – its daily use as a tool in coping with conditions regardless of its later use as evidence in war crimes trials and as illustrations of the deprivations and medical attempts to alleviate suffering.

Drawing as therapy

It was the British artist Adrian Hill, first commissioned artist by the IWM in WWI and later to teach a generation of British schoolchildren how to draw in his celebrated TV programmes, who first came up with the term 'art therapy'. His experiences in the trenches during the First World War led him to recognise the therapeutic value of art activity for war invalids and then, incapacitated by TB in 1938, he worked through drawing with wounded military at King Edward VII Hospital in Midhurst. In 1945 he published *Art versus Illness* and in 1964 formed, with the NHS developer of art therapy Edward Adamson, the Association of Art Therapists.

Hill knew from his own experience how drawing could be used to regain and maintain mental health and, although the diagnosis 'shell-shock' went out of favour it indicated a syndrome recognised by William Rivers at Craiglockhart Hospital during the First World War, respite home to soldier poets Siegfried Sassoon and Wilfred Owen. PTSD (Post-Traumatic Stress Disorder) was first classified as a diagnostic condition in 1981 but had been known throughout the two world wars and beyond as a condition suffered, sometimes years after the formative events, by military personnel. As a young art therapist in 2001, Janice Lobban met Far East prisoners of war at the offices of Combat Stress where she was to be employed for the next two decades. Working at Combat Stress, Lobban developed art therapeutic models in collaboration with these FEPOWs and other military veterans.[2]

Combat Stress is a charity founded in 1919 and earlier known as the 'Ex-Services Welfare Society'. It is the most prominent institution concerned with the mental and physical health of military veterans, and art therapy plays a core role in all the welfare courses offered. The centre operates on a three-stage art therapeutic approach – first to establish personal safety and security, next to explore through different themes the wider concerns and fears experienced by the veteran, with possible ways to resolve or mitigate their distress, and finally to integrate what they have learned into a more positive approach to life. All the FEPOW drawings, made years earlier, fit into this model and it makes sense of otherwise disparate works. The artists involved would not recognise the term 'art therapy' but every drawing, whether seen as distraction, entertainment or documentation, offered a validation of the artist's place in the unsettling surroundings of captivity and a way of giving order to an uncertain future.

Other Worlds and Soldiers' Flowers: art materials for the military

In 2010 the John Creasey Museum in Salisbury began a wide-ranging community project 'Other Worlds' to explore the world of the soldier through the visual arts. It encompassed art skills workshops, professional mentoring and an exhibition opportunity for active service personnel. Salisbury's local audience comprises a large number of soldiers and their families. I was able to join the curator Peter Riley when he initially welcomed a group of serving personnel to discuss their art backgrounds and how their Army experiences might be told through the visual arts. Later on, I was pleased to give them a guided tour of the art collections of the IWM. The servicemen selected war artists and artworks which resonated for them and facsimiles of these works

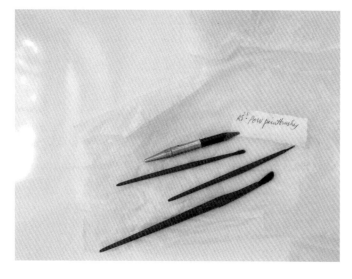

Figure 17. Pencil box, brushes and pencil stub in holder, kept by Gnr R. W. F. Searle in Changi camp (© the artist, permission The Sayle Literary Agency. IWM. IWM EPH.11503)

were shown alongside the soldiers' own works in the resulting exhibition 'A Briefing' (John Creasey Museum, 2011).

In parallel with this project an initiative was developed in co-operation with the Army Art Society to supply 20 communal packs of art materials to 40 Commando Royal Marines during their winter 2011/2012 deployment for Operation Herrick in Afghanistan. Using art materials was seen to be therapeutic, offering a way of defusing tension and of developing the skills of intent looking and understanding surroundings which are fundamental for artwork. Three experienced artists, Matthew Cook, Graeme Lothian and Dan Peterson joined 40 Commando Royal Marines in Afghanistan, demonstrating the use of the art materials and encouraging the serving personnel in identifying subjects. The resulting exhibition 'Soldiers' Flowers: Artists in Afghanistan' was shown in London in 2012. The catalogue shows a startling similarity with the subjects of FEPOW artists – portraits, cartoons and caricatures, landscapes, local flora, daily life on patrol, briefings, training. The material is now high-tech but the underlying need to record and to lampoon have not changed.

In 2012 the Combat Art Project built on this, aiming to supply portable bespoke art packs of sketchbooks, pens, crayons, watercolours and idea cards for each individual deployed by 40 Commando for their final tour in Afghanistan in 2012/2013. Resulting artworks were exhibited first in Taunton, the home of 40 Commando RM. The Army Arts Society, established by war artist Linda Kitson, was particularly committed to the provision of art materials for serving personnel.

One of the surviving FEPOW art materials collections is a hand-made wooden pencil box belonging to Ronald Searle (Figure 17). It contains paint brushes and tiny coloured crayons and a precious razor blade which Searle used to whittle and sharpen his few crayons. One of the artists commissioned by IWM in 2005 to respond to the 60th anniversary of the nuclear bombing of Japan looked at drawings and memorabilia dating from the FEPOW experiences. He responded immediately to the pencil box and particularly to the sharpening blade saying that he felt a live connection as one artist to another. Such recognition between artist generations can only be fostered by the Art Packs initiative.

That so many drawings have survived from FEPOW captivity is extraordinary. That such works, often small scraps of paper kept for years and hidden or buried, were retrieved and valued, is testament to the importance of drawing in captivity. The material now kept in public collections or family archives is only a part of the story. Other drawings were confiscated, lost, buried and never retrieved. It is a privilege to reveal what we can of hitherto hidden drawings and to celebrate these artists.

APPENDICES

APPENDIX I

Ashley George Old:
FEPOW Artist

Ashley George Old trained at the Northampton College of Art, where he was taught anatomy by Lewis Duckett MC, a World War I ambulanceman. Subsequently he worked for the famous commercial art firm Carlton Artists. During World War II, Ashley served in the Sherwood Foresters and was captured on the fall of Singapore, from where he was transported to a Japanese Prisoner of War camp in Siam (now Thailand). Here the prisoners were forced to build the Burma-Siam railway under almost unimaginable conditions of cruelty and hardship.

I knew Ashley from as far back as I can recall (I was born in 1957) until his death in 2001. He had a deep, close but platonic relationship with my mother from when they were teenagers to the moment of his death. I remember him as a special family friend from my earliest years. When he came to stay, the first thing he would say in the morning was: *"Any news?"*; it was much later that I realised this enquiry was a standard greeting from those who had endured imprisonment during World War II.

Ashley George Old, 1950s
(© courtesy of the Bartholomew family)

The years as a FEPOW made an indelible mark on Ashley and the way he coped with his feelings changed at different periods in his life. During the late 1940s and early 1950s, the letters he wrote to my mother show that he was suffering from what we now call Post Traumatic Stress Disorder. This subsequently led to him adopting a simple way of life (and sadly abandoning his art). From the late 1950s to the early 1980s this temporarily helped him find some peace. In a letter sent to me in the 1980s he says, *"I've had a wonderful life"*. Sadly, in his later years as his health declined, memories of his wartime torment seemed to take hold of him again and almost every letter to me reflected his intense hatred of his captors.

One nagging pain that he endured for over forty years was the thought that all the documentary art he had produced in the FEPOW camps had been lost. In 1985 he sent me a draft of a letter he intended to send to Australia House to try and find out if anyone knew what had happened to the works. That letter is shown below and explains how and why the art was created. Ashley had little hope of a helpful reply, but a few years later it was with delight and wonderment he learned his works had been found and were to be exhibited at the State Library of Victoria under the title 'The Major Arthur Moon Collection'. The tale of how these works were preserved and discovered is given in the exhibition catalogue (see extract below).

Almost every work in the extraordinary collection demonstrates the artist's clinical eye for detail and accuracy but also reveals the warmth and compassion of the man. Often the works are of horrific subject material but contain a haunting beauty. The catalogue cover shows a painting of a beckoning hand, titled 'Bomb wound (air attack)' and is compared in the narrative to Picasso's

'Guernica' as a truly extraordinary image of war. Ashley was invited to go to the exhibition but was too frail to do so.

In the letter Ashley wrote to me, he recounted being asked in Changi to do medical artwork in captivity:

> "Sometime after capture there was a very large art exhibition of POW work in which I submitted a very small watercolour painting of a young Scotch [sic] soldier with a ginger beard. It won first prize and next day a British medical orderly came to see me saying his boss an Australian surgeon – a Major Moon – wanted to see me.
>
> He said, 'You are just the man I need … lots of unusual wounds and diseases … want someone to represent them on paper', could I do the job? I instantly agreed, being delighted. Then he said: 'It will be very dangerous, you must never let the Japs find out what you are doing. So to make it easier I will put you into hospital with a fictitious disease … when can you start?'
>
> 'Tomorrow if you like?'
>
> 'Right! Go to such-and-such a ward and tell the medical orderly you have come to paint the wound on Private Orrey's ankle.'[1] I was always very happy painting … and doing a job I loved."

The following extract comes from the catalogue of the 1995 exhibition in Australia.[2] The exhibition marked the 50th anniversary of the ending of the Second World War and the release of captives in Far East captivity. Written by Moon's nephew Peter Jones in the introduction entitled, 'The other side of "MOONSHINE"', Jones quotes an extract from a letter written in 1973 to British FEPOW artist Philip Meninsky. In it Moon recounted how the medical artwork he had commissioned from FEPOW artists during captivity (among them Meninsky and Old) was hidden and eventually, after release, located and retrieved from hiding:

> "You may recall the difficulty I had in bringing these [medical illustrations] in a tin with other P.O.W. records and statistics when we left 'Tamuan' and went to our last distant camp up the north-east to 'Patchai' [sic].

*After liberation, we came down to Bangkok and I sent an N.C.O. who had
been with me, to recover the tin and papers buried under the hut at 'Tamuan'.
The camp had long since been deserted, huts pulled down, the area overgrown
and only bits of fencing, etc. left. He failed to find the hidden tin.*

*Fortunately, I was sent up there to see the Thai merchant, Boon Pong, who
had been an underground worker for us, and had been wounded in the chest
in an attempt to murder him after peace came. I was able to go to 'Tamuan'
and luckily, after a bit of digging, found the tin and contents intact."*

In my view, Ashley is one of the most important artists of the 20th century and
it is sad his work has yet to obtain the wider recognition it deserves. It is to be
hoped that this book and 'The Secret Art of Survival' exhibition, organised by
the Liverpool School of Tropical Medicine (2019–2020), will go some way to
redress this.

David Bartholomew
2019

···

Footnote:

To quote Peter Jones above, *"Each artist in his special way transformed deprivation
into bounty"*; the bounty perhaps being what both history and medical science
can learn from the skill of FEPOW artists.

Much more needs to be studied and understood about the life and art of British
war artist Ashley George Old, not least the importance to medical science and
to history of the skill of this humble and gifted artist. Like other great artists
in history, Old was not to enjoy the fruits of his creativity during his lifetime.
Posthumously, he has remained largely unknown, his work unacknowledged.

Old left a legacy of war art that speaks for itself. His portraits (by Old's
reckoning he did over a thousand during captivity) of ordinary men surviving
extraordinary circumstances, are treasured by the families who have inherited
them. Like this one, painted quickly one night in September 1945 in Rangoon

'A drunken British paratrooper' Rangoon, September 1945, watercolour by Ashley George Old (© *courtesy the Bartholomew family*)

after liberation. It captures a moment during an evening spent with a British paratrooper who Old, and his artist friend Philip Meninsky, came across while eating at a small Chinese restaurant in the war-ravaged city.

Old gave this painting to his 'Sweet Ruth' (this was how he always referred to his friend Ruth Bartholomew) sometime in 1980 with the following note, in which he had handwritten a description in block capitals, littered with frequent underlining and decorative sun rays around certain words (here in bold) for emphasis, on paper torn from a reporter's jotter. He explained how and when the watercolour was done and most particularly how it should be viewed. The note reads:

"IT WAS PAINTED IN RANGOON … <u>VERY FAST</u>, IN THE EARLY HOURS OF THE MORNING, IN THE HOME OF 'ALFRED' OUR (MENINSKY AND MINE) VERY GREAT YOUNG CHINESE FRIEND.
RANGOON HAD BEEN BOMBED, THERE WAS <u>NO</u> GAS OR ELECTRICITY. IT WAS PAINTED BY <u>ONE</u> CANDLELIGHT. SO, IF YOU WISH TO SEE ITS <u>VISUAL</u> **REALITY** <u>TAKE IT INTO A BLACK ROOM</u> & <u>PLACE JUST ONE LIT CANDLE TO RIGHT OF SITTER AND ABOUT 3 TO 4FT AWAY</u>, & BEHOLD – YOU SHOULD SEE THAT BLOOD RED COLOUR <u>LOOK</u> <u>LIKE</u> **LIVING** <u>FLESH</u>.
THIS IS <u>THE</u> PERFECT EXAMPLE OF WHY PICTURES SHOULD REALLY BE SEEN IN THE LIGHT THEY WERE OBSERVED, AND PAINTED IN.

YOU CAN NOW BETTER UNDERSTAND WHY BIG ART
EXHIBITIONS MAY BE UNFAIR TO SOME PAINTERS
BECAUSE THEY ALL GET ABOUT THE SAME KIND OF
LIGHTING.
THE SITTER WAS NOT MENINSKY BUT A TINY BRITISH
PARATROOPER – A <u>COMPLETE</u> <u>STRANGER</u> TO US. ALL
NIGHT THE DRINKING WENT ON – FIRST A TINY WHISKY
THEN A TINY CHINESE TEA, REPEATED INDEFINITELY –
THE TEA WAS TO KEEP US SOBER, <u>&</u> <u>IT DID</u>.
2 LOVELY LITTLE CHINESE SERVANT GIRLS, 11 YRS OLD,
KEPT BRINGING US THE DRINK – IT WAS OUR FAREWELL
PARTY – ALL FREE…
… REGARDING THE SIGNATURE [written in Chinese] – I
WROTE IT – <u>35 YEARS AGO</u> … THE FIRST LINE IS MY
SURNAME, THE SECOND RANGOON, THE 3RD LINE, THE
YEAR (FULL OF ADJECTIVES AND NOUNS)."

Through this book, and the Liverpool exhibition, LSTM has sought to locate
the whereabouts of more of these portraits, to create a virtual catalogue as a
tribute to the skill of George Old. In the canon of FEPOW art, Old's portraiture
stands as a remarkable example of the humanity of war and of endurance.
Portraiture was what he had wanted to go on to develop and perfect, once
liberated. But the ravages of his captivity, the demands he made of himself
to fulfil what was required of him, denied him that opportunity. He never
recovered from the psychological damage done by what he had witnessed and
recorded for over three years in the prisoner of war camps in Thailand.

As well as the medical art preserved by Moon, Old also left a vast private
correspondence of over 400 letters throughout his post-war life. These
handwritten letters were for Ruth, his lifelong confidante and friend. She kept
them, such was her regard for the writer and for the artist. This correspondence
gives an extraordinary insight into the blighted post-war life Old was forced to
endure, without the great love in his life, his art.

APPENDIX II

Family Recollections of Some of the Artists

Here are some personal recollections of FEPOW artists, by the people who knew them best. We were not in touch with all the families of the artists who featured in the enquiry, but we invited those we knew of to share some personal insights and reflections about their relative. The place names in brackets after the artist's name refers to the countries the FEPOW was held in during captivity.

BASIL PARRY 'AKKI' AKHURST (Singapore and Thailand), by his son David Akhurst

Dad was born 8 July 1920 in Heywood, Lancashire, and attended Heywood Grammar School with his younger brother, Cyril. After marrying Mary Johnson in 1945 they moved to West Kirby (in Wirral) for three years and then to Blackpool where he lived until his death.

Basil Akhurst 1939

First, he worked as a Fireplace designer for Sellars Fireplaces before setting up his own business as a Building Surveyor. During the 1950s and '60s he was a cartoonist for the Blackpool Evening Gazette.

Dad was very proud of his father, who was awarded the Belgian Croix de Guerre during WWI. This led Dad to enlist for the Royal Artillery in 1939. Dad weighed 16 stone but would return from captivity at just 8 stone. He would never talk about his war experiences, but I know he worked in the POW camp hospital and must have seen some horrendous things.

During the aftermath of the war Dad worked extremely hard – often 7 days a week – to establish his business and support his family, myself (David) born 1947 and Geoffrey (1949–2015). He died on 8 December 1989 aged 69.

STEPHEN CRIGHTON ALEXANDER (Singapore and Thailand), by his daughter Clare

Stephen Alexander was born in 1919 the youngest of eight children in a doctor's family in Clifton, Bristol. He had two years at Peterhouse, Cambridge before war was declared. Posted to the North Hertfordshire Yeomanry 135th Field Artillery, he reached Singapore shortly before the surrender, and from there he was sent to Thailand and the River Kwai. Six months after his return to England he joined the British Council and was posted to Colombia. While sailing to New York on the first stage of his journey he met his first wife Germaine Van de Wyck. They were married for 10 years and had four children. Apart from a London posting in the sixties, his working life was overseas – Medellin, Bogota, Tehran, Beirut, Hong Kong, Guyana, Barcelona, Caracas, Cyprus, Ankara and finally Madras.

Stephen wrote many interesting letters from abroad to his children, often filled with amusing illustrations. He was positive and enjoyed exploring new places

Stephen Alexander, 1940/41

and meeting new people. He was very interested in theatre and enjoyed all the arts and had a love of ancient parish churches. In retirement he returned to his roots and lived in Long Ashton near Bristol with his second wife Ruth. There he wrote his two books, *Sweet Kwai Run Softly* and *Foreign Strands*. He was very good at keeping in touch with his large family and old friends, many of whom had been with him on the Kwai. He had recovered well from his war experiences but never talked about them until later in his life and he found it difficult to show his emotions. He was always grateful to have survived.

HARRY BERRY (Singapore, Taiwan and Japan),
by his daughter Linda West

Harry Berry was not an artist, but he worked in partnership with Derek Clarke who was. Born in Islington, North London in 1916, he started his journalistic career on the London evening paper, *The Star* where he became a features' writer. He also played the piano in a dance band in his spare time. In April 1940, after only three months of marriage, Harry was called up, and served as a Gunner with the 5th Field Regiment in Malaya. Caught up in the Fall of Singapore, after a few months at Changi POW camp he was drafted to Taiwan, sailing on the hellship the 'England Maru. In 1943 he was sent to Japan, to Omori POW camp, near Tokyo. En route he met up with artist, Derek Clarke. The two became firm friends throughout their years at Omori. When Harry produced camp shows Derek designed the posters and programmes. They made a good team, helping to keep each other alive in appalling conditions.

In 1953 Harry joined British European Airways (BEA) and had a successful career in Public Relations. His POW diaries and letters were published posthumously in 2004, in *My Darling Wife. The true wartime letters and diaries of Harry Berry to Gwen 1940–1945*. As a tribute to their wartime and ongoing

friendship, and in memory of those who died in the war in the Far East, I also published (with his widow's permission) Derek Clarke's wartime autobiography, *No Cook's Tour*, in Japanese in 2019. Derek and Harry's friendship thrived until Derek's death in 2000. They never forgot their friends and comrades who fought, suffered and died in the Far East. Harry died in 2004.

DESMOND BETTANY (Singapore), by his son Keith

Born in Burnley, Lancashire in 1919, Des grew up the second of four children. At school he developed an interest in art and music but when he left he trained and worked as an analytical chemist in an artificial silk factory.

Early in 1939 he joined the Territorial Army and served in the 88th Field Regiment (Royal Artillery) as a Lance Bombardier in France and Belgium. He manned 25-pounder field guns, and after evacuation from Dunkirk was posted to southern England before being drafted to the Far East. He saw most of the major actions in Malaya prior to Singapore's capitulation in February 1942. Des recorded in art aspects of the outbound voyage, actions in Malaya and Singapore and his new life as a POW.

As a POW he kept spirits up by producing cartoons, some of which satirised his captors. He also became part of a production line making programmes for the many theatrical and concert parties. In contrast to much of the POW art which survives captivity, Des's work finds uplifting humour in the day-to-day existence of the POW. The spirit of light-heartedness helped Des and his mates keep a sense of optimism in the face of a brutal captor.

Not all his POW art survived the war.
A sketch book of political cartoons was
discovered by Japanese guards. Des
was required to explain this work, via
interpreters, to the Japanese commandant
and various senior officers. He was lucky,
in his words, not to have been given 'a short
haircut' as punishment. After the war, Des
studied at Leeds School of Art and was
appointed to teach art at a school in South
Shields. In 1958 he emigrated to Australia
with his wife and three young children. He
taught art in South Australia for many years, finally retiring as Acting Principal
of the South Australian School of Art in Adelaide in 1978. Des continued to
paint, and to teach informally, and enjoyed a fulfilling life. He passed away in
2000, at the age of 81.

GODFREY VERNON BIRD (Hong Kong), by his son Derek

My father was a very strong character, successful at school (Stonyhurst in
Lancashire) where he was captain of sport and deputy head boy. He trained
as an architect for seven years at the Royal Institute of British Architects
(RIBA) in London, during which time he joined the London Irish Rifles. He
left the London Irish with the rank of Captain and headed for the family firm of
architects in Shanghai and Hong Kong, Palmer and Turner (formerly Bird and
Palmer). His first job was to be the architect on site in Hong Kong for the new
Hong Kong Shanghai Bank building.

At the outbreak of war, he was conscripted to the HQ staff of General Maltby,
GSO3 Intelligence, with the rank of Captain, Royal Engineers. Following
the fall of Hong Kong, he was interned in Argyle Street Officers' POW camp
where he ran a 'service' communicating with agents on the outside, sending

Godfrey in Shanghai, 1934

and receiving news hidden in a hollow bolt on the garbage truck. This activity was eventually compromised and the GSO 1, 2 and 3 were taken in for questioning/torture. My father suffered what is now called 'waterboarding'. The other two (Lt Colonel Newman and Fl/Lt Ford) were executed by beheading and were posthumously awarded the George Cross, but my father survived to see the relief of Hong Kong. He was awarded the George Medal and returned to the UK where he worked as an architect for Courtaulds.

From John Warrack
[son of Godfrey Bird's close friend in captivity in Hong Kong, medical officer Captain Alexander Warrack RAMC]:

My only information re the artist, is my father's caption on the rear of the picture, 'My Bed Space' (Chapter 5, Figure 12), which says: *"The drawing was done by my friend Godfrey Bird. After I went to Japan Godfrey was taken out and tortured over the plans to get in touch with the British Aid Group in Chungking. Col. Newnham was shot. Godfrey survived. Newnham got the George Cross. Godfrey the George Medal. (The drawing was a birthday present)."*

He rarely talked about the picture, other than to always say *"my good friend Godfrey Bird"*.

When my father was transported to Japan, he did not know if he would ever see home again or Godfrey, because he knew of Godfrey's involvement with Colonel Newman, who was executed, and the links to the British Army Aid Group (BAAG, the paramilitary organisation run by British and Allied forces working behind enemy lines in southern China during the Second World War).

307

DEREK CLARKE (Singapore, Taiwan and Japan),
by Linda West, the daughter of Clarke's FEPOW friend, Harry Berry

Derek was born in 1921. He won a scholarship to Watford Art College but like so many other young men pre-war, he was not able to take up a place. After the fall of Singapore in 1942 and a brief spell at Changi POW camp, he was sent to Taichu, Formosa, which he described in his book as *"one long chronicle of disease, death, semi-starvation, heart-breaking toil and hopelessness."* In 1943 he was sent to Omori POW camp near Tokyo where he met Harry Berry. In the struggle to survive Derek and Harry entertained others with their songs, caricatures and sketches of characters in the camps (some of which were exhibited in the Imperial War Museum London in 2005).

His cartoons show defiance in the face of captivity: Derek sticking two fingers up at the Japanese (behind their backs!) and another (used as the cover image for his memoir) of his beating by a guard when Derek was caught smuggling stolen rice back to the camp. It was only by pilfering from the trucks they loaded and unloaded daily that men managed to survive the starvation rations. They knew, if caught, they would pay the penalty! After the war Derek

started working at Miller's studio in Watford painting pub signs for Benskin's a local brewery. He set up on his own as a commercial artist and later he and his wife Joan ran a studio at Thame, painting signs for among others, Ind Coope, Wadworth's and Samuel Smith. Derek illustrated his war time autobiography, *No Cook's Tour* (published posthumously by New Generation Publishing in 2004) which graphically describes the characters and scenes from captivity

Derek Clarke *circa* 1940

until liberation in August 1945. It was translated into Japanese and published in February 2019, his 25 fine and often humorous sketches of war time characters and scenes of Tokyo now able to be appreciated by the Japanese, in a very different city today.

Derek died in 2000 and is survived by his son who is married and has two daughters.

DONOVAN CLARKE (Singapore and Thailand),
by his son Michael and daughter Greta

Dad was a wonderful father, a quiet, kind gentleman who loved his pipe, smoking more matches than tobacco! Dad had time for us and we have lovely memories of the family playing games on a Sunday evening, and family walks and bike rides in the countryside. We had family holidays staying in a caravan at the seaside, travelling in the old Austin Seven.

A builder's labourer who became a self-employed painter and decorator, he always worked hard, had time for people and was well respected by his customers. He was a member of the Methodist Church and had a wonderful singing voice. His vegetable garden grew lots of fruit and veg and in the fifties, he also reared pigs and chickens. A salted pig was often hanging in the shed!

He painted on a Sunday morning. A member of the Oxford Art Society he often had his work selected for exhibition, with a mention in the newspaper which he enjoyed. His main media were watercolour and

Don Clarke 1941

pen and ink. He did landscapes but later while looking after Sybil, his wife, specialised in flowers and nature. He painted individual Christmas cards annually.

Dad didn't talk of his time as a POW when we were young – only to tell us that being a POW didn't mean he was a bad man. It wasn't until later in life that he began to speak of it. We do remember when he used to sit and shiver uncontrollably and Mum told us to leave him alone. This must have been bouts of malaria?

He didn't attend Remembrance Day services because he said he remembered his mates every day; he'd often say: *"I'll never ever forgive them – never, ever. I would, for what they did to me, but not for what they did to my friends!"*

JOHN FRANCIS CLEMENT (Singapore and Taiwan), by his son Frank

Dad didn't speak to us much about his time as a prisoner of war and managed to deflect any questions that we did have. We knew he had made several diaries with illustrations, but they weren't of great interest to the four of us as children growing up. However, some thirty years later one of his grandchildren,

Paul, wrote to him asking about his time as a prisoner of war and Dad made a tape recording, lasting 30 minutes or so, which provided a clear insight into his time not only as a FEPOW but also to his enlistment in the Army, through his training as a signalman, the ship journey to the Far East and his capture as a Japanese prisoner of war.

John Clement, 1946, after demob

The recording is a valuable reminder to us all of the six years out of dad's life that at first sight were fruitless. However, there does appear to be a positive side. On his return to civilian life, Dad decided he no longer wished to continue with his previous profession as an accountant. He felt that this required spending time looking backwards at accounts. He wanted to look to the future. So, he took the opportunity given to him after the war to retrain. He applied to Glasgow School of Art to study commercial art and follow his talent and passion.

Dad had an innate desire for 'lifelong learning' and instilled this in each of his children. As a family there was very little money, but Dad did what he could to support our sporting and creative interests. He firmly believed in the importance of education and the opportunities it could bring. Dad had high expectations of us all, supporting us throughout our learning and encouraging us to go on to further education at university or college.

Throughout his life Dad pursued his own continuous quest for knowledge. Despite having a chronic stammer, he changed career from a commercial artist to an FE College art lecturer. Even after retiring from teaching he undertook a degree course in the newly-introduced Open University programme.

After Dad passed away the full extent of his sketches and diaries came to light when my three sisters and I were clearing out some of his belongings. We decided to house them in the Mitchell Library in Glasgow where they can be accessed by anyone with an interest or undertaking research. The family wishes to express our gratitude to the staff at the Mitchell for taking such good care of Dad's possessions.

ERIC CORDINGLY (Singapore and Thailand),
by his daughter Louise

(Louise's father was not an artist, he was a Padre. He was given many items of artwork throughout his captivity)

When my father, Eric Cordingly, came home in 1945 he brought with him a typed diary of his experiences and also a wealth of artwork by fellow POWs: sketches, maps and paintings, particularly of the four chapels he'd created when he was an Army Padre. He obviously valued them because he had filed them away carefully until he died in 1976. But it wasn't until our mother died 35 years later that we opened the plastic bags which contained these treasures. It was a breath-taking discovery. The bright colours in the beautiful paintings and Christmas cards, the lively sketches and some jaunty cartoons, brought those lost years vividly to life before our eyes.

He didn't talk to us about his war experiences but every time we moved house he proudly displayed the carved wooden plaque of St George and the Dragon (made for his converted mosque in Changi POW Camp, Chapter 6, Figure 21) in the hall and we knew it meant a lot to him. He told us the story about how he'd lost it when they went up-country and was very indignant to discover that the Japanese guards had been using it as a dart board.

For our family these are priceless, tangible reminders of his experiences and we intend to keep them together as a family archive to pass on to future generations.

Padre Eric Cordingly, 1940

GEOFFREY SHERVILL COXHEAD (Hong Kong and Japan), by his son James

My father, Geoffrey Shervill Coxhead, was born on 10 May 1911 and brought up in Hinckley, Leicestershire, where his father was headmaster of Hinckley Grammar School. He studied geology and geography at Liverpool and London universities, and he had a natural talent for art.

He taught in Hong Kong before the war and was serving as a volunteer when he was captured on Stanley peninsular. He was transferred to Japan to work in a ship yard on the island of Innoshima. He was occasionally roughed up and suffered a fractured spine in a shipyard accident. He married Joan Gascoigne Osborne on 10 August 1946.

He never held a grudge against the Japanese and revisited the POW camp on Innoshima a couple of times after the war. Post-war my father was in education in the Colonial Service in Hong Kong, retiring as headmaster of Kings College School. He had a fantastic memory for quotations, poems and stories and was always cracking jokes or telling puns. He had a working knowledge in Cantonese and was Hong Kong chess champion twice. I remember learning to play chess using the hand carved chess set made by prisoners of war at Sham Shui Po camp in Hong Kong.

He loved hillwalking and passed this passion on to his children. He made many lifelong friendships as a POW including Raymond Smith and Terence Kelly. I'm still good friends with Raymond's son John Anton Smith! Dad died in July 2000.

Left: Geoffrey post-war; Right: Adam, aged 8, playing chess with Grandad, using the handmade chess set, 1996

313

WALTER SYDNEY CHARLES 'WALLY' CULLEN
(**Java and Sumatra**), by his daughters Jenny and Sara

Dad was the eldest of four boys, all of whom served in the Second World War and all returned home. He had a love of horses, riding from a young age with his father. He continued this interest after the war and horses were often a subject for his paintings.

Dad was a self-taught artist and records in his memoirs that while a POW he started doing cartoon sketches, while his friend Harold provided the captions. Needless to say, these cartoons weren't always complimentary to the Japanese and when guards found the drawings Dad received an 'almighty slap' for his efforts and the drawings were ripped up.

On returning home from the war, dad continued the family tradition as shopkeeper. His experience as a POW was not spoken about, and he had no interest in his war medals, which were only obtained later on his behalf by our brother. Jenny remembers seeing him have bouts of malaria when she was a child, wrapped in a blanket and shivering in front of the fire, but he never showed any anger or said any unkind words about his captors and it was only in later life that he wrote of his experiences.

Dad became a well-known local Kent artist, and regular exhibitor at art exhibitions throughout the county. His skill for cartoon drawing and caricatures was later put to good use, including illustrating a local book, a short story by Charles Dickens entitled, *The Tugg's at Ramsgate.*

Wally Cullen, 1940s

Once retired, he painted most days, and taught art to local art groups and a disability group.

He enjoyed the simple things in life, his family, his garden and his art. He was a man of great integrity, very loyal and always interested in people. He had that rare quality of being interested and interesting.

ANDREW ATHOLL DUNCAN (Java and Japan),
by his youngest daughter Jenny Grimshaw

Some people are made up of sharply contradictory truths. My father, certainly, was one such. Whether it was his POW experiences that made him the increasingly irascible, difficult and angry man he became in his later years, or whether actually it was precisely those terrible hardships which unlocked his enormous empathy and care towards others, I can't say; his Scottish Presbyterian father certainly had all the difficult aspects – and throughout his life – with none of my father's hardships to blame for them.

Whatever the truth, Dad relished his role as a family doctor, seeing it as his job to dispel fear and to protect every bit as much as it was to diagnose and to treat. He believed that depriving patients of hope was the cruellest thing any doctor could do. His patients, most of whom would have been astonished to discover how different he could be when among his family, loved him.

Like most children, I idolised my Dad, while understanding from a young age that he needed to be handled carefully to avoid his displeasure. One way 'in' was stamp collecting (one of his *many* collecting passions) and we sat together for hours

Atholl Duncan, Singapore, Sept 1941

at the dining table soaking off stamps and talking about the countries, and the nature and events depicted. He loved sharing knowledge and I learned a great deal with him. I was dreadful at maths and can still hear him patiently explaining *again* how some formula worked, always ending with *"get it now?"*

The images and writings he produced as a POW were technical in nature: meticulous drawings and plans of the camp and its huts, neatly written lists of the foods he desperately missed, pages of mathematical problems. His means of smothering his pain was immersing himself in fact and detail; he was no artist, and certainly no poet. But he was an instinctive rebel with a mischievous wit: one year he repeatedly sent formal sick notes to my sadistic form teacher, the reason given for absence always 'acute rhinitis'. Her name was Ryan. And he knew she'd 'get it'.

When dad died, my sister-in-law wrote: *"I have very clear and fond memories of your dad. I can picture him so vividly, walking up our garden path in his tweedy jacket with elbow patches, his gentle, kindly expression giving instant comfort and reassurance to over-anxious Mum and to me, her wheezy, gasping, asthmatic 7-year-old. Whenever we visited him in the surgery he would lean back in his chair – so at ease in his role – smile that lovely slow smile of his, with his elbows on the arms of his chair and his hands raised and clasped together."* This, above all, is how I remember Dad, too.

From Margaret (Jenny's sister): Dad was an engineer at heart who could make or mend virtually anything. He could never forgive the Japanese for the wanton neglect and waste of life that he had witnessed. It was the remarkable work done by POW doctors in captivity which left a lasting impression. He married Mum two months after arriving home and switched degree courses to study medicine, qualifying in 1950. He became a GP in Wirral in 1951.

In the early 1960s Dad trained as a volunteer civilian gliding instructor at RAF Sealand and spent 32 years teaching cadets at 2184 (Upton) Air Training Squadron the rudiments of flying. In 1973 his own flying days came to abrupt end when he was grounded following a mild heart attack. He died sixteen days after Mum, on 15 February 1997. It was the 55th anniversary of the Fall of Singapore, which seems a fitting coincidence.

HERBERT ELSEY (**Singapore and Thailand**), by Gaye Wolfe

In late 2018 I contacted Stewart Mitchell at the Gordon Highlanders' Museum, who told me this much about Elsey, the man who painted the portrait below that I inherited from my father, fellow FEPOW Peter Allen.

Herbert Elsey was born on 5 March 1917 and brought up in Huddersfield. He was one of many Yorkshiremen who enlisted with the Gordon Highlanders. He was a patient in Tarsao hospital camp in Thailand at approximately the same time, late 1943/ early '44, as my father Peter Allen. Interestingly, at the time of the fall of Singapore his local newspaper while reporting him missing also noted his artistic credentials as a 'former music hall artiste'.

Unfortunately, my father did not speak of Elsey or the sketch. However, I do know that Elsey's artistic abilities must have meant a lot to him as he kept the sketch on the wall in his office at Imperial College, London, where he was a Senior Lecturer and Researcher in Electrical Engineering.

Gaye Wolfe recalls her father, Peter Allen:
Dad was just 19 when he joined the Army in June 1939. He started his maths studies (for what was to be his future career) as a Far East prisoner of war (FEPOW) student of Changi prisoner of war camp's '18th Division University'. When he 'retired' from Imperial College he took a visiting Professorship at

Peter Allen 1940

Portrait of Peter Allen by H. Elsey, 1943/44

City University. My mother did not want the portrait (right, previous page) on display at home (probably due to the associated circumstances) and I later found it in his home desk. In 1994 in Singapore he spoke to an oral historian about his experiences as a FEPOW; he and I were in Singapore so that my father could complete research on the fate of fellow Royal Engineers, which he later published.[1]

In Thailand just before Christmas 1943 he was sent to Tarsao Hospital for a second time where he would have met Elsey. He was suffering from hepatitis (inflammation of the liver). But it was a pain in his knee that gave him what he later described as *"about the worst night"* of his life, before it burst open. It went septic and the tropical ulcer took months to get better. It's been suggested the portrait may have been a Christmas present. He mentioned the positive impact Colonel 'Weary' Dunlop made, arriving soon after Christmas and administering a cure for scabies that *"everybody was suffering from"*, which included an ointment made from truck grease and sulphur.

I know that my father would be pleased for this artwork to be used to communicate the FEPOW story, in honour of what his friends and comrades went through at the hands of the Japanese, especially those that did not return. The *circa* 1940 photo of my Father, newly enlisted, shows what a good likeness the portrait is, as well as highlighting the visible effects of the ill health he was suffering as a FEPOW. I only now realise how incredible it was that this picture was preserved and kept hidden from the Japanese. I hope that in time more information will come to light.

BASIL FERRON (Singapore and Thailand), by Steve Smith

(whose grandfather, Cecil Bertrum Lucas, was a fellow FEPOW)

Basil Ferron was Anglo-Indian perhaps from Ceylon, had black curly hair, and was a medical orderly. These are things my grandfather told me about him. He also said that Basil was quite small, had rather delicate features and that he took the leading lady roles in many of the camp entertainments. Basil had had access to paper as he was the medical orderly in camp. His pictures were hidden in the bamboo in the roof of a building.

My grandad was a lorry driver in the camp in Thailand and he would be sent out to get supplies. He would drop off any medical items to Basil and over time they built up a relationship. They would sometimes share stolen food, for example eggs; grandad said he would have cooked on the engine of the lorry.

On a visit to the UK soon after repatriation, Basil visited my grandad as he wanted to introduce his fiancée. He gave grandad all his artwork and asked him to look after them. He never returned so they stayed first with grandad before eventually coming to me.

And, from Emeritus Professor Sears Eldredge, in Chapter 7 of his e-book, *Captive Audiences: Captive Performances:*

> *"Basil Ferron, an Anglo-Indian who impersonated the movie star Dorothy Lamour, became the Harboured Lights' primary 'actress.' Pritchard described Ferron as 'a very small chap … slight … and could pass for a girl easily.'* Fergus Anckorn [the magician known as Wizardus] *saw him as 'a gorgeous looking Indian girl … flashing eyes and all the rest of it.'"*[2]

GEOFFREY BARLOW GEE (Singapore and Thailand),
by Jill Flemming, the daughter of Jack and Vera Mayne

(Geoffrey sketched this portrait for Jack of his young wife Vera from a photograph while both men were in Chungkai camp in Thailand).

When I was a little girl, I remember seeing the portrait of my mother hanging in the front room at my maternal grandparent's house. The front room was only used for special occasions. Although my grandmother never spoke about the portrait I believe it meant a great deal to her, especially as my mother died from multiple sclerosis in 1956 (aged 40), something she had lived with for many years. To my father this portrait was obviously special. It was copied from one of at least two photographs of her that he had taken with him to the Far East in 1941. Reading the letters that I have, they were a very loving couple.

Geoffrey
Gee, 1939

Vera, 1944

I did not connect the portrait with his captivity until the FEPOW research
conference in Liverpool in 2015, when Meg Parkes mentioned artists in
captivity and spoke about Geoffrey Gee. My husband Richard said, *"We have
one of his pictures hanging on the landing,"* and told me it was the portrait of my
mother. It is pleasing to have such a good likeness of her hanging on the wall of
the stairway and looking happy. I was only six years of age when she died, and I
only remember her being ill.

I am so pleased that my father and Geoffrey met whilst at Chungkai camp and
he was able to copy that photograph so beautifully. I will be forever grateful.

MAURICE GREEN (Singapore and Thailand), by his son Mike

My father was born 29 May 1916 in Curepipe, Mauritius, where his father
was a colonial policeman. The family returned to England in 1920 settling in
the Waterloo district of north Liverpool. In 1930 Maurice joined the Army
as a 14-year-old 'boy soldier' being educated and trained at Beachley Army
Apprentices College, near Chepstow. In 1934 he enlisted as a Sapper in the
Royal Engineers (RE). He married Doris Irene Rose in July 1940 and by 1941
he was Company Quartermaster Sergeant of 287th Field Company RE.

As part of the British 18th Division, 287th Company (which also included his younger brother) were drafted overseas, eventually reaching Singapore on 13 January 1942. They were immediately engaged in combat with Japanese forces in Malaya. The brothers were together on the 15 February the day of the British surrender, initially going into captivity in Changi POW camp. Maurice was sent to Thailand and his brother to Formosa and Japan. Both survived.

Like most returning Japanese POWs, Maurice suffered from the after-effects of many illnesses and injuries, including the loss of an eye and all his teeth. For the rest of his life he had many recurring bouts of malaria and severe nightmares. He remained in the Army post-war, serving in the UK and Gibraltar. His final posting was as Regimental Sergeant Major, Singapore Engineer Regiment and for his service he was awarded the Meritorious Service Medal. He retired from the Army on returning to the UK in 1960.

In civilian life he worked in Liverpool companies, as well as serving as a special constable becoming Superintendent and second-in-command of Merseyside's Special Constabulary.

He was a member of Bootle Masonic Lodge since the 1930s, in retirement his involvement became considerable, eventually serving the Lodge an unprecedented three times as its 'Worshipful Master'. This and his great interest in the Far Eastern Prisoners of War Association, kept him busy. Although in later life he talked about his POW experiences he bore no great ill-will towards the Japanese in general. He spoke highly of

Maurice Green just disembarked
SS *Tegelberg*, Liverpool
11 October 1945

several individuals who had shown kindness but expressed hatred for others and, like many FEPOWs, had a strong dislike of the Korean guards.

My personal memories of my father are of a man with a very positive attitude to life, extremely smart in appearance and bearing. He was organised and precise in everything he did, polite, considerate and well-respected. A true gentleman. He and Doris celebrated their 60th wedding anniversary in July 2000; a month later Maurice died, aged 84 years.

LIEUTENANT COLONEL A. A. JOHNSON MC,
4th Suffolk Regiment 18th Division (Singapore and Thailand),
by his daughter Wendy Bird

(NB Lt Col. Alec Albert 'Ack Ack' Johnson, born in May 1897, was not an artist, but he encouraged many who were and who arrived in his camp in Thailand to use their skills to record his collections of flora and fauna)

My first clear memory of my father, Lt Colonel A. A. Johnson MC of the Suffolk Regiment, was when the Post Office boy came on his bicycle to tell my mother that my father was 'Missing Presumed Dead' during the battle of Singapore Island. About three weeks later another telegram arrived saying he had been injured and was a prisoner of war. News then was very sparse indeed, so much of the following was what I learnt in retrospect. I do know now that the played cricket with, or against, G. W. Swanton while he was in Singapore. That would have pleased him.

When he arrived home, I understand that he talked non-stop for two days and then would never speak about the horrors again but did have nightmares for very many years and frequent bouts of malaria.

White Coolie by Ronald Hastain was published in 1947 and gave a very interesting account of Camp 226K (now I understand called Johnson Camp) in his book. The fighting was now over but conditions were dreadful. It seems that AAJ felt that it was very important that POWs should be kept busy and as well as possible. Cholera and other tropical diseases were rife. Much time was spent building

shelters and improving conditions in the camp. Kersey, who had been father's batman in India and China in the 1930s found my father and asked to be his batman again. Later, when the camp was much improved, he was instrumental in building my father's orchid house and many POWs collected 'orchids for the colonel'. Meanwhile, AAJ was collecting butterflies which he somehow stored in a tin box. Kersey also played an important part in organising and taking part in the concerts and other entertainments.

When the war ended AAJ spent some time in hospital in Rangoon where he showed the butterflies to Lady Mountbatten (Chapter 3, Figure 9). He was in one of the last ships to arrive back in Liverpool. Back in the UK, AAJ was put in charge of various German POW camps where he encouraged the inmates to keep busy. I have a picture of sea eagles and a beaded fire screen of a sunflower that were made for him by POWs.

SERGEANT JACK KEMP (Singapore and Thailand), by his daughter Jill Upcraft

Being born in 1939 and just six and a half years old when I first met my father, I will never be quite sure what are true memories and what I was told as time passed. I do know that my father came from generations of fishermen at Lowestoft in Suffolk. Also, that he was Head Boy at his school, and on leaving had been given a junior reporter's job on the *Lowestoft Journal*.

Like his brothers, at the outbreak of war he joined the services. Some went in the navy but Jack and his younger brother joined the Army. My mother told me that after Dunkirk local children were evacuated from coastal towns and we moved to her sister's pub The Duke of Cambridge in Plumstead. Dad was

given compassionate leave in June 1941 on the death of his youngest brother Ken who was killed in action. His last visit was his embarkation leave 14 Nov 1941, then not to be seen again for four years.

My first sight, in January 1946, was of a little yellow man covered in tropical ulcers and suffering from malaria. In his hand he was holding a banana, something I had never seen before. He helped in the pub for six or seven months before he found a job as a clerk in Woolwich docks. Later, he got a job in the drawing office of Siemen's Engineering in London. It was not long after that we all moved back to Lowestoft. He again got a job working in the drawing office at Brooke Marine on the construction of Russian trawlers.

He was always a quiet person, never talking about his prisoner of war days. He was happy drawing posters and cartoons for people, as a hobby. But he never told anybody about maps and the butterflies, moths and flowers he painted, or anything else that happened in the prison camp.

After his wife's death he came to live with us at Southwold. At that time my husband Frank was working for the Japanese company Sanyo and had several Japanese mates. Jack could still speak to them in Japanese and was happy to take many a whisky and soda from them.

Jack died in May 1990 loved by all who knew him. He never complained about anything and found life too short to argue with people about religion and politics.

MAURICE HENRY KINMONTH RAF Medical officer flight lieutenant, No 242 Squadron

Our father's character bore the marks of two strong influences; his Roman Catholic family and the Japanese POW camps.

Maurice was the second of four children. His father, a General Practitioner in Co. Clare, Ireland, moved the family to London (1921) to escape the troubles. His sisters said Maurice was sensitive and artistic; he studied Medicine at St Thomas's, with his elder brother, both becoming surgeons.

Maurice married Stella (1947), had Fred and Ann Louise (1949 and '51) and moved to Leicester (1952) as Consultant plastic surgeon, where Katherine and Patrick were born. I remember him as relentlessly cheerful and active; skilled in reconstructive hand and burns surgery, sailing, shooting wood carving and salmon fishing. He nursed Stella at home in her final years. Everyone admired a full life lived despite a stint in hell.

Maurice said little of this until retirement. Stella spoke of his nightmares. Maurice told us amusing tales of camaraderie, chess and bridge, fishing competitions, carving, and hidden radios. Captured March 8th 1942 in Java (Bandoeng) he worked in POW hospitals and camps at Tjimahi and Batavia, operating with ingeniously devised instruments and great commitment; he once donated his own blood while operating on a haemorrhaging patient.

On release in August 1945 Maurice weighed 8st 6lb and had just been ordered to dig his own grave. We still have the small oak box he carved 'in the jug' and his oak leaf for being 'mentioned in dispatches'. We are proud of his survival.

Ann Louise for the Kinmonth family
August 2019

Maurice Kinmonth, sailing.

FRED MARGARSON (Singapore and Thailand), by his son Rod

Fred was born in Grimsby on 20 April 1918. He had no formal art training but was adept at sketching. After leaving school he started a plumbing apprenticeship before the war intervened and he joined the RAF, becoming a Flight Sergeant with 232 Squadron. In November 1941 he married Yvonne Smith shortly before being sent overseas. Captured at the Fall of Singapore he was sent to Thailand where he worked on the building of the Thai–Burma railway. For a while he ran the workshops at Chungkai Hospital camp and could make all manner of surgical instruments and equipment needed by the doctors.

After repatriation he found adjustment very difficult and it took quite some time for him to get his sense of humour back. In March 1946 he set up a plumbing business in Grimsby, teaching himself about heating systems. He took on an apprentice and very soon he employed several time-served plumbers. He had the reputation locally for solving heating & plumbing problems that others could not solve. The company is still trading as Fred Margarson Ltd and is run by his grandson.

He enjoyed sailing and bought a 4-berth boat which he navigated to Holland from England, and back. He loved motorbikes having raced at Cadwell Park before the war. In the 1960s he spent three years with his son Rod, putting together a Velocette 250 MOV. He despised the Japanese and would never knowingly buy anything made in Japan. It took him a long time to talk about his experiences and then

Fred Margarson, Ouston, summer 1941

he never really went into the atrocities at any great length. He did not suffer fools gladly but had a fabulous sense of humour, being an excellent joke and story teller.

He was a well-respected businessman and in later life became a Freemason. He and Vonnie had one son and were happily married for 59 years. Fred died on 8 December 2000 aged 82.

GEOFFREY CHARLES MUNTON,
by his daughter Sally and son Andy

Sally: Born on 3 November 1918, Sapper Geoffrey Charles Munton served in the 560 Company Royal Engineers. During his time as a FEPOW he made dozens of drawings and I recently deposited his whole archive with the Imperial War Museum. Goodness knows how he got the lot home, since retribution was swift and brutal if prisoners were found with pencils and paper, and my father said he frequently buried his belongings.

Interestingly these are mainly images of home – portraits of Churchill, George VI, plans and drawings for a dream house he would like to build, self-portrait and portraits of friends and film stars of the day. Images of home too, e.g. Ely Cathedral, an old-fashioned Lincolnshire signpost (where he lived), a drawing of the company motif, and a mat, made from dyed bits of wool and cloth and embroidered from the drawing design. That said, as he was involved with the building of the Changi Lychgate, there is a sketch of that and the burial ground too, and a map of Singapore from 1942/3.

Geoffrey Munton, 1939

My father, by some miracle, finally made it home after six months' convalescence at a Red Cross Hospital in India, though he was plagued by consequential ill-health and nightmares for the rest of his life. He died on 19 August 1993.

From Andy: My father was born in Greetham near Oakham in Rutland, where his father was a stonemason (he also worked on the great North Road). They moved to Cranwell in Lincolnshire when he was a small boy (about seven years old) and this is where he spent his childhood. Although he did well at school financial pressures meant he left school when he was 14 and followed his father into the building trade – by 1936 at the age of 17 he was foreman working with building contractors developing the rapidly expanding RAF Cranwell.

He joined the Royal Engineers in 1939 and he was in such poor health by the end of captivity it was December 1945 (some 4 months after VJ day) before he arrived back in the UK. A recently published biography of former medical officer, Captain Bill Frankland (*From Hell Island to Hay Fever*) – he was the camp doctor who twice saved Dad's life – contains an extended section 'meeting an old friend' where Bill recalls his memories of my father in the camp highlighting Dad's ability to overcome and survive the most catastrophic health problems.

On his return to the UK his health remained poor for some time with malarial attacks and rheumatoid arthritis. He later recounted the lack of understanding he and many FEPOWs faced when they got home. Within weeks of his return his former employer, Hoskin's the builders, were pressurising him to return to work, implying that he was malingering by taking time-out. He decided at that point he has had enough of answering to authority and would be his own boss. By 1947 he started in business with himself as the bricklayer and his friend as labourer. He married in 1949, moved to Digby village where he built his own home. Over the next 26 years he built up his own building and international haulage business (which at its peak employed 120 people).

In 1973 he sold the haulage business to P+O and in 1975 had a serious heart attack and had to wind down his business. In his retirement he opened up more and more about his experiences as a FEPOW.

REGINALD NEWMAN (Singapore and Borneo),
by his daughter Janet Fursier

Reginald Newman was my father and I was so privileged to have such an inspirational role model. He was born in Newport, Monmouthshire on 15 July 1918. Divorce soon followed, and his mother moved her family to Cardiff, near her younger sister. Her brother-in-law ran a successful general building works company and became the 'replacement father' to Reg and his brother. His influence on Reg was enormous and engendered a 'can do' attitude from an early age.

After leaving Cardiff High School for Boys he joined the Civil Service in 1936, working in the Ministry of Labour. A surprising choice perhaps as I knew him as a very practical man (or was this the result of his captivity?). Following conscription into the Army on his 21st birthday, he manned anti-aircraft guns on the south coast and then, as a newly-commissioned officer, was drafted to the Far East, ostensibly to defend Singapore. But Singapore fell whilst they were still at sea, so they were diverted to Java. A severe bout of malaria and a narrow escape, courtesy of his men, from a failed defence of Kalidjati airfield, contributed to his war time experiences. Failing to be rescued from Java as promised, they were ordered to surrender. Thus, began almost four years of captivity, in Tangjong Priok, Changi jail in Singapore and approximately three years in Kuching, Borneo, during which he rose to the rank of captain.

Post-war he married the sister of a school friend. He had returned to the civil service and gained promotions up to manager of a region of mid-Wales by 1958. He never mentioned his war time experiences to me and I only learned later of his nightmares in the early years of his marriage. As a child I was never allowed to say 'I can't do' anything. His mantra was that 'you didn't know until you tried, and if you fail, try again!' He was very supportive, kind, hard-working; he could be quick-tempered but was always ready to forgive and admit if he was wrong or had made a mistake. He had a great sense of humour and was always prone to teasing in a gentle, humorous way.

He joined the long-running Newtown Amateur Dramatic Society as an actor, stage designer and general factotum. Later as chairman, he instigated the

purchase of an old church school, designing alterations to the lay out and manufacture of the stage and raked seating. Completed in 1968/69 this remains his main legacy, the Powys Theatre in Newtown. Sadly, he died very suddenly in 1972, aged 53.

In 2009 the society staged a comedy written by Reg whilst he was a POW to honour him and to celebrate 75 years of the society's existence. He was highly respected in the local community and many people in the town still speak of him with affection despite it being almost 50 years since his death. His legacy lives on as I am now Chairman of the Dramatic Society.

WILLIAM 'BILL' 'NOSHER' NORWAYS (Singapore and Thailand), by his son Toby

Bill Norways was taken prisoner by the Japanese in Singapore when the British surrendered on 15 February 1942. He began his captivity in Changi where he taught advertising and art in the Changi 'University'. After spells in various work camps, he was transported to Thailand in May 1943 as part of H Force. Bill worked on the railway throughout the worst of the 'speedo' campaign, where he contracted cardiac beriberi, bronchitis, malaria, and dysentery. He was returned to Singapore in April 1944 and spent the remainder of his captivity in Selerang and Kranji hospital camps. His artistic skills were utilised by the camp medics to sketch records of tropical diseases. Upon liberation, he was shipped on the SS *Tegelberg* to Liverpool, docking in October 1945.

On his return to England, Bill resumed his career in advertising, achieving several senior positions, including creative director at McCann-Erickson and becoming a board member of C.J. Lytle Advertising. He took early retirement

in 1982 and moved to Cornwall with his third wife Sonja. He died from lung cancer in September 1986.

Like many FEPOWs, Bill rarely talked of his wartime experiences. Unusually, however, he bore little animosity towards the Japanese, preferring to blame 'war' as the true evil. Bill's attitude was influenced by his early days of captivity in Singapore, where he struck up a friendship with one of his Japanese guards, Kameo Yamanaka. The guard would share his food rations and smuggle Bill pencils to continue his artwork. The two men corresponded after the war, between Cornwall and Tokyo.

In 1983, three years before Bill's death, he wrote to Yamanaka enclosing the following poem:

> *Our world decreed*
> *That we should meet*
> *As enemies,*
> *Without a common tongue;*
> *But, prompted by*
> *An even greater Power,*
> *Our hearts conversed*
> *And softly spoke of Peace.*
> *Dear God,*
> *Who Brothers made of us,*
> *Touch all men's souls*
> *So Mankind may be thus!*
> *Kameo Yamanaka – Bill Norways*
> *Singapore 1942*

Bill's letter concluded: 'Please let our children, and their children, and their children, preserve our friendship for all time.'

In 2015, Bill's son Toby started a Ph.D., revisiting his father's letters and over 200 pieces of artwork that Bill managed to bring home from the Far East. He located the Yamanaka family and flew out to meet them on their fruit farm outside Tokyo. He discovered that Yamanaka had died many years previously, though Bill's former guard had engraved the poem in granite on the Yamanaka family shrine.

ALFRED NOWELL HAMILTON PEACH (Java),
by his daughter Trish Groves

Our father's love for birds, captured in his photos and in his collection of antiquarian books, was beautifully described in this abridged piece in *British Birds (1978)*.

On board MV Cilicia L–R S/Ldr John Stewart Tupholme(pilot), W/Cdr Alan Stanley Giles (padre), Fl/Lt Basil Arnold Stoll, Fl/Lt Maurice Henry Kinmonth (MO), **Fl/Lt A. N. H. Nowell Peach (MO)**, S/Ldr John Lillie, Fl/Lt Frederick Alistair Forbes (MO), Fl/Lt Patrick Joseph Connolly, W/Cdr William Trefor Hugh Nichols. *(Photo courtesy estate of Nowell Peach)*

"… Nowell's notes told me that he qualified as a doctor of medicine at Bristol in 1937 and became a Fellow of the Royal College of Surgeons in 1948, but carefully omitted the period spent in a Japanese prisoner of war camp that must have been pretty grim yet did not sour him.

He is now in general practice in Horsham with a surgical appointment. Anyone who has seen him disentangle a small bird from a mist-net cannot fail to agree that neurosurgery is the poorer. I have long had the impression that patients are admitted to his list only if they agree to tell him about any nests suitable for photography.

In the field he is not only an indefatigable worker and tireless erector of difficult hides, but is a most cheerful companion who, while contributing his fair share of blasphemy about failures, seems able to bring home more good results than expected from few opportunities. He has been a valued member of the Zoological Photographic Club for many years, and his portrait of Tengmalm's Owl is, I think, one of the loveliest bird photographs ever taken.

In one long session in a hide, Nowell became aware of an increasing state of alarm of a hoopoe which refused to go down into the nest. He was forced to take a step which all conscientious bird photographers are loth to do: he got out of the hide and found that a large snake had entered the underground nest. Violent action on Nowell's part resulted in the regurgitation of two very bedraggled youngsters. One was paralysed and seemed beyond hope. After some weeks of forced feeding in an aviary both recovered and bred two years later."

(M.D. England, *Brit Birds* 1978 71:258–66, abridged by Trish Cooper)

RICHARD 'DICKIE' PHILPS (Java and Haroekoe),
by his daughter Vicky Taylor

Frank Richard Philps was my father. I have two brothers. He was talented and innovative, a devoted husband for 54 years and a caring father. Always resourceful, he lived life to the full and could not tolerate time wasters.

On returning after the war he was awarded the MBE (Military Division) in 1946. His intention was to continue his career as a surgeon, having qualified

MBBS immediately before the war, but was so debilitated by severe malnutrition and TB that this became impossible. He studied for his DPH (Diploma in Public Health) and qualified in 1947.

Dickie Philps in 1940

Following a thoracoplasty (operation to remove ribs) he obtained his MD in 1952. He became a pathologist and leading cytologist, winning many accolades. He strove all his life to do the best possible and expected his children to do the same. He was a strict disciplinarian, would not tolerate food waste and expected all of us to use our time wisely.

When ill health forced his retirement in 1973, he devoted his time to photographing and filming wildlife and wrote a children's book *Watching Wildlife*. He made several wildlife films for the BBC, being awarded their Nature Film Prize and the Council for Nature's Film Prize[1].

When no longer managing to carry his heavy photographic equipment, he set his mind to watercolour painting and woodwork. He exhibited at the Royal Institute of Painters in Watercolour in London, and had his paintings hung by the Federation of British Artists. He made several tables.

He didn't mix socially with former FEPOWS, apart from a couple whom he had befriended, one of which was Leslie Audus with whom he worked while in the Spice Islands. He never spoke to us of his experiences during the war, having written them down on his return and subsequently published in *Prisoner Doctor*.

A much-loved amazing man.
Richard Philps died on 16 October 1995.

---

1 Editor's note: see Philps' film, made for the BBC 1 in 1977, 'The Magic of a Dartmoor Stream' which documented kingfishers and other wildlife that inhabited the banks of the River Lyd in Devon: https://www.youtube.com/watch?v=iHkF9glPQ9o

NORMAN HICKEY 'FREDDIE' POWER (Java and Japan),
by his daughter Maddy and son Justin

Freddie married Audsley Knowles Cullen in February 1949 in Coventry. He'd first met Audsley, a New Zealander and a Red Cross occupational therapist, when he was hospitalised in New Zealand after his release from captivity in September 1945, prior to his return to the UK in 1946.

Their children – Charlotte, born in 1950, Madeleine in 1951 and brother Justin in 1958 – all remember Freddie as very easy going: *"We wouldn't have been aware of any immediate 'post war' problems and our childhoods were not coloured by his experiences."*

He was very amusing, didn't always take life too seriously and was very involved in any theatricals staged in Zentsuji POW camp in Japan. *"He sometimes talked about the war, usually when he had a couple of gins inside him, and always regarded his fellow Zentsujians as the lucky ones."*

He forgave the Japs on the basis that they were savages who didn't know what they were doing (but detested the Germans because they were a Christian nation who did). He was a very heavy smoker and used to relate the story from captivity of swapping a rarely acquired pig's trotter, which he had won by pulling the long straw, for 20 cigarettes. Although starving, the thought of eating a pig's trotter was unbearable!

Freddie Power, summer 1946

Justin remembers: NHP was an amusing man, convivial and a great raconteur. While he didn't talk about his WW2 experience unprompted, he wasn't one of those that wouldn't discuss it at all, and if you asked he would certainly tell you about his time in captivity. After all the trauma it is surprising perhaps how undamaged he seemed to be. His health though had taken a hit, and the list of edibles that gave him grief seemed to grow as he got older. Fortunately, this didn't affect his consumption of gin, which he maintained at a level of enthusiastic moderation until his death. He carried on with his cartooning for special family occasions – notable birthdays, the passing of exams, and the births of grandchildren. His cards were much anticipated and added greatly to the celebration at hand.

Freddie died on 7 February 1992, in his 75th year.

DESMOND PYMENT (Java and Borneo), by his son Mike

It's a shame that the children of FEPOW inevitably say the same thing, *"I wish I could have talked to Dad about his experiences before he died"*.

Dad was a very modest quiet man and the war was rarely talked about. I probably found out more after he died, when I came across his drawings and letters – especially his letters home after he was liberated. They contained in equal measure, tear-jerking moments and his inexhaustible sense of humour. He loved drawing cartoons, and one of his letters home to his mother and father included a cartoon at the end of the letter, of dad being examined by an Australian Army

Desmond Pyment

doctor. The doctor had written 'BARMY' across Dad's condition paper, and Dad's caption was *"it took me a while to realise this meant British Army!"*

Dad was a forgiving man, and on one of the rare occasions that he spoke about those horrific times I asked him if he was bitter about the treatment he received from the Japanese. His reply was, *"what is the use of being bitter, it would only hurt me and would not change anything"*. The only mention of a regret was when I was racing motorcycles in the 1970s and he expressed sadness that the best bikes of that era were Japanese.

Dad eventually returned home in very bad shape suffering the effects of stomach ulcers and malaria. He returned to college and completed his studies to become an architect. He married Mum and moved to Reading where he raised my sister and I. He loved gardening, he would spend all his free time in our garden which had a field attached. He turned this field into an allotment and grew copious amounts of fruit and vegetables, filling the freezer and ensuring that nothing was ever wasted. I am sure this was a reaction to his time as a FEPOW.

We talk about pressure on us today. I cannot comprehend what those extraordinary men and women had to endure so that we can enjoy the freedoms we have, they must never be forgotten.

STANLEY RUSSELL (*Java and Sumatra*),
by his daughter Anne and his grandaughter Lizzie Oliver

Anne: May 2019 saw myself and my daughter Lizzie in The Hague to view my father's drawings held there. A long-held wish, how deeply satisfying it was to find ourselves on the plane on the way to Schipol Airport. From there to The Hague via train, through the agricultural lands of The Netherlands. And then the exciting walk to the Museum, taking pictures on arrival, standing with heart in mouth, knowing where my beloved Dad's drawings were at rest, and were I would for the first time see them for *real*. I describe this journey a little, because it is part of the story of how this need was met, how this expectation and desire to view his pictures of such a tortuous time, took place. How the feelings were building from the moment I left my home at 7.30am.

Perhaps I want to bring forward the intensity and focus of the adventure, resulting in more than ever I was expecting. As soon as I saw the instantly recognisable drawing style and scripts around them, it was as if my father was about to walk into the room. I wanted to hug them to me. However, we were left to view them quietly. Their importance became quickly evident in my emotions of respect and admiration, their immediacy hitting me as if they had been drawn but yesterday. Their accuracy in a few pencil strokes depicting the daily events of such a brutal life. To therefore not be ignored. I did not want to shelter myself from their impact.

Without this artwork we are left conjuring up, and probably hiding from, the realities of the resilience, the pain, the discomfort, the horrors that these brave men endured. With this artwork we are given full realistic knowledge. We can feel with them. Comfort we could not give at that time, is mentally given in our thanks at their efforts. Or that is how it is for myself. Gratitude comes from the artwork visions presented, that Dad and his comrades succeeded for us. They did not give up in their endeavours. Emotionally, it brought such an enormous sense of belonging to this man who, long before I was born, put his skills and effort to record his life as a soldier-prisoner.

Lizzie: My grandfather's experiences as a prisoner of war on the island of Sumatra were the original inspiration for my Ph.D. studies and subsequent book. During my research, I had the good fortune to meet the late Terry Hadoke. His uncle Patrick died in the sinking of the *Van Waerwijk*, 26 June 1944, whilst en route to the Sumatra Railway. Terry had been looking for information about his uncle's time as a POW, and it was he who discovered the treasure trove of artwork that my grandfather, Stanley Russell, created in Medan (1942–3). That artwork is now held in Museon (in The Hague) as part of a huge collection of items from the camps across the Dutch East Indies.

My conversation with Terry before he died was a prime example of why POW artwork remains so important today. He told me that my grandfather's pictures had helped him to understand what life had been like for his uncle. As much as he acknowledged the deprivation and the brutal manual labour that the men had carried out, Terry was looking for something else. Through the art, he had appreciated learning about the beauty of the natural landscape on Sumatra, the joy of Judy the dog and her reassuring presence among the men, and the characters who sang around the piano during camp concerts. Terry saw the comedy in the cartoons that my grandfather drew, and it brought him some comfort that his uncle Patrick shared the last days of his life with men who could find laughter in such darkness. It was by looking at my grandfather's artwork that the myriad threads of a deeper, human story had come to life.

By undertaking the dangerous work of recording the events that took place around them, FEPOW artists like my grandfather not only made it possible for us to understand a little more about this history. They shone a light on what resilience really means, the importance of looking after each other, and remembering to appreciate the simple things in life. I remain deeply thankful, and humbled, to have learned his story.

HARRY SILMAN (Singapore and Thailand),
by his daughter Jackie Passman

When my father died, he was not a fragile sick man of 94, but a kind, caring, wise, funny human being who was an integral part of all our lives. He was genuinely interested in people. Even on a casual level, while many of us listen to others with half an ear, Dad would ask pertinent questions and share our pleasure or give considered advice. He was a very good conversationalist and it was a pleasure to be in his company.

Dad cared about each member of his family, including, as he put it, everyone mad enough to have married into it. He asked searching questions so that he knew what all our various jobs entailed and would recognise the possible implications of current events on the work we all did. He derived tremendous pleasure from the achievements of his children and grand-children, and from the cuteness of his great-grandchildren. Our happiness was his happiness, our sorrows equally his sorrows. He had an open mind, embracing new ideas and technology with enthusiasm. He was totally fascinated by the power of the internet, and quickly understood that Google could find details on all medical problems however obscure.

Harry Silman, 1940

He could always see the funny side of life. I know his positive outlook and sense of humour helped him (and many others) to survive the war years. He made light of his wartime experiences to us children, joking about the hardships and privations as if they were mere inconveniences. It was quite a shock when we read his diary, to find out what really happened in this period of his life. Until the very last few months of his long life, I remember Dad as always smiling, quick with a pun or corny joke. He taught us how to laugh at ourselves. He died on 9 May 2005, aged 94.

RONALD JOHN 'JACK' SPITTLE (Singapore), by his son Brian

The clearest images I have of my father are of him hunched over a microscope in his study or wading into some pond, insect net bobbing about him, in search of specimens. He had a passion for natural history – an obsession more like, my mother said – dating from childhood.

During captivity he put it to good use by making notes on the birds at Changi and Kranji, publishing them in 1950 in the *Bulletin of the Raffles Museum of Natural History* in Singapore (https://lkcnhm.nus.edu.sg/app/uploads/2017/06/21brm184-204.pdf). It was a passion and discipline he sought refuge in after the war, throwing himself into his research, career and marriage, more or less in that order.

My early memories of my father are of a caring but emotionally distant figure. Aside from the gaunt appearance he was in relatively good physical shape on returning home. But he suffered a great deal from on-going anxiety, acute loss of concentration and sudden mood swings. He needed complete quiet at home and we moved house several times because of some or other noise irritant in the vicinity. As the only child I was presumably one of those irritants and once

Jack Spittle, late 1930s

I started school I was often shipped off to my grandparents during the holidays. In due course I was sent to boarding school.

After the war my father was lucky enough to build a career consistent with his passion, working as a river pollution prevention officer, first in Worcestershire and then in Devon. He resumed a long-term study of a heronry near Henley-on-Thames, which had begun during his teenage years and did not end until he was in his eighties; his POW notebooks include early drafts of the monograph he would complete fifty years later. He also participated in a number of entomological research projects including the mapping of insect life on the Isle of Rum for the Scottish Nature Conservancy. His own research on the aquatic ecology of Devon streams is now housed at the Plymouth Museum.

My father never fully recovered from his time in captivity though his nervous condition moderated somewhat. He rarely talked about his experience and as a child I was told never to ask him about it. But then a year or two before he died he started to talk to me about his time in Singapore. Clearly, the memories were still painful. And yet, he had no personal bitterness towards the Japanese. In his view, neither side had a monopoly of right or wrong.

Died 28 September 2004 (aged 90).

ERIC STACY (Singapore and Thailand), by his son Jeremy

My memories of him are as loving father (and loving husband to my mother), fully committed to his Christian faith. He was extremely reluctant to talk about the war.

He trained as a chartered architect and was 30 when the war broke out. He became a Lieutenant in the Royal Engineers, supervising the construction of pillboxes.

He arrived in Singapore just two weeks before it fell and when he was held captive in Changi POW camp he helped the chaplains to design and construct temporary churches, not just the building but the furnishing of them as well. He was in one of the parties sent up to complete the building of the Burma Railway at the beginning of the rainy season and spent eight months in the jungle.

The conditions were so appalling that only 50% of his force survived. After the war he moved to the Acoustics section of the Building Research Station in the UK and supervised projects including the sound insulation of schools under the flight path of Heathrow airport and improving the acoustics of the Albert Hall. He married and had two children and turned from painting to woodcarving in his spare time. He was also very involved in his local church and contributed both professional architectural advice and woodcarvings for the building. He rarely talked about his experiences as a prisoner, but when his grandchildren asked him to write down some memories for a school project he told them this story:

"One day in August 1945 we were told Japan had capitulated and we were free. We all stayed up late discussing the wonderful news, but when at last I went to bed I could not sleep because of a stomach pain which had come on

Eric Stacy in 1949

quite suddenly. The next morning, I joined the sick-parade queue, waiting in the hot sun for an hour to see the medical officer. He whisked me off at once to the operating theatre in our improvised hospital, having diagnosed acute appendicitis. That same day, within two hours of my 'coming to' after the operation, a medical orderly offered me a meat pasty, part of a first consignment from the Red Cross. It was the first meat I had tasted for nearly two years. Scrumptious! The doctor was horrified when I told him I had been given such solid fare so soon, but I thrived on it. I was soon on my feet and enjoying the new freedom to come and go as we pleased. The badly sick were soon flown out to better-equipped hospitals, but the moderately fit had to wait four or five weeks for ships to be assembled to take us home. In the meantime, we could go for a stroll or a swim or perhaps visit a warship in Singapore harbour. It was on board a British battleship that I had my first hot bath for 3½years!"

He died in 2004 aged 95.

FREDERICK STALLARD (Singapore and Taiwan), by his grandson Ben

Although I didn't see my grandfather a huge amount growing up, I remember he was always very jovial and chatty and loved spending time his family. I remember him as very religious and he went off to pray in the afternoon and always said grace. Later I learned that his faith was what saw him though and it continued to be into his old age. He wrote a note in his book to my mother '*my life depends on 3 F's – faith, family and friends*'.

Revd F. H. Stallard, *circa* 1941 pre-embarkation

I know he suffered nightmares for a long time and was insistent on finishing food at mealtimes – which he called a *"Stallard plate"*, but generally had a positive outlook post war. Being a priest, I think he found his work in camp obviously incredibly hard and tough, but in the end, it was the ultimate calling for him. I think he found comfort in the fact that he was actually useful to people who needed him most, at that time.

His drawings were of people and characters rather than the difficulties and traumas of prison camp. Having a creative outlet clearly helped him through these most difficult times. He died on 13 March 2003.

HERBERT 'BERTIE' UPTON (Java and Sumatra), by his son Richard

Bertie, my father, qualified as an architect in 1934 and became a Fellow of RIBA. In 1939 he was working for the Public Works Dept in Malaya and on 12 September that year Bertie joined the Malaya Royal Navy Volunteer Reserve (RNVR) and was gazetted Lieutenant on active service. He commanded a minesweeper – HMS *Rahman*.

In March 1942 HMS *Rahman* was sailing from Batavia to Colombo (Ceylon) when she was attacked by Japanese destroyers off Java. When it was obvious that

HMS *Rahman* was not going to escape, Bertie went down to the engine room to scupper the ship so that the Japanese would not get the magnetic minesweeping gear. He managed to get away from his ship but became submerged in the sea. On reaching the surface he could neither see nor hear and he believed himself dead until he thought to touch his face and found it completely covered by his uniform cap!

Herbert Upton

From 1942 to 1945 Bertie was a prisoner of war in Japanese prison camps. He was the senior officer of a draft of POWs in transit from Java to Sumatra in a Japanese prison ship, *Junyo Maru*, on 19 September 1944 when the ship was torpedoed by a British submarine. He toured the ship before it sunk and ordered the Japanese captain and guard commander to leave the ship which they did before it was sunk. Out of 2,000 British prisoners only 700 reached the shore. He was 'Mentioned in Despatches' for his distinguished service.

During his time as a prisoner in Tanjong Priok Transit camp north of Batavia (now Jakarta) he designed a chapel for the prisoners and designed and made two faux stained-glass windows. These windows still exist and can be found in the Anglican Church of All Saints in central Jakarta, where they have been in safe-keeping since being removed there in late 1943. They have been reproduced and are on display at the FEPOW Memorial Building at the National Memorial Arboretum in Staffordshire. The story of the chapel and windows is well documented on the LSTM and COFEPOW websites.

JOHN 'JACK' WILBYE BENSON WHITE (Singapore, Thailand and Burma), by his daughter Julie Aldridge

As with most children of FEPOWs I never heard my father talk about his experiences, apart from a few anecdotes about tricking their captors. My parents had several books written by former prisoners which I read when far too young – maybe 8 or 9, but we never discussed them. I did however see the sketches but did not understand the chronology of his time in captivity until I did research with the help of the Thailand–Burma Railway Centre

Jack White, 1940

(TBRC) in Thailand! It was particularly moving when I made the 'pilgrimage' to see the site of the Chaungauya camp through the metal fence of the Burma border.

My father was a quiet, diligent and very kind man, who did not express emotions easily. I have all the letters he wrote to my mother on the voyage out, and the 22-year-old who jumps out of the paper full of feeling, love, anxiety and ambition, really never came back. He wrote excitedly from Cape Town (en route to Singapore) where he had family, of emigrating there after the war, but he settled for a steady life in Southend which my mother found too narrow at times.

This life however was comfortable until they made the decision to travel to Singapore and Thailand with friends (a fellow FEPOW) to revisit the past. I can't remember when this was but probably around 1990. They never made it: he became physically ill with unexplained stomach trouble and dizziness. Medical investigations found nothing; it was clearly PTSD. He was referred to Combat Stress and had more than one respite visit to their centres – with art therapy. However, he became frailer, withdrawn and unable to eat. He saw doctors who diagnosed dementia, which he certainly did not have, and the medication they tried made him even more ill. In his last few weeks he was emaciated and depressed, and he eventually died of pneumonia on December 10, 2001 at the age of 82.

A small point: he could not bear to waste food, and always needed to know there was enough to eat in the house. My mother put this down to the years of starvation. She never forgave the government for refusing sufficient rations to help returning POWs to recover!

I started research with one of my oldest friends whose father was also on the Railway – we lived very close to them, but neither of us believes that the two men ever talked together of their experience.

WILLIAM CARTHEW WILDER (Singapore and Thailand), by his son Anthony

Dad was a quiet, shy man, but this was underpinned by a tenacity of purpose – a stubborn determination to achieve whatever he set out to do. His schooldays taught him little except how to survive adverse circumstances and this proved useful in his POW experience. He also had a great sense of humour, and this ability to see the funny side of almost anything was another mechanism for survival.

His teaching was characterised by a strict attention to sound drawing, tempered by a kindness that needed few words. He continued to teach at Culham College of Education near Abingdon until the college closed (in 1977) when he was 62. After a brief period of school teaching he taught adult education classes at Sunningwell School of Art until he was nearly 80.

My mother, Joan, was also an art teacher and while they were very different characters, they balanced each other well and were totally dedicated to each other. Their painting work was extensively exhibited locally especially through Reading Guild of Artists and in projects for Wallingford Museum. As Dad's fiancée, Mum had very little news of his circumstances after he was taken prisoner and what little information she did receive was often 18 months out of date.

In the early 1980s, Dad returned to Singapore and Thailand travelling along the railway he had helped to build. This time Mum was with him. He said it was good to *"see it all from the right side of the fence"*! While he never forgot his comrades who didn't return, he refused to carry that burden of bitterness. Over the years he taught a number of students from Japan. He always treated them with unfailing courtesy and would not blame the next generation. I am sure all this helped him to lead a long and fulfilled life.

Will Wilder, 1940s

THOMAS 'TOSS' WILSON (Singapore and Thailand),
by his sons Tom and Liam and daughter Maura O'Hara

Toss was a much-loved husband and father who was very caring, patient and down-to-earth. He did not talk about his war-time experiences, not to his children anyway, and we do not know what he may have told his wife Nan – it was certainly never discussed in our presence. We were just so thankful that he survived and came home at all, even though painfully thin. He and Nan purchased a house in Portstewart (Northern Ireland) and this became the family home for the next 43 years.

He gradually regained weight and strength, enjoyed a game of golf, and started to integrate in the local community. But for many years he would not purchase any goods manufactured in Japan, for understandable reasons (although his attitude even to this did soften in later life, when he bought a Japanese car!).

Both he and Nan had loved their life in Malaya before the war, so when he was asked to go back in 1946 and help with the restoration of civilian government, it was no surprise that he agreed to do so. Unfortunately, this did mean that we three children did not see as much of our parents as most other children would, as they were only able to return on extended home leave for about six months every third year, although Nan usually stayed for longer after Toss had returned to Malaya.

Toss had a great sense of duty and would go out of his way to help others. This manifested itself again later, after his retirement, when he volunteered to work in a local Health Centre in Portstewart twice weekly and was elected to the local Coleraine District Council where he served for 8 years. He also served on the Northern Health and Social Services Board.

Thomas 'Toss' Wilson, Malaya, 1933

He continued to enjoy his golf, photography (he possessed a movie camera from the late 1930s) and started going to adult art classes. When later his wife Nan's health started to deteriorate he cared for her at home, apparently having vowed to himself to make amends to her for all the time – 21 months – when he was in captivity and she did not know whether he was alive or dead.

Notes

Introduction

1   Lancashire Infantry Museum, Fulwood Barracks in Preston, home to the FEPOW archives of the 2ⁿᵈ Btn The Loyal Regiment. *NIB* is just one of the highlights of the Lancashire Infantry Museum's collection.

2   T. Bowden, *Changi Photographer* George Aspinall's Record of Captivity, Times Editions (1997).

3   S. A. Eldredge, *Captive Audience/Captive Performances*, Ch.1 'in the bag'. https://digitalcommons.macalester.edu/thdabooks/22/

4   J. B. Chalker: Interview with M. Parkes (2007) LSTM records.

5   J. and S. Dewey, *PoW Sketchbook, a story of survival* (2014), p. 18.

6   Dr. Khan's PhD thesis title – K. Khan, 'Psychiatric Morbidity amongst ex-Far East prisoners of war more than thirty years after repatriation,' PhD thesis (University of Liverpool, 1987).

7   www.captivememories.org.uk

8   Birds of Malaya went into two further editions post-war, which Molesworth also illustrated. The only copy of the First edition is held by Madoc's daughter.

9   See www.singingtosurvive.com for more about the Vocal Orchestra music created from memory by Dryburgh and Norah Chambers.

Chapter 1: Documenting Captivity

1 IWM Art LD 7342 1–22.
2 Programme shown to Meg by Roger Jackson at a talk she gave at Blackpool Central Library in February 2016. Reunion held at Norbreck Castle Hotel Blackpool from 15–17 June 1956. Roger is the son of Charles William Jackson 88th Field Regt, from Blackpool, and has a large archive of memorabilia left to him by his father.
3 A British scientist with a flair for theatricals at Nakom Paton, who had been a seasoned producer-director in Kuala Lumpur pre-war; see S. Eldredge, *Captive Audiences/Captive Performers*, chapter 8, page 317, for more information about the concert parties and theatricals in camps in Singapore and in the Thai–Burma railway camps; https://digitalcommons.macalester.edu/cgi/viewcontent. cgi?article=1011&context=thdabooks
4 IWM Documents 66/308/Box 6.
5 J. B. Chalker, *Images of War* (2007) p. 119.
6 The Lancashire Infantry Museum at Fulwood Barracks in Preston has a large archive of FEPOW artwork.
7 J. B. Chalker: Interview with M. Parkes (2007) LSTM records p. 15 Chalker transcript; see also M. Parkes and G. Gill. *Captive Memories. Starvation, disease, survival.* (Lancaster, 2015) p. 72; also S. Eldredge, p. 403, for full description of the production and design of the poster and to read Chalker's hilarious account
8 S. Eldredge, *Captive Audiences/Captive Performers* ebook (2014) p. 331.
9 Ennis secretly performed over a hundred post-mortems while at Changi and kept notes.
10 'The R.A.M.C. in Thailand P.O.W. Camps', *Journal of the Royal Army Medical Corps* (April 1946) Vol. LXXXVI, No.4 pp. 139–70.
11 www.captivememories.org.uk
12 www.captivememories.org.uk
13 Currently, quarterly newsletters are produced by the Java 1942 Club, COFEPOW, the Researching FEPOW History and the Malayan Volunteer groups, the Association of Birmingham FEPOW, the FEPOW Fellowship Welfare Reunion Association, as well as a regular FEPOW newsletter by Pam Stubbs, widow of FEPOW Les Stubbs. All have been active supporters of LSTM's FEPOW art enquiry.
14 https://bspittle.wordpress.com/2009/05/02/ronald-john-jack-spittle/

Chapter 2: The 'Unrecognised' Artists – Part I

1 Bettany's website: www.changipowart.com
2 www.lstmed.ac.uk/FEPOW
3 Plarr's Lives of the Fellows https://livesonline.rcseng.ac.uk
4 *Captive Memories* p. 68–69.
5 The chapel was included in the 1946 book, *The Churches of Captivity in Malaya*, by former FEPOW padre J. N. Lewis Bryan.

6   M. Parkes, and G. Gill, *Captive Memories* pp. 88–91; more info www.captivememories.org.uk

7   See Williams' private papers in IWM (ref 53/1/1).

8   Discovered among the Private Papers of Lieutenant Ronald Williams RA at the IWM

9   COFEPOW stands for the Children and Families of Far East POW; manage the FEPOW memorial building and archives on a voluntary basis; viewing of the archives by appointment only.

10   www.captivememories.org.uk

11   In the 1950s Fletcher-Cooke became a Member of Parliament and wrote a memoir entitled, *The Emperor's Guest*, first published in 1972 by Leo Cooper.

12   A. Turbutt. Interview with Meg Parkes (2009) LSTM records

13   'Magic of a Dartmoor Stream' BBC 1, 1977 see You Tube: https://www.youtube.com/watch?v=iHkF9glPQ9o

14   In 1955 Bell was to realise his dream, first conceived in captivity, of establishing the Bell Language School and by 1972 had set up the Bell Educational Trust Limited, which is still based in Cambridge; Bell Foundation https://www.bell-foundation.org.uk/about-us/our-history/

15   F. Bell, *Undercover University* (1990) p. 48.

16   The full-size caravan was made using Newman's drawings and notes, by Will Hardie for 'George Clarke's Amazing Spaces', Channel 4, Series 6, Episode 9, WW2 special December 2016. https://www.channel4.com/programmes/george-clarkes-amazing-spaces/on-demand/62966-009

17   Peter Winstanley: http://www.pows-of-japan.net/articles/82.htm, found in Articles … other stories, entitled: 'Australian sailor with RN captured Banka Island', Bob Miller.

18   *The Tuggs's of Ramsgate* was published originally in 1889. Re-published for its centenary 1989 by Lytehouse Limited in Ramsgate, this latter edition is an A4 landscape, glossy hand-back book beautifully illustrated throughout with Wally Cullen's work.

19   The brothers lost touch when John was sent first to River Valley Road work camp in Singapore before being shipped to Formosa (Taiwan) in the October. In February 1945 he was moved again to Japan from where he was liberated in the September.

20   https://bspittle.wordpress.com/2009/05/02/ronald-john-jack-spittle/

21   Nephew of well-known late-Victorian artist, Frederick Elwell, Beverley museum collection.

22   In Liverpool in September 2012, the Researching FEPOW History Group organised a special afternoon of FEPOW entertainment history entitled, 'An Afternoon at the Theatre'. The guest speaker was American Emeritus Professor Sears Eldredge. author of *Captive Audiences/Captive Performers*, the definitive work on FEPOW entertainments in Singapore and Thailand.

23   http://eresources.nlb.gov.sg/infopedia/articles/SIP_487_2004-12-23.html

24   W. Hammond, The Changi Murals (Singapore 2002).

25 J & S. Dewey, PoW *Sketchbook, a story of survival*, (1985) (colour version 2014).

26 IWM Documents.26443 (Papers of G. C. Munton).

27 Correspondence with Sears Eldredge.

28 Full title, *'Don't ever again say "It Can't be Done"', The Story of Changi Industries Inc.*

Chapter 3: The 'Unrecognised' Artists – Part II

1 Article about Meninsky, IWM Art Dept files.

2 News cutting 1950 held in the IWM Art Dept, reporting on Old's award to study at Camberwell School of Art.

3 Contact fepow.project@lstmed.ac.uk

4 Information gleaned from Liberation questionnaire; also L & P. Stubbs, *Unsung Heroes of the RAF* (2002).

5 S. C. Alexander. Interview with Meg Parkes (2007) LSTM records.

6 Fergus was well-known as a magician and would often be asked to do tricks for the Japanese commander in camp. He was the youngest member of the Magic Circle at the age of 17 and when interviewed in 2007 was the oldest member. See P. Fyans, *The Conjuror on The Kwai* (2011).

7 This text is taken from the catalogue for the 'Flora and Fauna' exhibition at the Sladmore Gallery in London in 1970.

8 Sears Eldredge, Chapter 12a.

9 P. Fyans, *The Conjuror on the Kwai*.

10 See article by Sears Eldredge, 'We Girls: Female Impersonators in prisoner of war entertainments' (2014) https://novaojs.newcastle.edu.au/ojs/index.php/pes/article/download/133/107

11 W. Pearson, *Expended Portion*, 2018 published by Fizzer's sons Neil and Malcolm; based on Fizzer's diaries; page 169 Fizzer recalled the Victory Concert. This memoir is a rich and informative biography of one of the main characters in FEPOW theatricals in Singapore and Thailand.

12 Jim also noted that other British artists in Argyle Street, Lt Alexander Skvorzov (a white Russian who took British nationality) and R. Parkinson, also contributed, designing advertisements for wine promotion.

13 See film 'A War Story' https://www.nfb.ca/film/war_story/, written and produced by Anne Wheeler, daughter of Canadian RAMC medical officer Major Ben Wheeler. This film 1981 B&W film charts Major Wheeler's battle to keep men alive in Kinkaseki in Taiwan.

14 Records the stories of the Taiwan camps – www.powtaiwan.org

15 This is where American airman Louis Zamperini USAF had been tortured under the reign of terror of the infamous guard, Corporal Watanabe known as 'the Bird'. For more about Watanabe see: Wade, Tom Henling, *Prisoner of the Japanese from Changi to Tokyo* (1994); also, Hillebrand, L. *Unbroken*, (2012) Louis Zamperini; also a feature film of the same name, directed by Angelina Jolie.

16 Charles Frederick Mummery, qualified in dentistry at Edinburgh, Malaya pre-war, joined the FMSVF and later attached to 2nd Btn The Loyal Regiment. See *In Oriente Primus*, Moffatt J., and Riches, P., for further information.

17 J. Moffatt, and P. Riches, *In Oriente Primus,* (2010) for information about the Malayan Volunteer Forces.

18 Sears, Eldredge, 'Chapter 1. *"In the Bag": Changi POW Camp, Singapore'* (2014), p. 20. Book Chapters. 22

Chapter 4: Camp Life – A Pictorial View

1 Colonel C. Owtram. *1000 Days on the River Kwai. The secret diary of a British Camp Commandant.* (Barnsley, 2017).

2 J. Coast. *Railroad of Death.* (London, 1947), p. 68.

3 B. Akhurst. Liverpool School of Tropical Medicine LSTM records.

4 For more information on the Sumatra Railway see: H. Hovinga. *The Sumatra Railroad. Final destination Pakan Baroe 1943–1945.* (Leiden, Holland 2010); and: E. Oliver. *Prisoners of the Sumatra Railway. Narratives of history and memory.* (London, 2018).

5 D. Fogarty. Interview with M. Parkes (2008). LSTM records.

6 A. Turbutt. Interview with M. Parkes (2009). LSTM records.

7 M. Parkes and G. Gill. *Captive Memories* pp. 27–8.

8 M. Parkes. *Notify Alec Rattray.* (Hoylake 2002), p. 155.

9 D. Arkush. Interview with M. Parkes (2007). LSTM records.

10 G. Gill and M. Parkes. *Burma Railway Medicine. Disease, death and survival on the Thai–Burma Railway, 1942–1945.* (Lancaster, 2017), pp. 46–7.

11 C. H. D. Wild. Narrative of F Force in Thailand, April–December 1943. LSTM records.

12 H. E. de Wardener. Interview with M. Parkes (2007). LSTM records.

13 G. P. Adams. *No Time for Geishas. Journeys of a Far East prisoner of war.* (London, 1973), p. 54.

14 L. Toseland. *River Kwai Yasumee Nai!* (Northamptonshire, 1994), p. 53.

15 D. J. Morley. Interview with M. Parkes (2008). LSTM records.

16 J. T. Tidey. Interview with M. Parkes (2008). LSTM records.

17 J. Chalker. *Burma Railway Artist. The war drawings of Jack Chalker.* (London, 1994), p. 35.

18 C. Lyons. Imperial War Museum Sound Archive (IWM-SA) 10752/3, pp. 25–6 of typescript.

19 D. Fogarty (2008).

Chapter 5: Medicine and Art in Captivity

1   For more detail on these and other diseases affecting Far East POWs – see G. Gill and M. Parkes *Burma Railway Medicine – disease, death and survival on the Thai–Burma Railway 1942–45* (Lancaster 2017), pp. 61–96.

2   T. Wilson and J. A. Reid, 'Malaria amongst prisoners of war in Siam ('F' Force)'. *Trans Roy Soc Trop Med & Hyg* 1949; 43: 257–72.

3   H. E. de Wardener. Interview with M. Parkes (2007). LSTM records.

4   H. E. de Wardener and B. Lennox. 'Cerebral beriberi (Wernicke's Encephalopathy)'. *Lancet* 1947;1: 11–17.

5   F. Whalley. Imperial War Museum (IWM) 98/79/1. A retrospective (written in the 1990s) but vivid account of life and death on the Thai–Burma railway.

6   J. Markowitz. 'A series of over 100 amputations at the thigh for tropical ulcer'. *J Roy Army Med Corps* 1946; 86: 159–70.

7   Captain Harry Silman. Diary. IWM 66/218/1. p. 160.

8   Captain C. D. Chilton. Annual Report – V.D. and Scabies Department – Roberts Hospital. Period 20.2.42 to 15.2.43. National Archives (NA) WO 222/1383. pp. 134–6.

9   D. Arkush. 'Dentistry in a POW camp in the Far East'. *British Dental Journal* 16 August 1946: 128–9.

10   Wilson and Reid (1949).

11   Major T. M. Pemberton. Various records. IWM P437.

12   S. Cairns. Interview with M. Parkes (2008). LSTM records.

13   J. Chalker. Interview with M. Parkes (2007). LSTM records.

14   D. Arkush (1946).

15   L. J. Audus. *Spice Island Slaves.* (Surrey, 2001).

16   Blood transfusion appreciation note. Chungkai camp 17 October 1943. LSTM records.

17   J. Markowitz. 'Transfusion of defibrinated blood in POW camps at Chungkai and Nakom Paton, Thailand.' *J Roy Army Med Corps* 1946; 86: 187–9.

18   For more detail of Gordon Vaughan and his self-retaining ileostomy tube, see: M. Parkes and G. Gill. *Captive Memories* pp. 127–9.

19   Private G. Chapman. Report on the work of the Nakom Paton Camp Scientist, April 1944 to August 1945. NA WO222/1389.

20   J. Chalker (2007).

Chapter 6: Maintaining Morale

1   See also Daily Mail article December 2014: https://www.dailymail.co.uk/news/article-2880666/I-tortured-sadistic-prison-camp-guard-Angelina-Jolie-blockbuster-British-victim-Bird-reveals-Japanese-psychopath-crucified-soldiers-got-excited-saliva-bubbled-round-mouth.html

2 J. B. Chalker, published by Leo Cooper (London 1994); also repeated in *Burma War Artist* (2007).

3 L. Reynolds, *Down to Bedrock The diary and secret notes of a Far East prisoner of war chaplain, 1942–45* (2013) Art Angels Publishing. Louise also published *The Changi Cross A symbol of Hope in the Shadow of Death* (2015) and *Eric and Scrunchball* (2017), a children's book written and illustrated by her son and daughter, about Cordingly's dog.

4 *Down to Bedrock*, p. 131.

Chapter 7: Finding a Voice – Changing Post-War Attitudes

1 R. W. F. Searle, *To the Kwai and Back: War Drawings 1939–45* (1986).

2 Lobban, J., *Art Therapy with Military Veterans: Trauma and the Image*. Routledge (2017).

Appendix I

1 Three watercolours by Old of Orrey's ankle are among dozens of digitised images of Old's artwork, available online at: http://search.slv.vic.gov.au

2 'Prisoner of War Art from the Burma–Thai Railway Camps', an exhibition of medical artwork created by British artists in captivity in Thailand during the Second World War, The Queen's Hall, State Library of Victoria, Australia, 4 April–21 May 1995. A copy of the catalogue is in the Art Department of the IWM and with the author.

Appendix II

1 Full transcript of this article is at: https://www.cofepow.org.uk/armed-forces-stories-list/18th-division-royal-engineers

2 There are more references to Ferron's theatrical prowess, both at Nong Pladuk and later at Ubon camp, in Eldredge's e-book.

Acknowledgements

This book, and the research that underpins it, has been generously supported by many individuals and institutions over the past 12 years and more. It is the result of the Liverpool School of Tropical Medicine's (LSTM) FEPOW art research enquiry.

Firstly, sincere gratitude must go to all the Far East prisoner of war (FEPOW) veterans who, in myriad ways, have provided a broader understanding of their experiences. Veterans interviewed for LSTM's FEPOW oral history study (2007–2010) shared their memories as well as the many small and sometimes curious mementoes of their years in captivity. The variety and quality of the artwork and the artefacts revealed is what initially sparked our interest and the need to see if there was more to be found.

Sincere thanks go to all the families of FEPOW artists, and to the private collectors of FEPOW art, who have helped in our search for this material. Relatives of FEPOW artists welcomed our enquiries, often expressing surprise that anyone should be interested. Many of them, and private collectors, loaned material for the 'Secret Art of Survival exhibition' (Liverpool 2019–2020) and gave permission for these and other images to feature on LSTM's FEPOW website – www.captivememories.org.uk. This will provide a lasting legacy long after the exhibition has finished.

FEPOW families were keen to ensure that we gained a broader perspective and insight and responded enthusiastically with information required during the various stages of the enquiry. The authors are indebted to all those who have given permission to reproduce many of the images that appear in the book. Please note, the families of the artists or executors of the artists' estates, retain copyright to the images in this book. This artwork cannot be reproduced for any reason without their permission.

The authors wish to thank all the institutions, owners and individuals who have given permission for the use of images in the book. We have made every effort to contact copyright holders for the use of images; omissions and corrections will be made in subsequent reprints or editions.

Sincere thanks go to the Wellcome Trust for awarding a travel grant that enabled visits to both institutions and individuals that had FEPOW artwork in archives and private collections. Travelling all over this country and abroad in 2012–2014 Meg was privileged to meet more FEPOW veterans, some of the last few eye witnesses to this history. All were in their late 90s or centenarians and were keen to support the project.

The institutions visited were both large and small and included museums, libraries and regimental headquarters. Curators, archivists and librarians were not only knowledgeable but without exception helpful. Visiting one collection often led to another thanks to assiduous librarians keen to help us in our mission. We have endeavoured to follow up all leads regarding contemporaneous FEPOW artwork. It should be noted that artwork created from memory in later post-war years was not included in this enquiry.

The following list of institutions is by no means exhaustive and inevitably some 'gems' will have been missed along the way. Sometimes there was the frustration of travelling long distances to see a specific item by arrangement, only to find on arrival that it was either missing or had been returned to the owners! But such irritations were balanced by making wonderful discoveries on at least three occasions.

The authors are most grateful to the Trustees of the Imperial War Museums for allowing access to the collections and to each of the copyright holders; Museon in The Hague, Netherlands for their assistance; to the National Army Museum for permission to reproduce the watercolour 'Mr Stanley' in the book.

In addition to these institutions, we have also consulted: the Wellcome Library, British Red Cross Archives and Clavell Library at The Royal Arsenal Woolwich, all in London; the Museum of Military Medicine; Cambridge University Library and Cambridge City Archives; COFEPOW archives in the FEPOW Memorial Building at National Memorial Arboretum in Staffordshire; the archives of the 2nd Loyal Regiment at the Lancashire Infantry Museum, Fulwood Barracks in Preston; the Second World War Experience Centre near Wakefield; the Fusiliers Museum of Northumberland at Alnwick Castle; the National Museum Scotland and the National Library of Scotland, both in Edinburgh; the Gordon Highlanders Museum and Archives in Aberdeen and Glasgow's Mitchell Library which houses the Glasgow City Life archives. The authors are grateful to all these institutions for access to their collections and for their assistance.

There were also overseas visits to view known FEPOW artwork collections: Changi Museum and the National Museum, both in Singapore; the Anglican Church of All Saints in Jakarta, Indonesia. Preparations were greatly assisted by the kindness of administrators, archivists and librarians at all the locations.

Many other people have supported this work, and in myriad ways, ensuring that our efforts bore fruit. Special gratitude goes to Keith Andrews, Annie Lord, Rachel Mulhearn and Janice Lobban for their unfailing and invaluable assistance and advice at different stages. There are too many others to name individually, but they know who they are: the teams who run, and the members who make up, the British FEPOW clubs and groups; fellow researchers, academic and family historians around the world, those who run FEPOW descendants' groups, websites, small museums and larger collections, who have kept us informed of items of interest and contacts for further investigation; and everyone who has helped to promote the research enquiry, the exhibition and this book, we are indebted to you all for your unfailing support and help.

The curatorial staff and librarians at IWM deserve special mention. The late Rod Suddaby and our co-author Jenny Wood, were two of IWM's own, both unstinting in their support for this research. Geoff and Meg have worked closely with many others over the past 13 years and longer. They were generous with their time and have assisted greatly throughout the FEPOW art enquiry.

The staff at LSTM across all departments have been extremely supportive. They are proud of the FEPOW work done at LSTM over many decades. Looking a little further back, tribute must also be paid to the late Dr Dion Bell, Reader in Tropical Medicine and Honorary Consultant Physician. It was Dion who led the FEPOW project at LSTM from the early 1970s. He knew some of the clinicians who treated FEPOW patients at Liverpool in the early post-war years, notably Professor Brian Maegraith who was Dean of LSTM from 1946 to 1975.

Dion also briefly worked alongside one of the hitherto unknown FEPOW artists discovered during the enquiry, LSTM's Professor Thomas Wilson who held the Chair of Hygiene from 1962–1971. On one occasion in the late 1960s, Dion accompanied Wilson on a trip to Thailand. Dion Bell carried the torch, lit by LSTM clinicians in the 1940s and 1950s, eventually passing it on to Dr Geoff Gill who led FEPOW medical research studies at LSTM.

The exhibition, 'Secret Art of Survival. Creativity and ingenuity of Far East POW 1942–1945', was the result of LSTM's FEPOW art enquiry. The partnership between LSTM and the University of Liverpool's Victoria Gallery & Museum (VG&M) to bring this previously unseen record of captivity and survival together, ensured that this extraordinary visual history could be seen together for the first time. Up till 2013 LSTM's FEPOW clinical, scientific and medical history research was carried out while LSTM was affiliated to the University of Liverpool and so it is fitting that the university's gallery and museum is hosting the exhibition.

Our thanks go to the Lottery Heritage Fund for the generous grant funding for the exhibition, and to the staff of VG&M who back in December 2016 committed to host the 'Secret Art of Survival' exhibition and who worked tirelessly to deliver it.

Lastly, we are once again indebted to our publishers Palatine Books, to Anna, Lucy and Srishti and the rest of the team, for their invaluable advice and support throughout the making of this book.

The research that has informed *Captive Artists* (and the exhibition) honours the memory of all those held in Far East captivity – the artists and those whom they documented, the men who survived, and the many thousands who did not.

Meg Parkes
July 2019

Index

bamboo and atap 89, 145, 99

bamboo, 232, 237 (needles), 282 (walking stick), 284 (tubes)

Ban Khao camp, Thailand 138

Ban Pong POW camp 120, 127, 142, 198, 280, 285, 288

Bandoeng POW camp, Java 26, 65–66, 68, 82, 254, 235

Bangkok 27, 100, 128, 143, 274, 283, 299

barber's shop 206

Barn Theatre, Sime Road POW camp 119

Barnes, A/Seaman R. D. ix, 64, 160

Bartholomew, David 132, 299

Bartholomew, Ruth 274, 300

Batam Island (transit camp) 76

Batavia (Jakarta) 21, 58, 66–68, 75, 78, 81, 208, 325, 344

Batu Lintang POW camp Kuching 93, 208

Beales, Fl/Lt C. RAF dental officer 88, 90

Beaumont, Major, RASC 184

Beckerley, LAC J. ix, 64, 118–119, 248, 252

Bell, Dr Dion 7, 33, 37, 51, 362

Bell, Lt 2nd Btn The Loyal Regt 184

Bell, Lt F. 93, 353

benjo hut 176–177, 206

Berry, Gnr H. W. 174–175, 248, 304–305, 308

Bettany, L/Bdr D. ix, 31, 46, 52, 63–64, 99, 122–125, 154, 237, 257, 305, 352

Bettany, Keith 305

Bevan, Capt. G. A. J. ix, 64, 166, 168–169, 257

bird photographer 92, 333

Bird, Capt. G. V. ix, 15, 64–65, 156–157, 201–202, 206, 306–307

Bird, Daphne 15

Bird, Derek 15

Bird, Wendy 139, 322

birds xii, 67, 75, 91

Birds of Malaya 15, 351

Birmingham FEPOW Association 10

Blackpool Evening Gazette 36, 38–39, 227– 303

Blackpool Regt 38, 280

Blakang Mati, Singapore 117

blood transfusions 237–238, 256

blood typing 239

Boie Glodok Jail, Java 76, 81–82, 98, 208

Bolitho RN, P/O W. 95

botanical studies 69, 217

botany 69, 72, 250

Bourke, Bill 14

Bowen Road Hospital, Hong Kong 156

Bradley, Capt. J. 102

Brazil, L/Bdr R. G. ix, 64, 145–147, 248, 273

Brennan, Jim 111

British Army Aid Group 307

Brook, Maddy 335

Brown, Band Sgt B. W. 46–48

Brown, John 169

Brown, Richard 46

Bryan, Revd Lewis (padre) 81

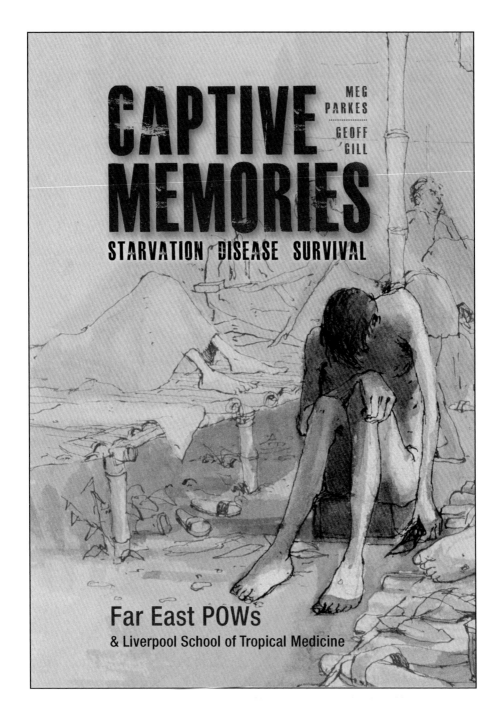

Also available in the series, *Captive memories*, £12.99,
visit **www.carnegiepublishing.com** or call the
publishers on **01524 840111** to obtain copies.

BURMA RAILWAY MEDICINE

GEOFF GILL
MEG PARKES

DISEASE, DEATH AND SURVIVAL ON THE
Thai-Burma Railway, 1942–1945

Also available in the series, *Burma Railway Medicine*,
£14.99, visit **www.carnegiepublishing.com** or call the
publishers on **01524 840111** to obtain copies.